IMAGES
of America

Geauga Lake

The Funtime Years 1969–1995

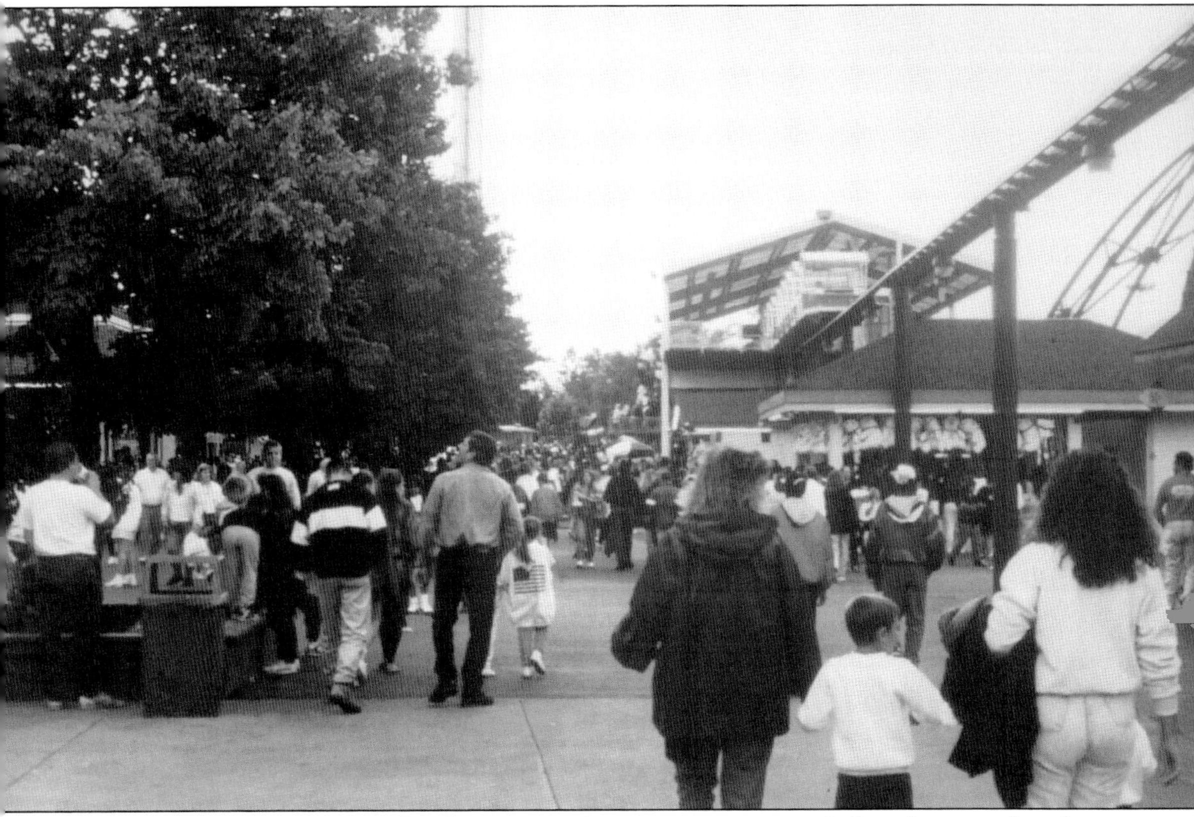

Geauga Lake was a popular destination for group picnics, and this photograph, taken on Cleveland Clinic day in 1993, shows how big the crowds could get during the Funtime years. (Jim Futrell collection.)

ON THE COVER: The Big Dipper was Geauga Lake's most iconic ride and a favorite for generations of thrill-seekers. (Dave Hahner collection.)

IMAGES
of America

GEAUGA LAKE

THE FUNTIME YEARS 1969–1995

Jim Futrell and Dave Hahner
Foreword by Jeff Lococo

ARCADIA
PUBLISHING

ISBN 978-1-4671-1389-2

Published by Arcadia Publishing
Charleston, South Carolina

Printed in the United States of America

Library of Congress Control Number: 2014954049

For all general information, please contact Arcadia Publishing:
Telephone 843-853-2070
Fax 843-853-0044
E-mail sales@arcadiapublishing.com
For customer service and orders:
Toll-Free 1-888-313-2665

Visit us on the Internet at www.arcadiapublishing.com

To all of those who visited Geauga Lake and SeaWorld Ohio over the years, this book is for you. May your fondest memories of summers past be rekindled.

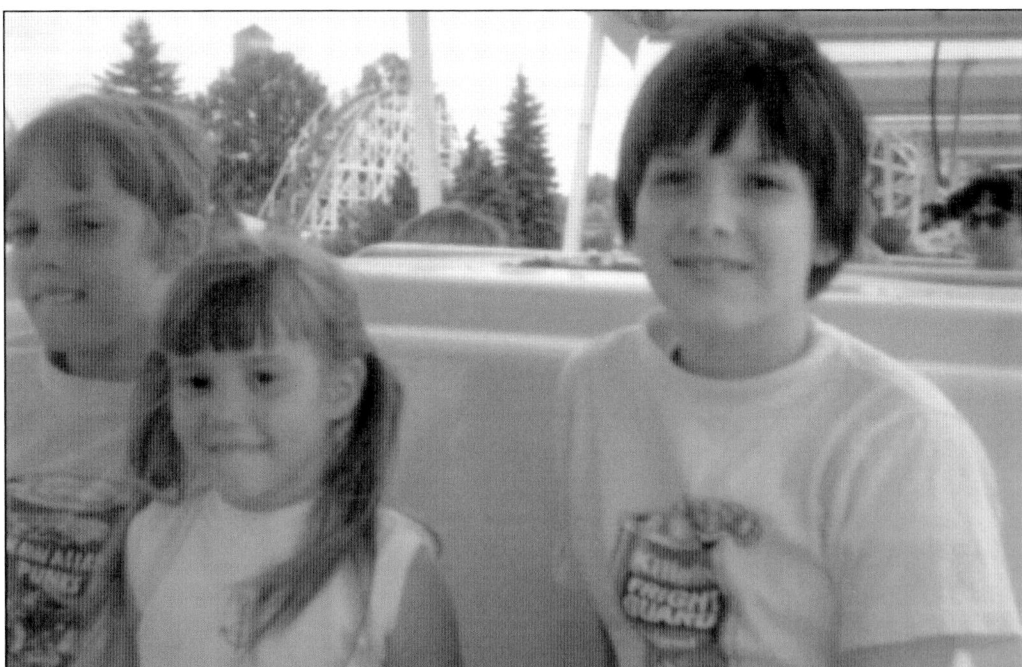

Author Dave Hahner (right) enjoys Geauga Lake's monorail during a childhood visit in 1974 with his brother Tom Hahner and sister Kelly Hahner. (David and Kathleen Hahner collection.)

Contents

FOREWORD

On a cold winter day in December 1999, I sat in a construction trailer on the shores of Geauga Lake. The park was being transformed into Six Flags Ohio, and I was in charge of bringing the project on line. We were going to compete with the big boys, and Geauga Lake was to become a true destination. I was lucky enough to be a part of fulfilling my uncle Gasper Lococo's vision for Geauga Lake.

As a 13-year-old kid in April 1969, my family and I were his guests for opening day. Gasper had just left an executive position at Cedar Point to pursue his dream of becoming an owner of a park. He and his friend Earl Gascoigne and business partners Milford Jacobson and Dale Van Voorhis formed Funtime, Inc. with the support of Dick Blake and Allen Gulker of the Ohio Company. There we were, the entire Lococo family and a host of other close friends, thinking my uncle had truly lost his mind on a venture that seemed far-fetched at best. The weather was cold and only a couple hundred visitors showed up. Neither the fresh paint on the Big Dipper nor the new monorail ride seemed compelling enough for us to believe this whole idea was going to work.

But Gasper and Gascoigne had a brilliant plan to bring a national brand, SeaWorld, to Aurora, Ohio. It was not too long before Shamu played to thousands of fans watching the shows and wondering about the great-looking amusement park across the lake. They knew that the draw of SeaWorld was the market dynamic they needed to grow Geauga Lake into a major amusement park.

Fast-forward to March 2000, and Gaspar's son Augie and I are at Geauga Lake discussing plans for opening day. I was departing for a new job with Great Wolf Resorts, and Augie was appointed to take over as head of development. He was now responsible for having the park ready for the inaugural year of Six Flags Ohio.

It was a great run through Geauga Lake's glory days. How fitting that Augie got to be the one to put the final touches on what was truly one of America's classic amusement parks. I will forever be grateful for the chance to be part of this history and proud that my uncle and his partners got to see their dreams become a reality.

—Jeff Lococo

ACKNOWLEDGMENTS

As with any book of this nature, we would like to thank everyone who helped us create this memory of Geauga Lake during the Funtime era, from 1969 to 1995. Many people gave us their memories as well as images that we were permitted to use within the book. Big thanks go to Lee Bush and Richard Hershey of Amusement Park Books for their contributions of historical images from the early years of Geauga Lake. Others graciously provided images from their collections as well as personal photographs from their many visits to both Geauga Lake and neighboring SeaWorld that were not part of Jim's or Dave's personal collection. We would like to give a huge thanks to Michael Horwood, Sam Shurgott, Joel Styer, and Sarah Windisch for the use of their images within this book, as well as a thanks to Duane Marden of rcdb.com for his assistance. This book would have certainly been more difficult to produce without their help. Also, a huge thank-you goes to Jeff Lococo for writing the foreword.

Tim O'Brien's book *The Wave Maker* (Ripley Publishing, 2005) was used as a reference for selected material in this text.

We would also like to thank our families: Jim's wife, Marlowe, and their sons, Jimmy, Christopher, and Matthew; and Dave's wife, Theresa, and son, David. Without their support, enthusiasm, and patience, this book would certainly never have gone forward. We would also both like to thank our parents, Jim and JoAnne Futrell and Dave and Kathy Hahner. Both sets of parents helped nurture our passion for amusement parks by taking us on various trips to parks throughout the country as children and encouraged our enthusiasm as adults. For that, we can be forever grateful.

INTRODUCTION

The shores of Geauga Lake in northeastern Ohio have served as a summer escape for almost 150 years. During that time, the lake's attraction has pretty much remained the same—a place to escape on a hot summer day. While this appeal has been a constant, the personality of the land surrounding the waters has changed many times.

In the years following the Civil War, Geauga Lake first became a destination as a quiet picnic grove. By the 1880s, railroad excursions brought thousands of people to what was then a thriving summer resort complete with hotels, dancing, and boating and a roller coaster, carousel, bowling alley, and roller rink. After a period of neglect, Geauga Lake was transformed into a modern amusement park in the 1920s featuring mechanical rides and a huge swimming pool. In more recent years, one of the largest theme parks in the country dominated the shores. Today, a water park still provides that cooling escape.

But for many people, it was the period between 1969 and 1995 that holds the fondest memories. This was the time that Geauga Lake was a thriving, growing, regional amusement park owned by Funtime, Inc., a local company.

To fully appreciate the impact Funtime had on Geauga Lake, one has to look at the amusement industry in the late 1960s. It was a time of profound change in which large, corporate-owned, carefully planned theme parks that looked to Disneyland for inspiration were opening throughout the country and coming to dominate the industry. Meanwhile, the large family-owned amusement parks like Euclid Beach in Cleveland, Ohio; Riverview in Chicago, Illinois; and Fontaine Ferry in Louisville, Kentucky, that had defined the industry for decades were fading away in the face of aging facilities, declining neighborhoods, and family succession issues.

By most accounts, Geauga Lake was doomed to a similar fate. In the 1960s, the Schreyer family, which had been involved in the park since 1920, was aging and had no heirs, the buildings were worn out, and few new rides had been added. While most of Geauga Lake's other local peers, including Brady Lake, Craig Beach, Idora Park, and Meyers Lake, quickly became memories, Geauga Lake was able to defy the odds, modernize, and grow.

This was due to the ownership of Funtime, formed in 1968 by four executives who had been part of the transformation of Cedar Point in Sandusky, Ohio, from a fading relic into the leading amusement resort in the Midwest. They knew how important it was to continually invest in improving the park, and during their ownership, they invested \$40 million to modernize and expand Geauga Lake. Over that period, attendance increased from 250,000 to 1.1 million while revenues grew from \$795,000 to nearly \$24 million.

But Funtime also knew that constant reinvestment would not be enough, as the park operated in one of the most competitive regions in the country, with dozens of amusement parks—large and small—operating within a short drive of Geauga Lake. As a result, what really set Geauga Lake apart during the Funtime era was the innovative thinking that allowed it to stand out in a crowded marketplace. This included recruiting SeaWorld to open a marine life park on Geauga Lake property; being the first amusement park in the world to have two looping roller coasters;

pioneering fall events with the introduction of Oktoberfest; developing Boardwalk Shores, the first full-scale water park to be integrated into an traditional amusement park; introducing the Euroracers go-cart ride, the first extra-charge attraction at a pay-one-price amusement park; adding the Texas Twister, the first top-spin ride in North America; and its creative use of promotions such as free pizza day, free children's admission, the world's largest root beer float; free bungee jumping, and carload days.

Sadly, Geauga Lake is now gone, a victim of the corporate consolidation wave of the 1990s and 2000s. The Wildwater Kingdom water park is now the sole remainder. But, the intent of this book is not to mourn Geauga Lake's demise but to celebrate a time when Geauga Lake was a creative, scrappy competitor in one of the nation's most competitive amusement park markets.

Enjoy reliving the memories of *Geauga Lake: The Funtime Years.*

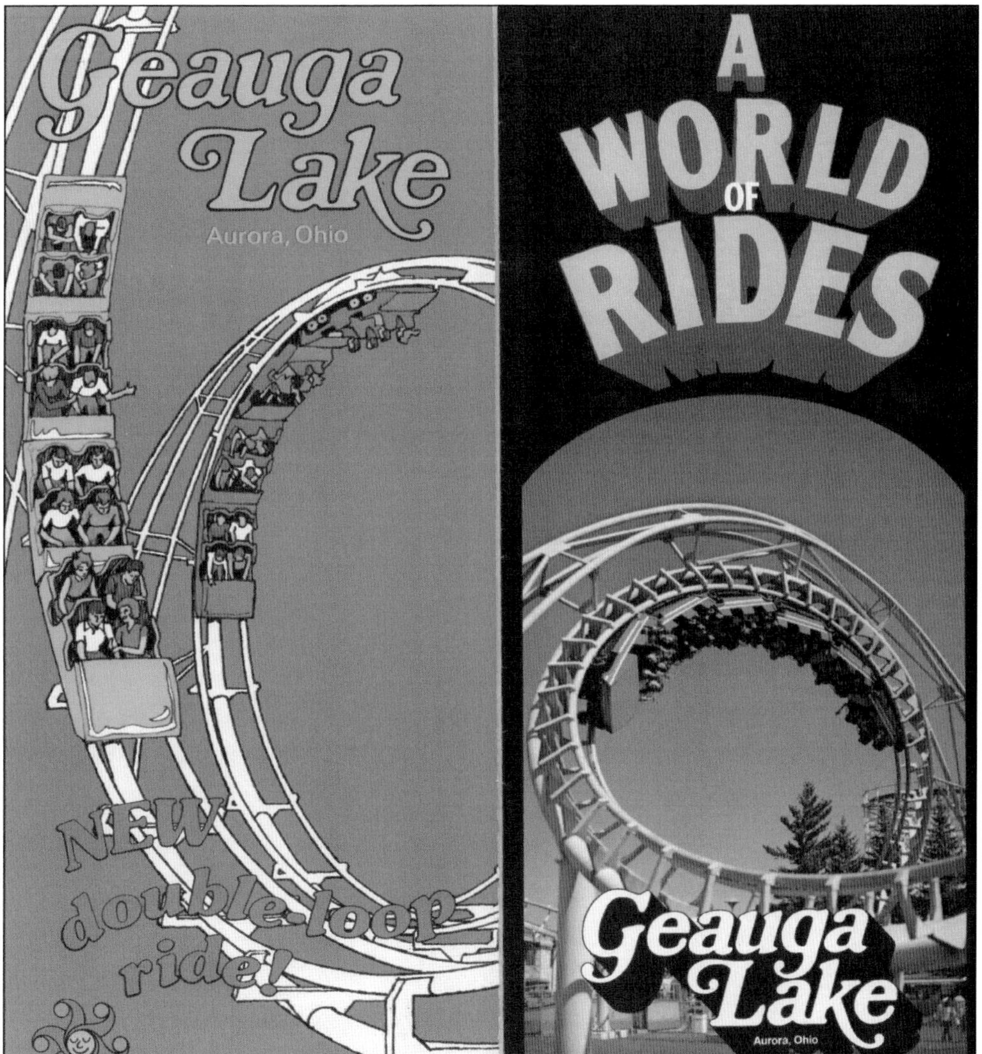

Every spring, Geauga Lake's new brochure would start appearing around Ohio and Pennsylvania, signaling the season was just around the corner. The brochure on the left promotes the opening of the new Double Loop roller coaster in 1977, while the one on the right, from 1979, invites people to enjoy "a world of rides." (Jim Futrell collection.)

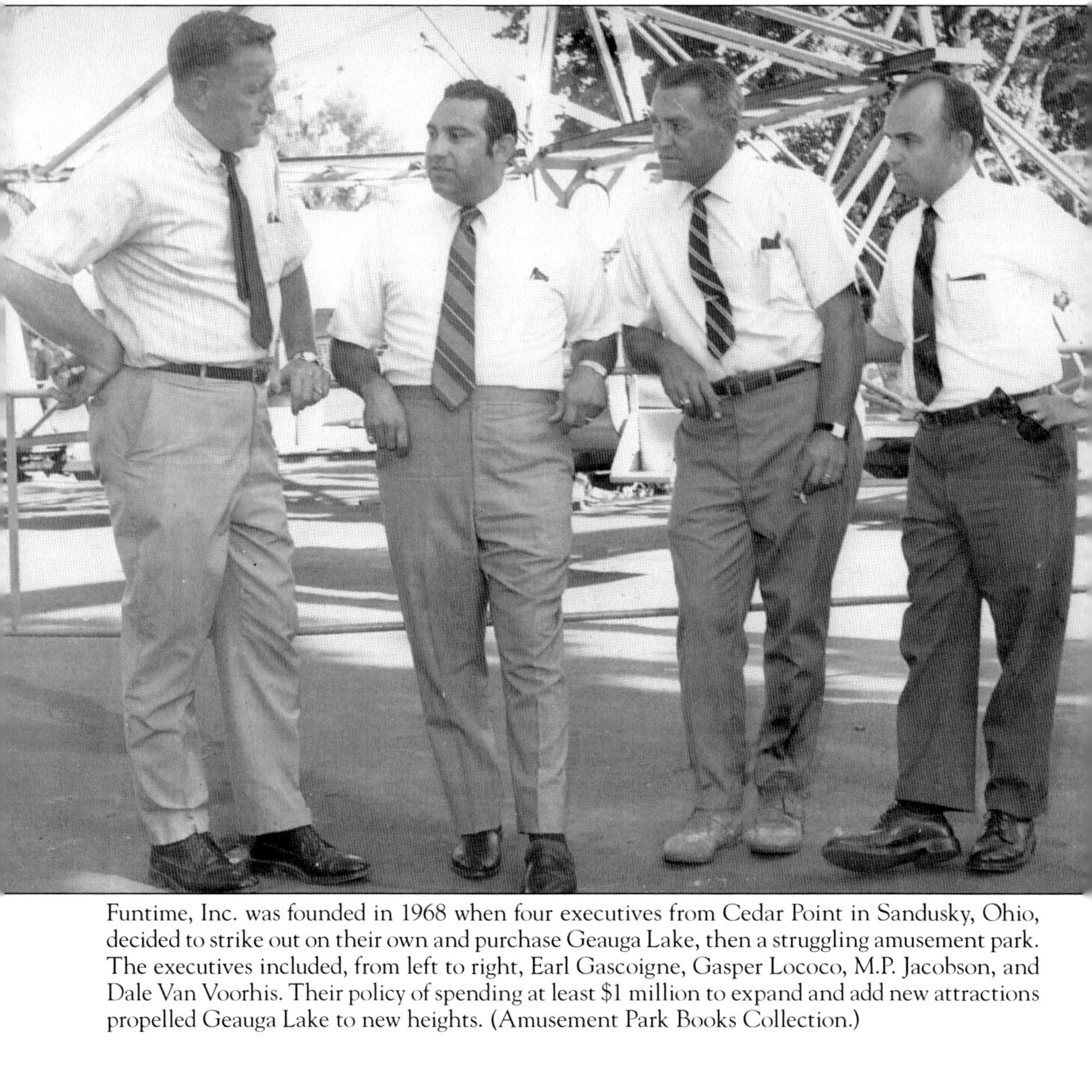

Funtime, Inc. was founded in 1968 when four executives from Cedar Point in Sandusky, Ohio, decided to strike out on their own and purchase Geauga Lake, then a struggling amusement park. The executives included, from left to right, Earl Gascoigne, Gasper Lococo, M.P. Jacobson, and Dale Van Voorhis. Their policy of spending at least $1 million to expand and add new attractions propelled Geauga Lake to new heights. (Amusement Park Books Collection.)

One

Prologue 1870s–1968

During the Ice Age, retreating glaciers sculpted the landscape of northeastern Ohio, leaving behind hills, rivers, and lakes. One of the lakes, best known as Geauga Lake, was a pristine 55-acre spring-fed body of water that early on became known for its purity and depth.

Toward the end of the Civil War, a group called the Geauga County Pioneers began holding picnics at the lake. By 1872, with recreation becoming an increasingly important part of American culture, Sullivan Giles came to the shores of Geauga Lake and opened a picnic area. The first ride, a primitive merry-go-round, appeared in 1876. Soon after, Kent's Grove opened adjacent to Giles's facility. By 1885, Kent's Grove had expanded, opening the Kent House hotel, a skating rink, and an early roller coaster, a "circular track several hundred feet around." Other attractions included boating, dancing, bowling, concerts, and strolling through the wooded grounds.

As the 20th century dawned, increasing competition started to impact the resort. As Kent's Grove fell under new ownership in 1900, newspaper accounts said much of the lake had been "stolen back again into nearly its original state of rustic simplicity." The old resort was in a state of decline.

That changed in 1920 when the Geauga Lake Amusement Co. started acquiring property. A new dance hall was opened in 1921, and in 1925 a $500,000 expansion converted Geauga Lake into a modern amusement park with the addition of seven rides, including the legendary Big Dipper roller coaster.

World War II brought its own challenges, including a 1942 tornado that knocked over a portion of the Big Dipper and wartime restrictions that limited operations to weekends and picnic days. But with the war ending, Geauga Lake once again began expanding. New rides were added, including a Wild Mouse roller coaster in 1958 and a kiddieland in response to the postwar baby boom. But the park began to struggle in the face of changing consumer tastes, aging ownership, deteriorating facilities, and a 1952 fire that destroyed several buildings. By the mid-1960s, like so many of its peers, Geauga Lake was struggling.

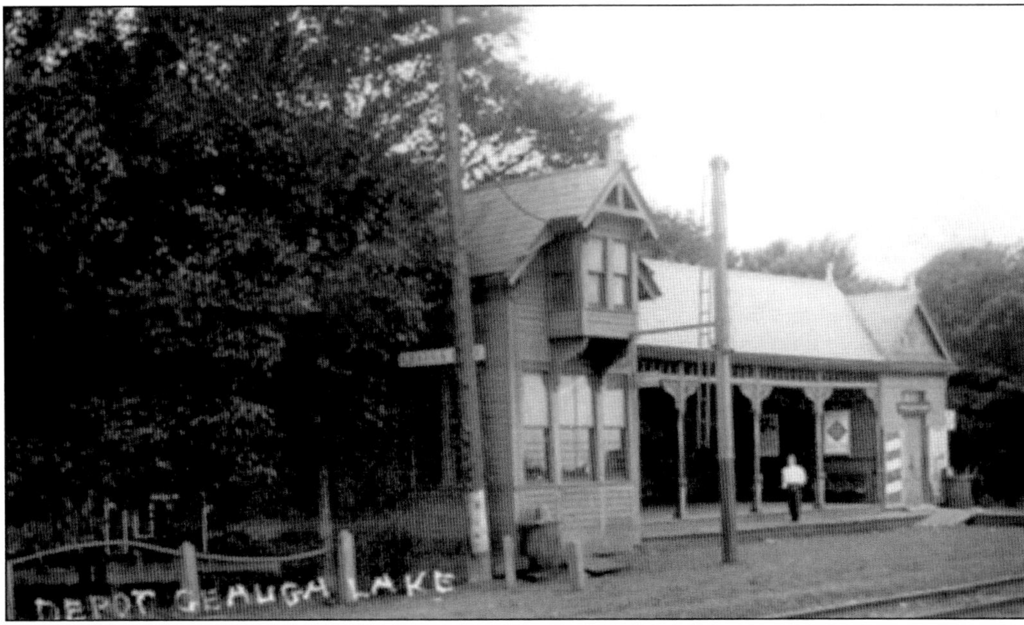

Railroad tracks first rolled past Geauga Lake in 1856. Soon, railway excursions were a popular summertime diversion, and by 1884 the New York, Pennsylvania, & Ohio Railroad was selling 60,000 tickets a year to the burgeoning resort. In 1885, a new depot—one of several that would serve the masses over the next few decades—was constructed to serve the growing crowds. (Jim Futrell collection.)

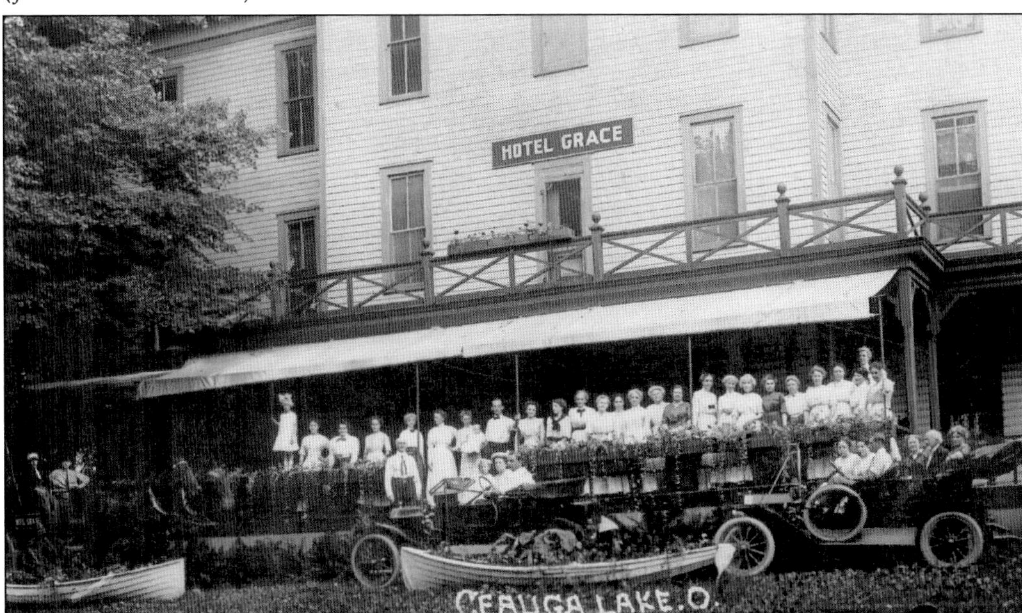

With railroad service, Geauga Lake soon grew into a thriving summer resort. Kent's Grove was mentioned as early as 1880. In 1885, proprietor A.G. Kent undertook a major expansion that included the construction of a new hotel, roller rink, billiard hall, and bowling alley. The Kent House hotel, in later years called the Hotel Grace, was a popular destination for resort-goers. (Jim Futrell collection.)

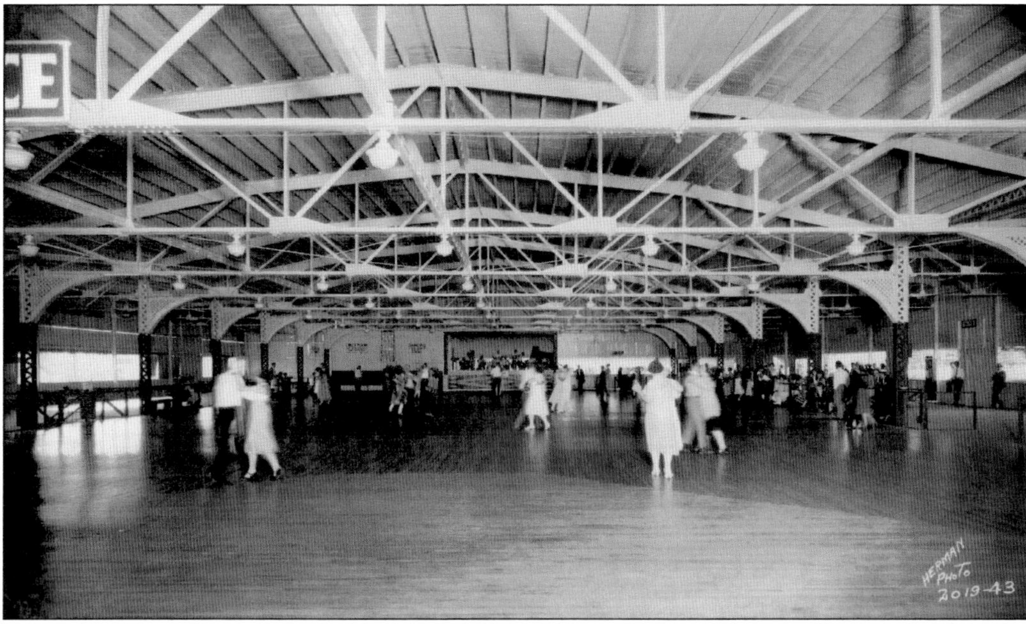

By the early 20th century, the park had fallen on hard times, but in 1920 the Geauga Lake Amusement Company, headed by bowling alley proprietor William Kuhlman, acquired the park and slowly began creating a modern facility. While the park at the time was, according to an article in the *Cleveland Plain Dealer*, little more than a "body of water, cider mill, and apple orchard," one of the company's first moves was to construct a new ballroom. (Amusement Park Books Collection.)

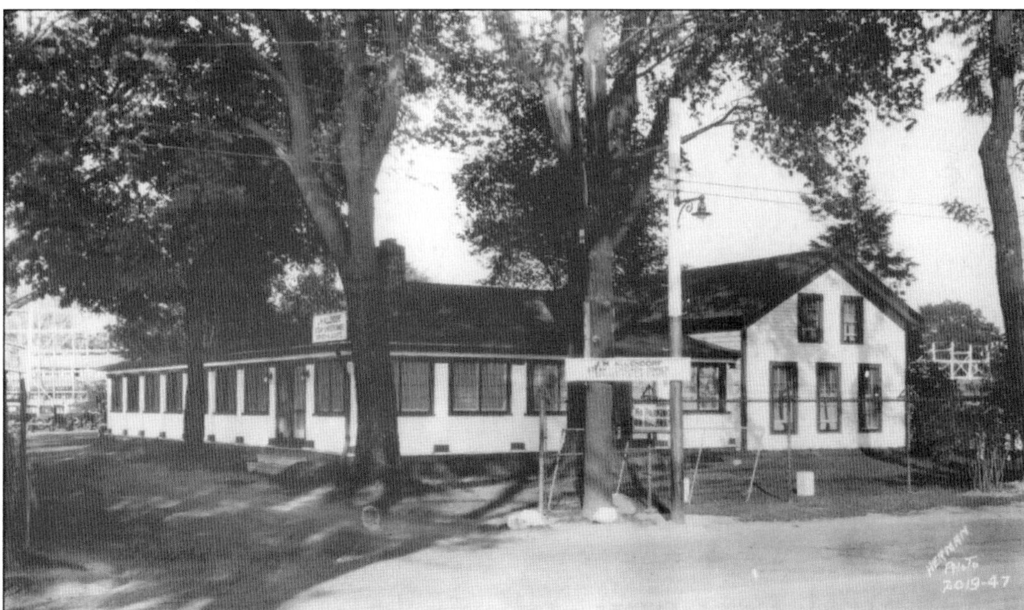

In 1921, the Geauga Lake Amusement Company purchased the property of Lela Selover, which adjoined its existing holdings. The five-acre parcel included 500 feet of frontage on the lake. Selover's former home was converted into a dining room, which greeted visitors for several years. (Amusement Park Books Collection.)

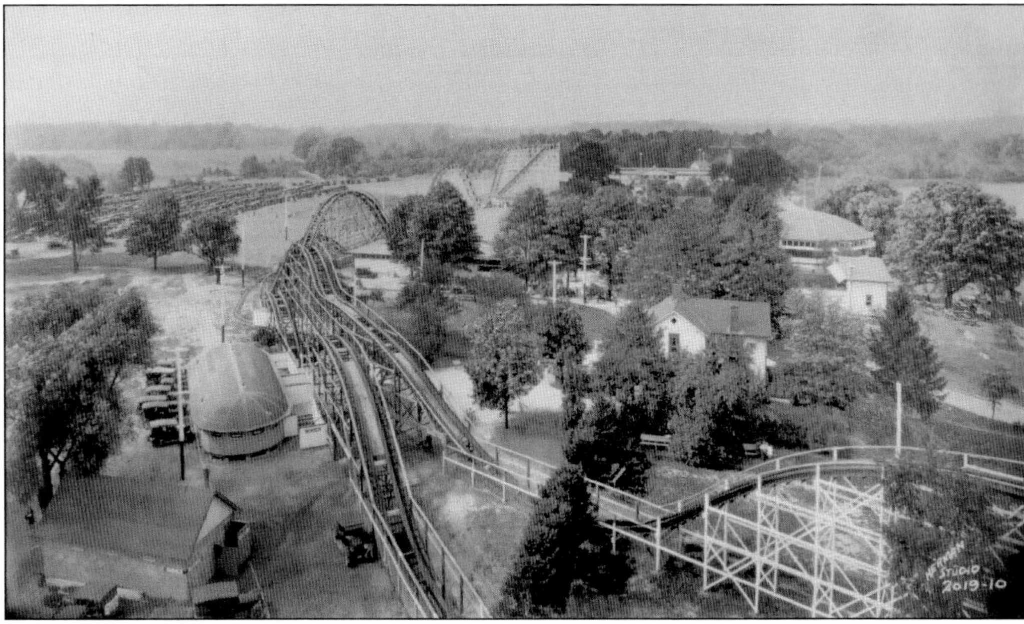

In 1925, Geauga Lake began to resemble the park that people know today when it undertook a $500,000 expansion to transform it from a sleepy summer resort to a modern amusement park. With the growing popularity of the automobile, the park featured a parking lot for 5,000 cars, seen in the top left of the above image. As was the trend in the industry, rides were the focus, with seven being added. Most notable was the Sky Rocket roller coaster, what became the park's most iconic ride. It was built by John Miller, the most innovative and prolific roller coaster designer of the era. The 65-foot-tall ride featured nearly 2,700 feet of track and was known for its series of large drops and the distinctive park entrance through the second hill. (Both, Amusement Park Books Collection.)

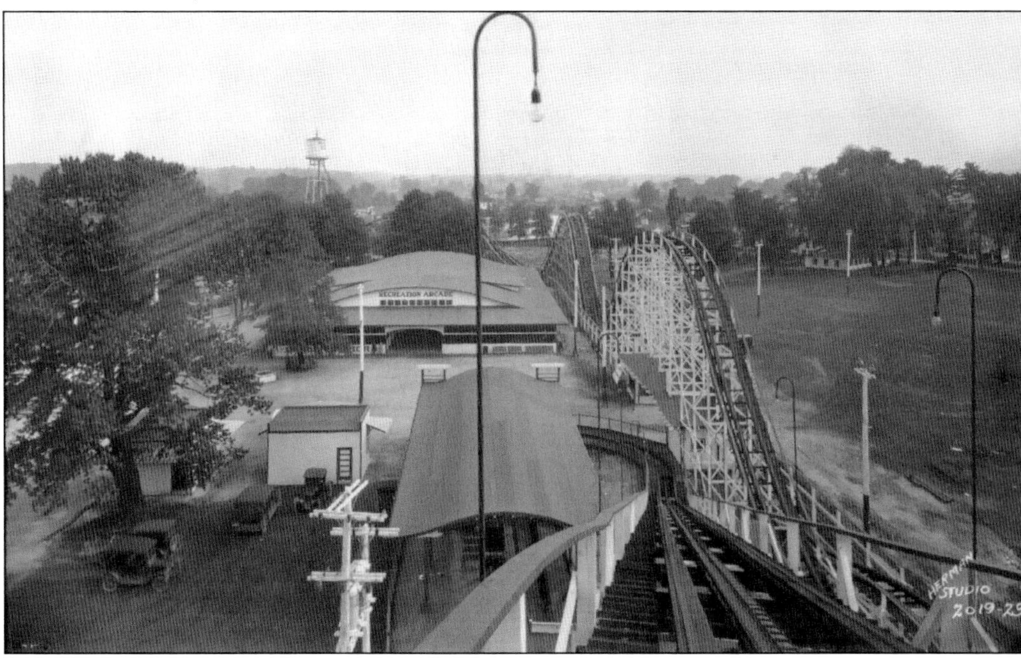

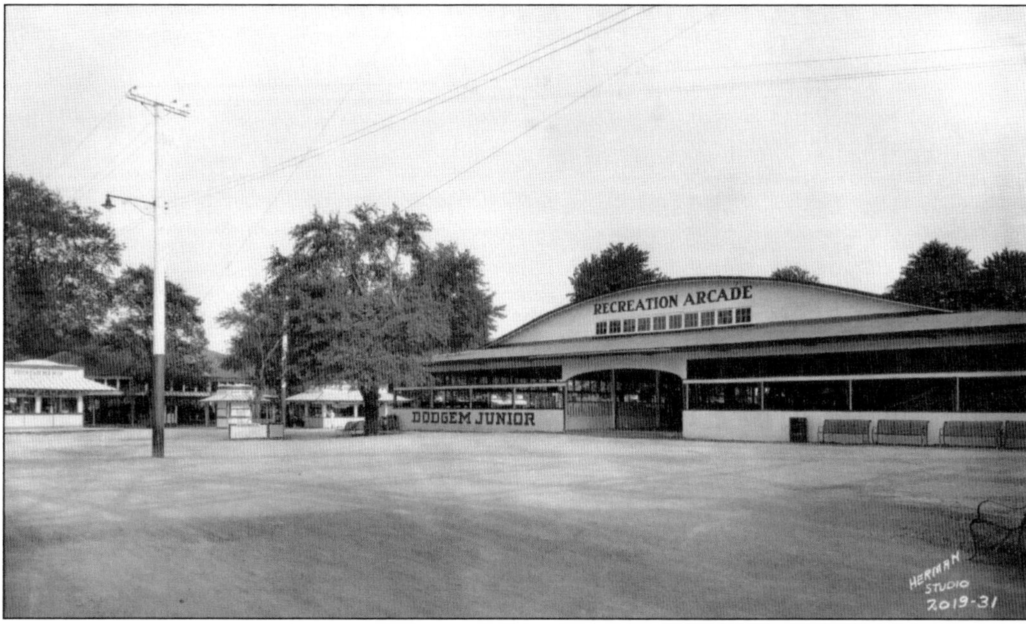

Once entering the reconstructed park, visitors encountered the recreation arcade. This sprawling building was one of Geauga Lake's most enduring structures, lasting until the conversion to Six Flags following the 1999 season. In the early years, the arcade was home to skill games, arcade games, Skee-Ball alleys, refreshment stands, and the Dodgem Junior ride. (Amusement Park Books Collection.)

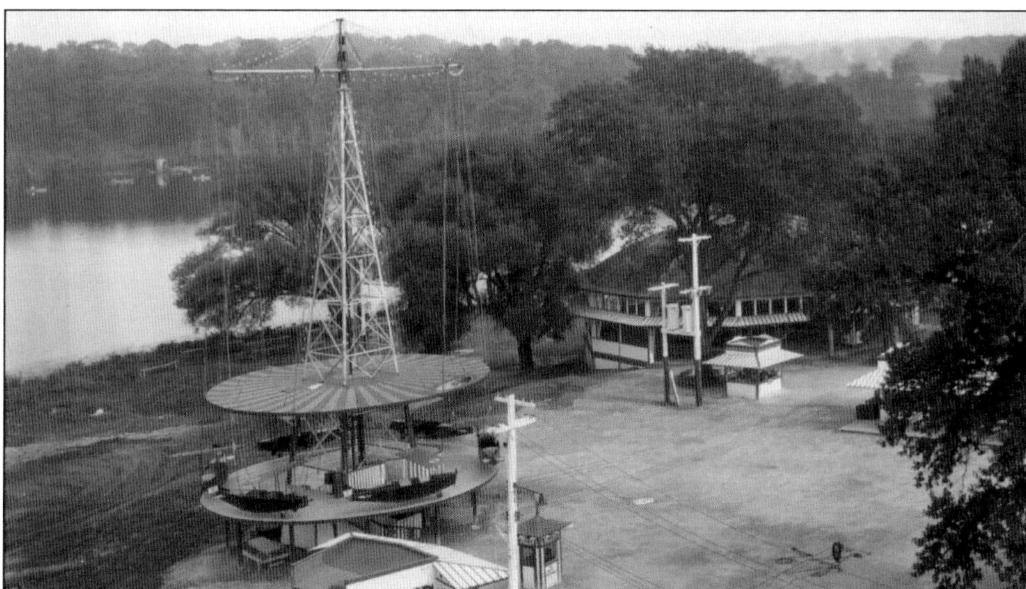
The lake remained a focal point, with several rides and attractions erected near the shore, including the aerial swing. Built by Traver Engineering of Beaver Falls, Pennsylvania, the ride took advantage of the public's fascination with flying, featuring six airplane-shaped cars circling the tower. In 1946, the planes were replaced with stainless-steel rocket ships, creating the ride that so many people remember fondly. (Amusement Park Books Collection.)

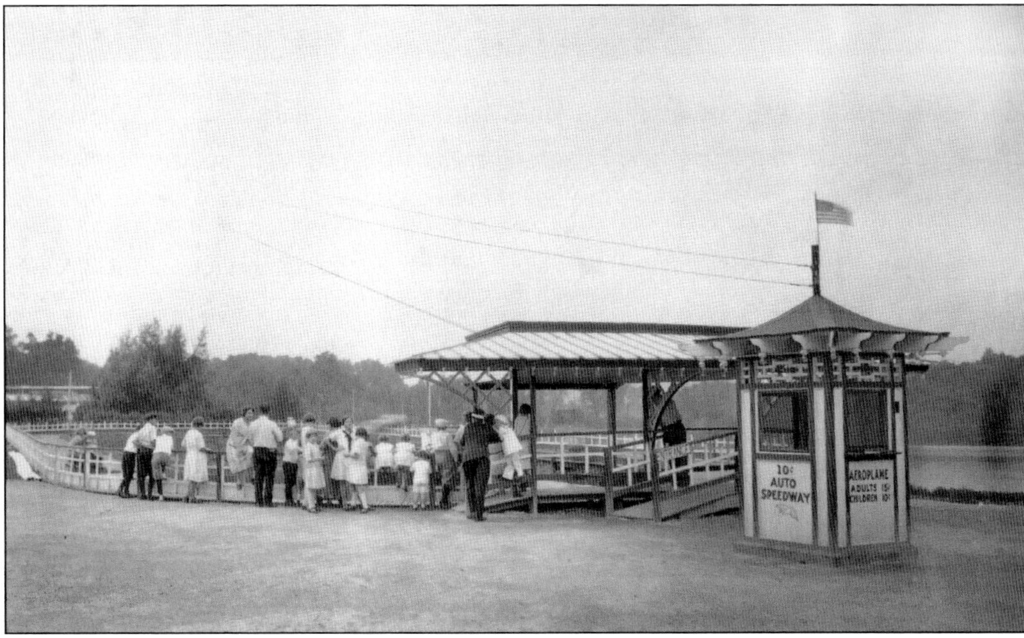

In 1925, the Auto Speedway was next to the aerial swing. Invented just one year earlier by the Custer Specialty Company of Dayton, Ohio, the Auto Speedway consisted of small battery-powered cars traveling around an oval-shaped wooden track. A popular ride in the 1920s and 1930s, the Custer Car was the first example of an auto-based amusement ride, a forerunner of today's turnpike and go-cart rides. (Amusement Park Books Collection.)

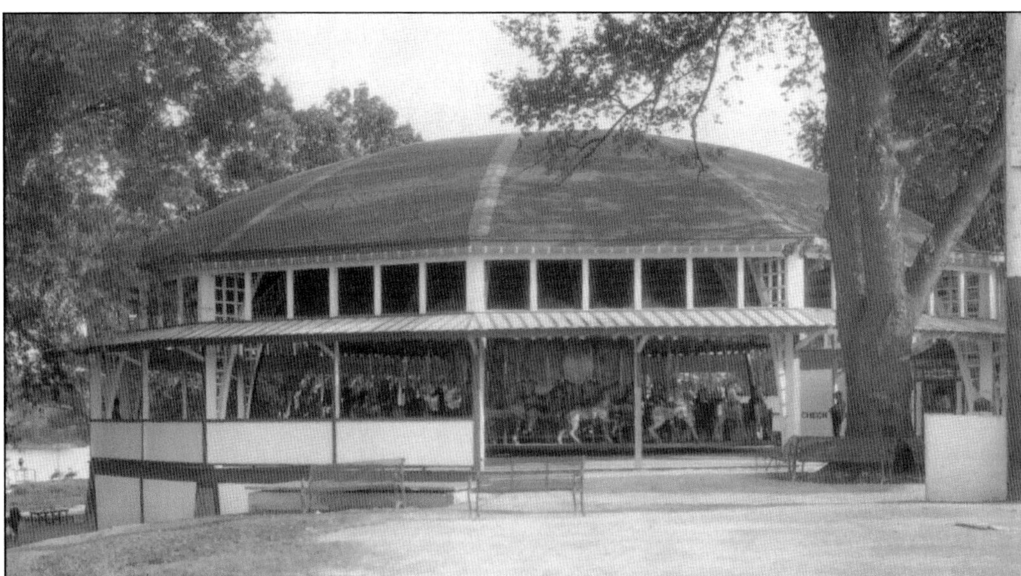

Also located along the midway was a large carousel building. The carousel that most visitors to the park fondly remembered would not appear until 1937. That ride was originally carved by Marcus Illions for the 1926 Sesquicentennial Exposition in Philadelphia, Pennsylvania, and was later placed in storage and acquired by Geauga Lake for $35,000. (Amusement Park Books Collection.)

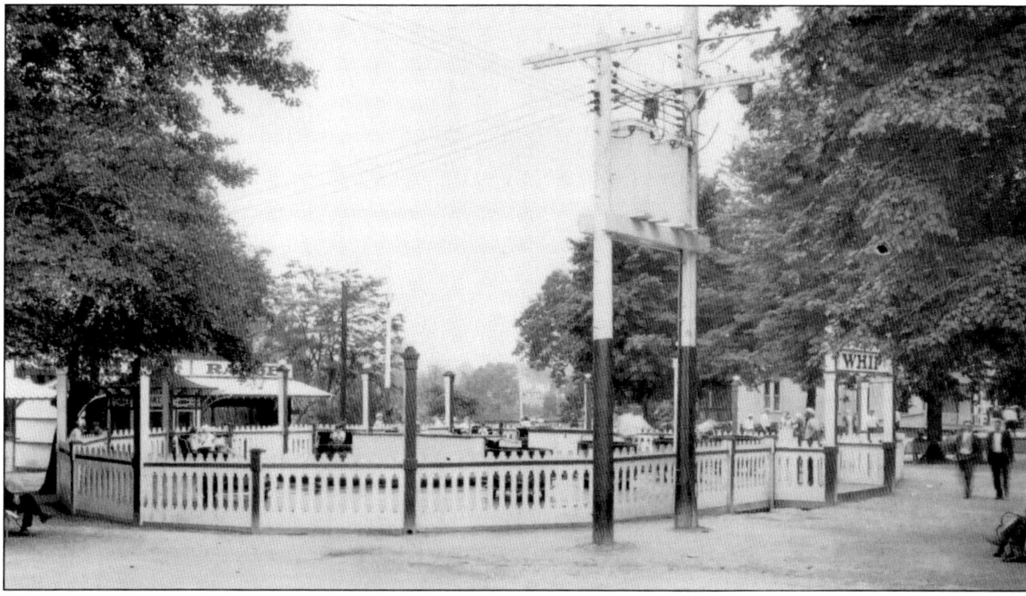

The Whip was another longtime fixture on the midway. Invented in 1918 by William F. Mangels of Coney Island, New York, it is considered one of the first flat rides to operate at amusement parks, the forerunner of today's spinning rides. Geauga Lake's, known for a time as the Snap, operated until 1971. (Amusement Park Books Collection.)

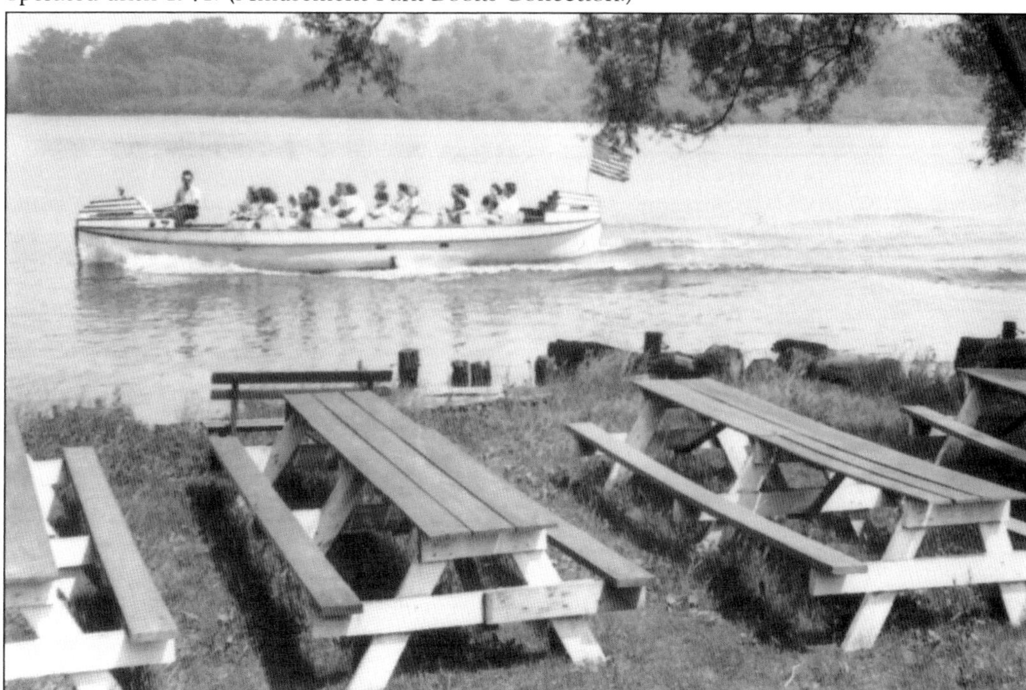

Even with all the new attractions, the 1925 expansion did not forget the traditional appeal of the lake. A broad lawn spread out along its shore, where visitors could picnic and play games. A dock featured rowboats for rental, and a motor launch plied the waters. (Amusement Park Books Collection.)

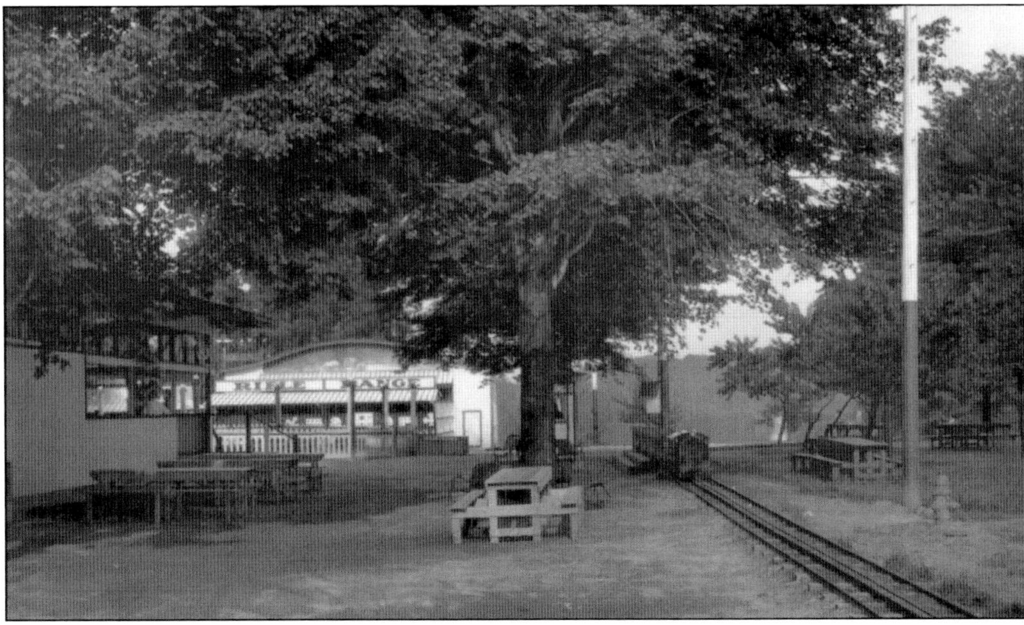

At the end of the midway, Geauga Lake featured what was promoted as the largest rifle range in the nation. Unlike today's shooting galleries, Geauga Lake's featured real rifles. In later years, patrons could also enjoy a pistol range. To the right of the rifle range is the miniature railroad, which circled the grounds, traveling past the Sky Rocket and along the lake. (Amusement Park Books Collection.)

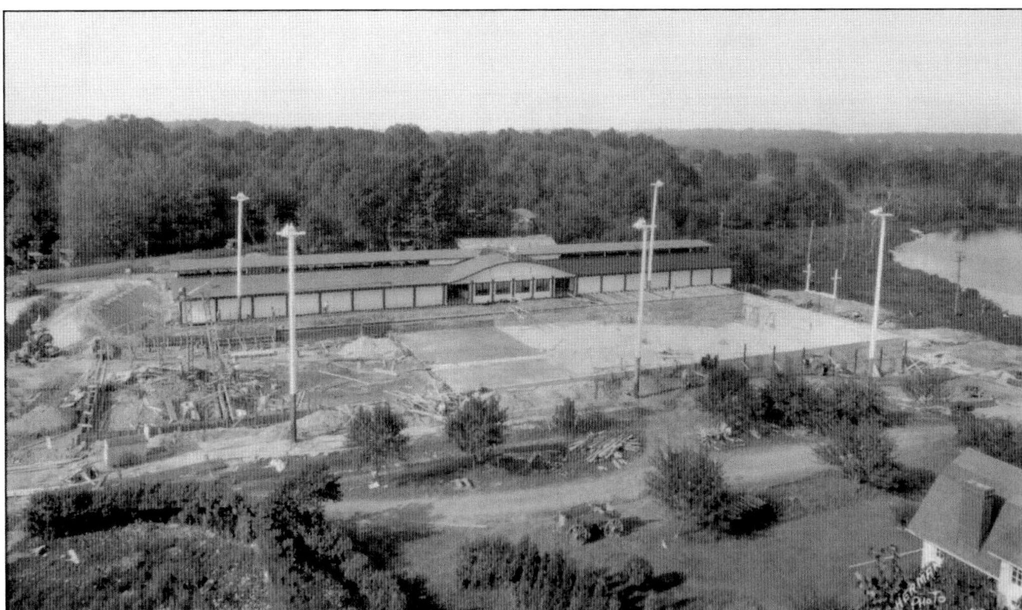

Due to the depth of the lake, swimming was not permitted. Instead, the expansion included the construction of a 350-by-100-foot swimming pool. The pool was still under construction when Geauga Lake opened for the season, but it soon became one of the most popular attractions in the park. In 1926, Johnny Weissmuller set a world record for the 220-yard freestyle in the pool. (Amusement Park Books Collection.)

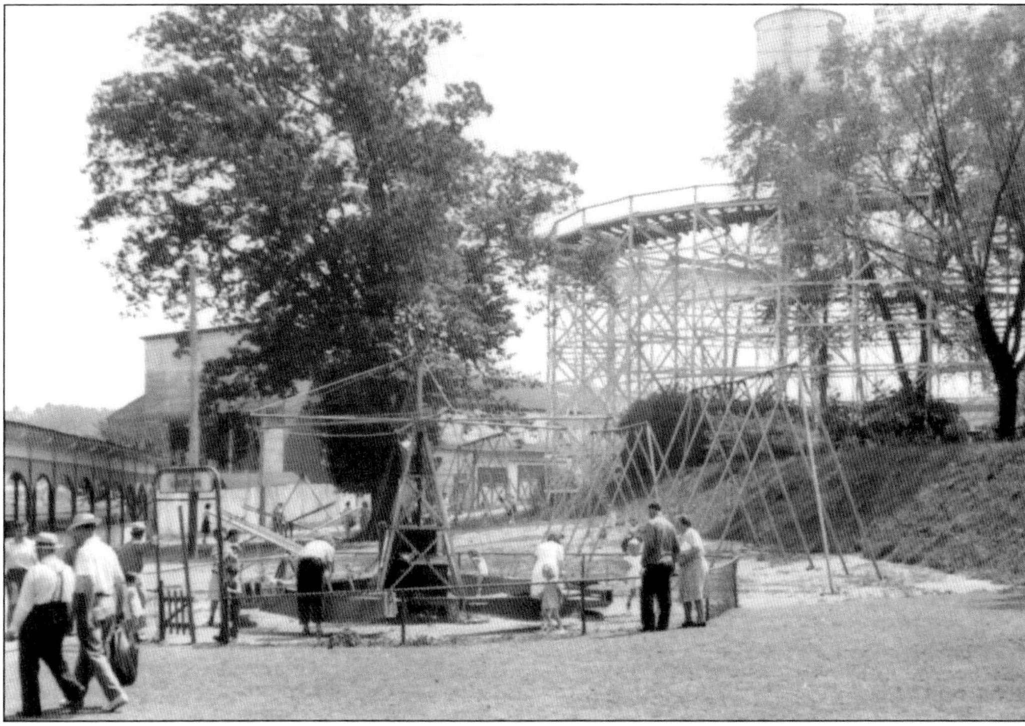

Geauga Lake also made sure to entertain its youngest visitors. At the far end of the park, near the turnaround of the Big Dipper, a children's playground was added. As kiddie rides became more popular in the 1920s, the area grew into a full-blown kiddieland that lasted until the late 1960s, when Funtime developed a new one. (Amusement Park Books Collection.)

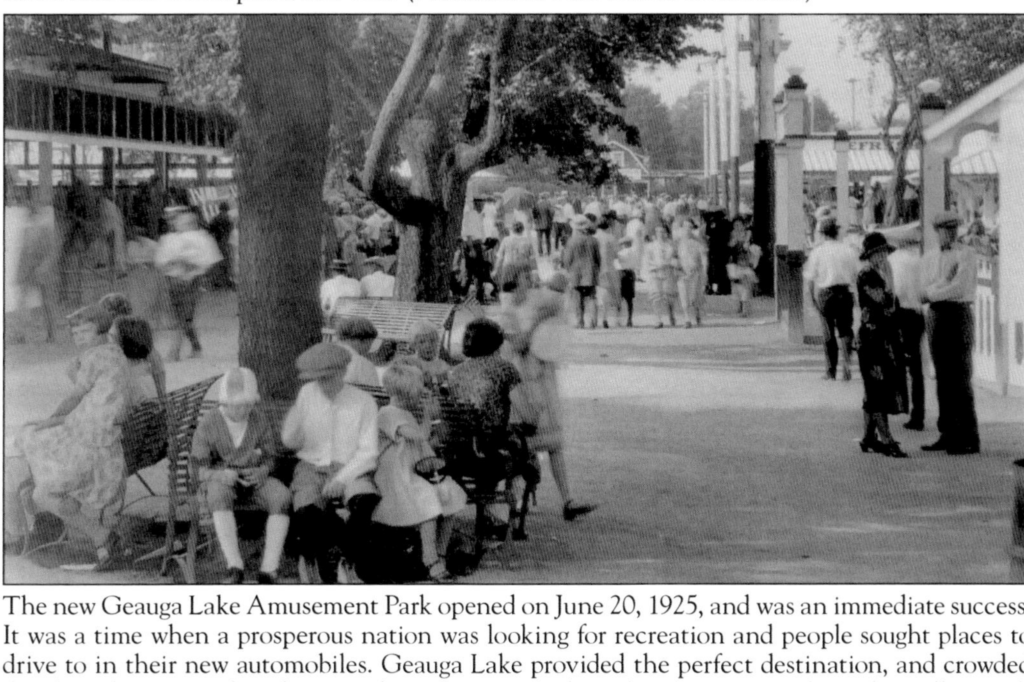

The new Geauga Lake Amusement Park opened on June 20, 1925, and was an immediate success. It was a time when a prosperous nation was looking for recreation and people sought places to drive to in their new automobiles. Geauga Lake provided the perfect destination, and crowded days like the one in this photograph were commonplace. (Amusement Park Books Collection.)

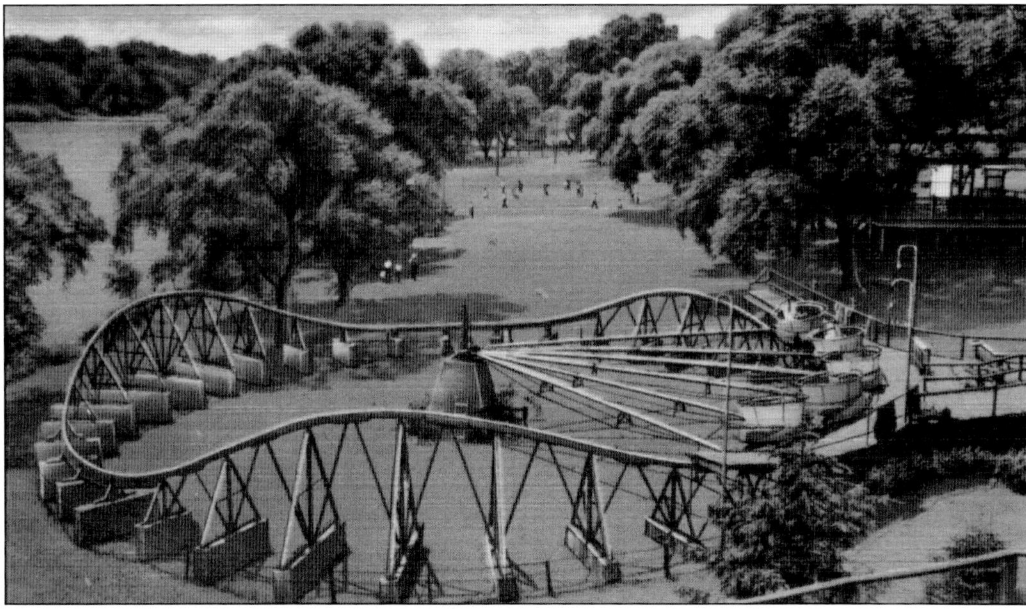

One of the first rides added following the 1925 expansion was the Tumble Bug. Located along the lakeshore, the Tumble Bug consisted of five circular cars that traveled along an undulating circular track, 100 feet in diameter. Manufactured by Traver Engineering of Beaver Falls, Pennsylvania, the ride was invented in the mid-1920s and operated at Geauga Lake until 1977. (Jim Futrell collection.)

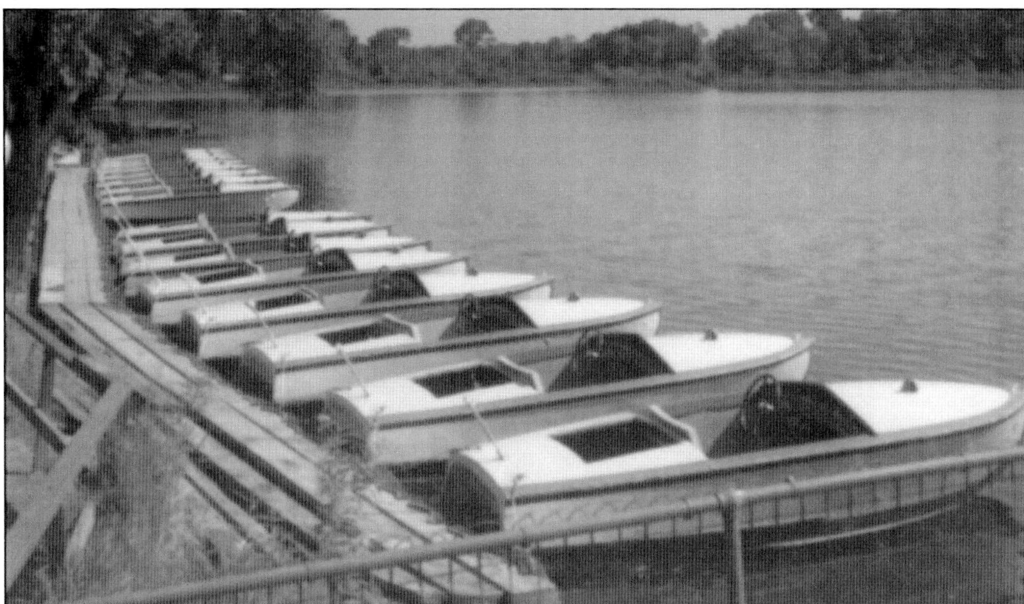

Despite the addition of a large collection of modern mechanical rides, the appeal of the lake never waned. One of the most popular of many different boat rides was the U-Drive Boats, slow-moving two-passenger watercraft that customers could drive on their own in a section of the lake. Added in 1941, they were a popular attraction until the mid-1970s. (Amusement Park Books Collection.)

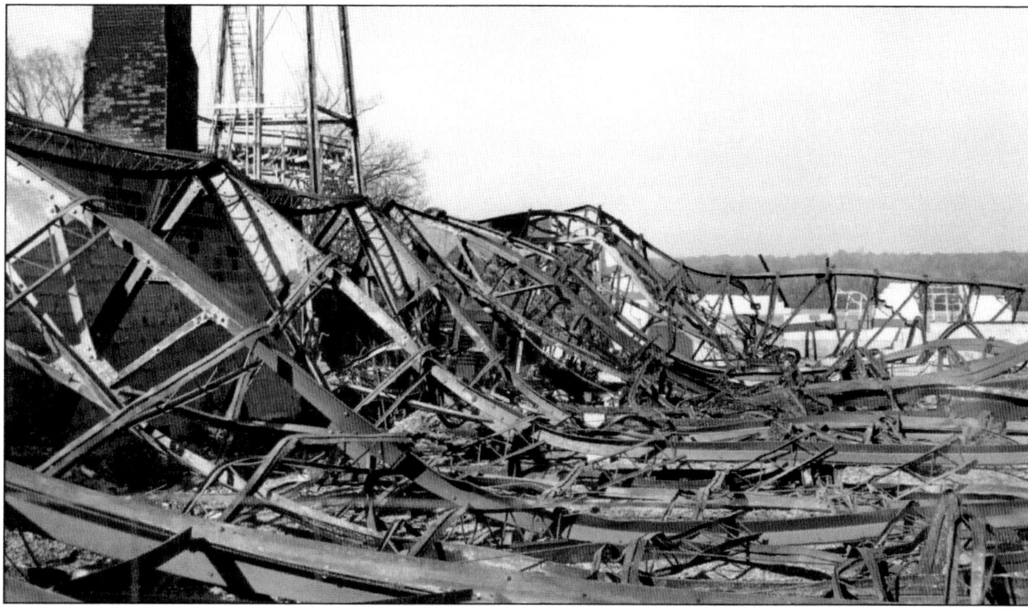

On April 9, 1952, just before the start of the season, a major fire destroyed the bowling alley and original 1920 dance hall. It had been converted into a roller rink in 1941 following the opening of a new ballroom. It took firefighters from six communities to keep the fire from spreading to the Sky Rocket, just 39 feet away (to the left just beyond the water tower). Damage was estimated at $200,000. (Amusement Park Books Collection.)

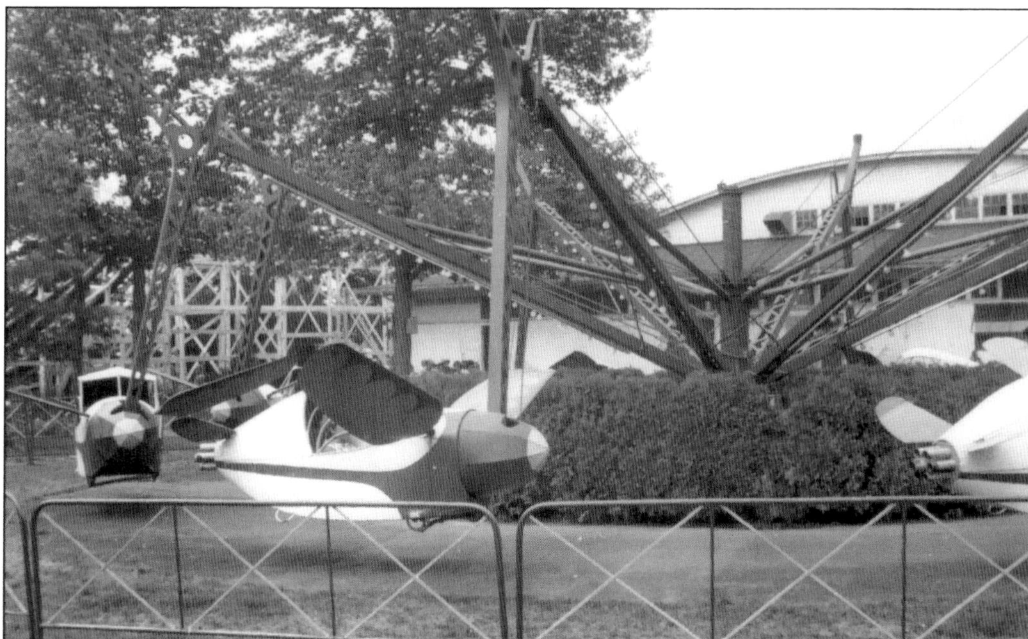

Despite the fire, Geauga Lake continued to expand. In 1952, the park added the Fly-O-Plane. It was built by Eyerly Aircraft of Salem, Oregon, and was one of the first participatory rides in which customers could flip the planes completely upside down. Later relocated to Geauga Lake's western area, it remained a midway staple until 1985. (Amusement Park Books Collection.)

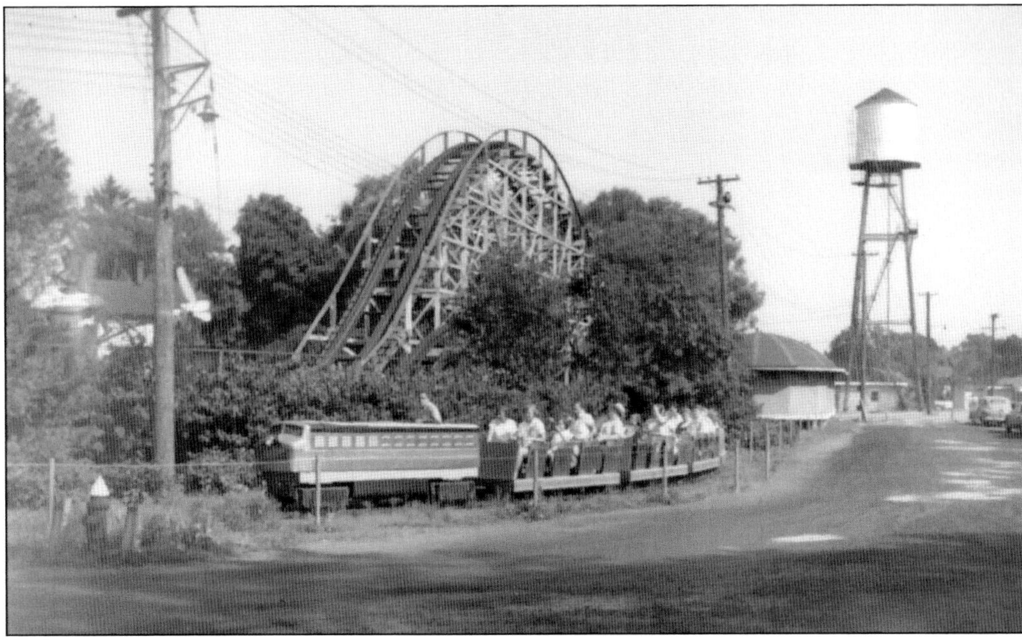

Geauga Lake continued its expansion in 1953 with four new rides, including a new train ride that traveled the length of the roller coaster. The train was manufactured by the National Amusement Devices Company (NAD) of Dayton, Ohio, one of the largest manufacturers of amusement rides in the mid-20th century. It operated until 1981. (Amusement Park Books Collection.)

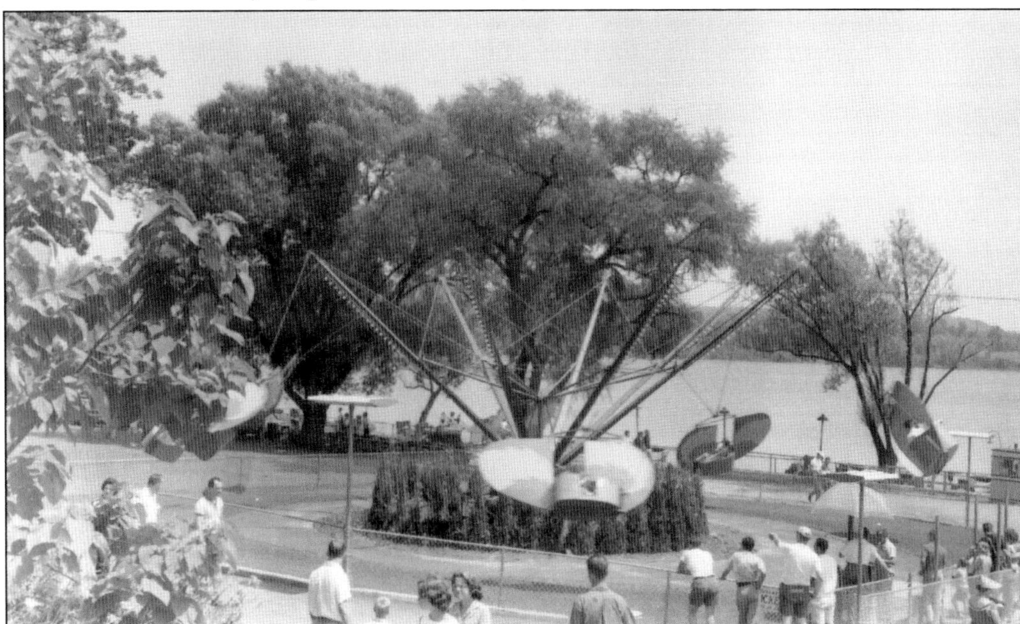

The Flying Scooter joined the lineup in 1958. Built by the Bisch Rocco Company of Chicago, Illinois, the Flying Scooter was unique in that people could control the motion of each tub. Originally on the lakefront, the ride was relocated to a new midway area next to the Corkscrew in 1984 and then the western area, where it operated until the 1999 season. (Amusement Park Books Collection.)

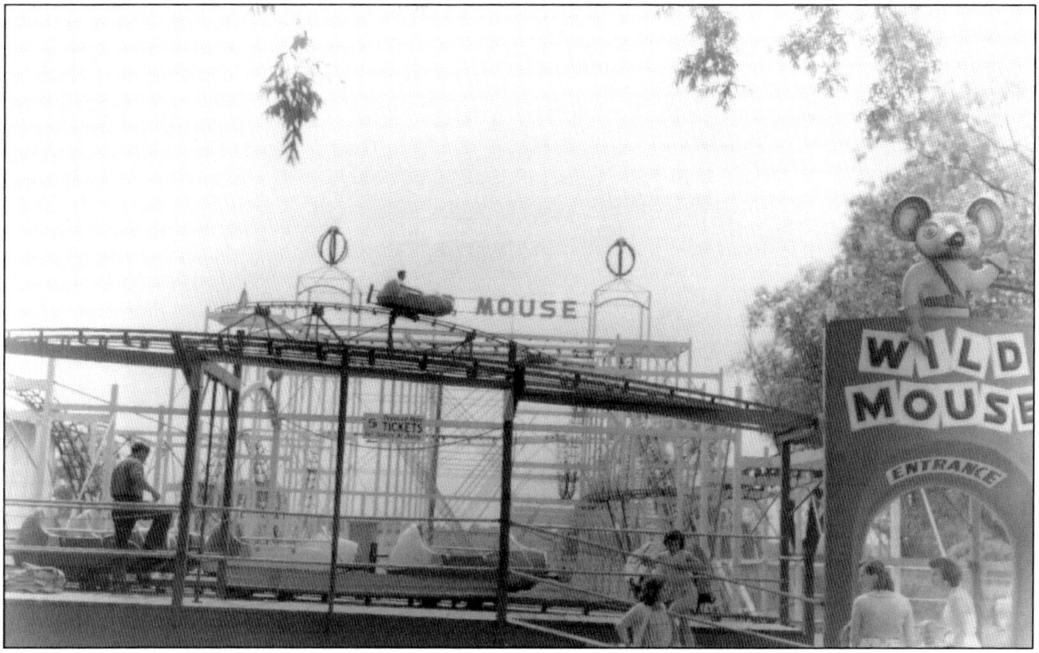

Geauga Lake gained a new roller coaster in 1958 when the Wild Mouse opened. A popular attraction in the late 1950s and early 1960s, the Wild Mouse featured a steel track with a series of hairpin turns providing the illusion of falling off the edges. The Wild Mouse was a midway staple through the 1970 season. (Amusement Park Books Collection.)

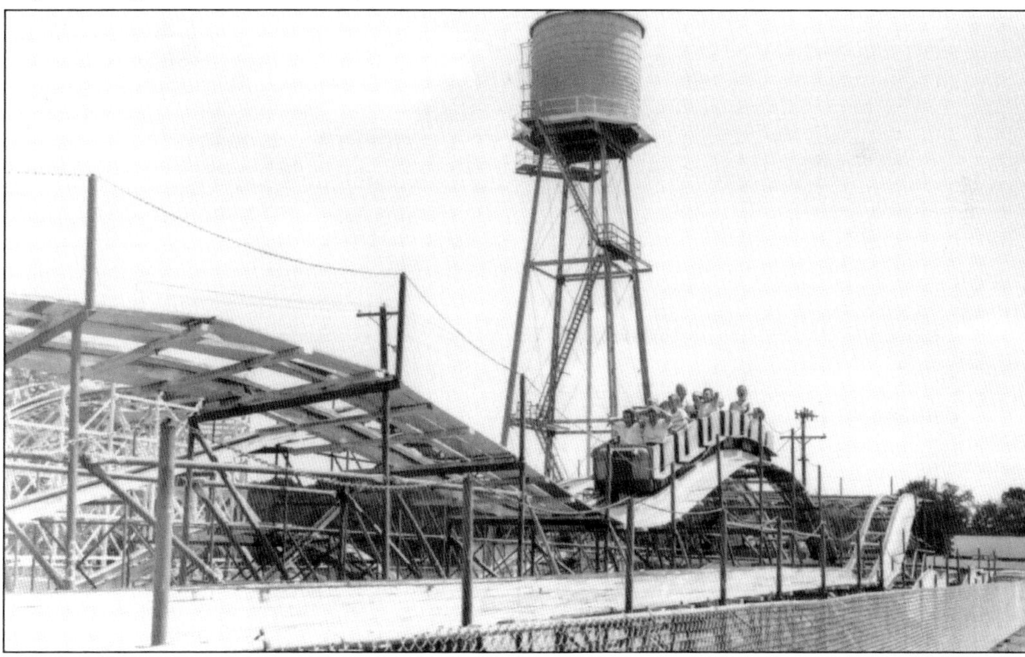

With the postwar baby boom in full effect during the 1950s, Geauga Lake also added a roller coaster for its smaller riders—the Little Dipper. Constructed by NAD, the oval-shaped wooden-track ride stood about 25 feet tall and provided a great introduction to roller coasters for the park's youngest visitors. (Amusement Park Books Collection.)

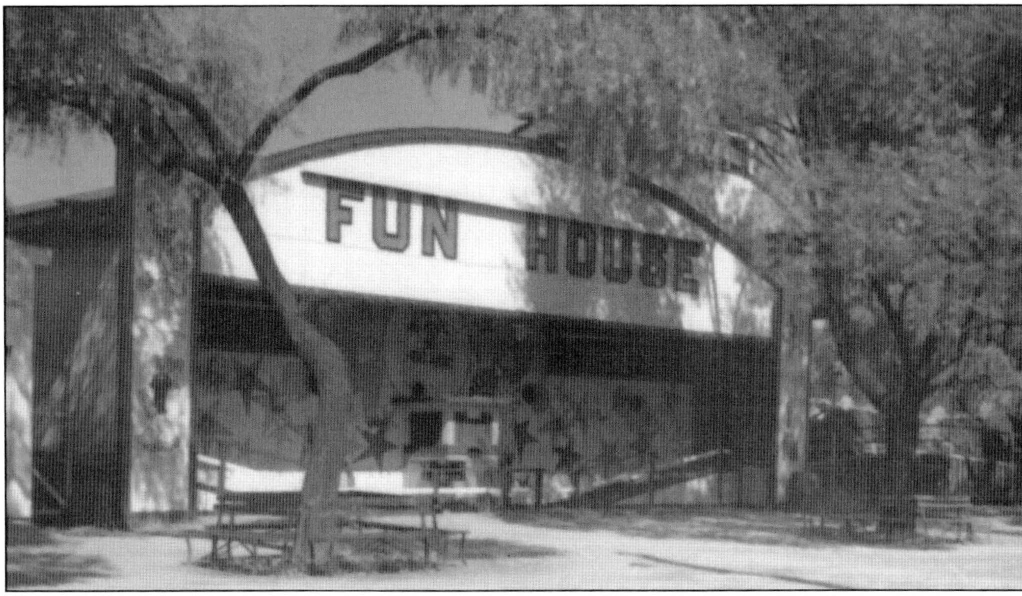

For many years, the Fun House was a staple on Geauga Lake's midway. The walk-through attraction featured a variety of elements, including the rotating barrel, human roulette wheel, and shaking floors. In 1977, the attraction was converted into the Palace Theater, which remained until the park closed. (Amusement Park Books Collection.)

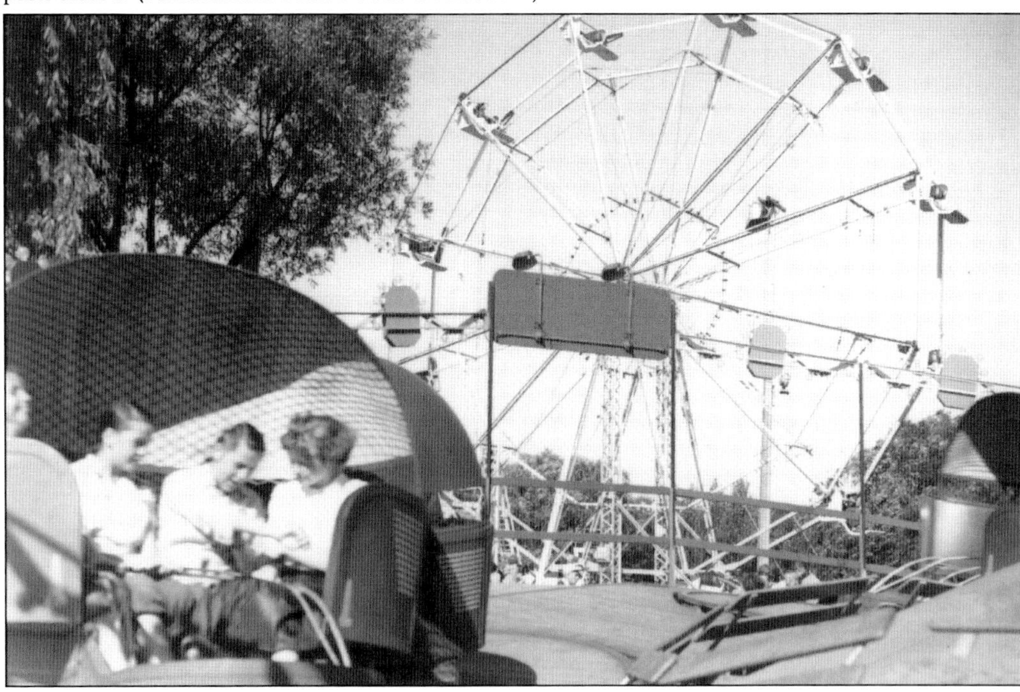

For many years, two midway staples occupied the area between the Fun House and swimming pool. The Tilt-A-Whirl in front was built by Sellner Manufacturing of Faribault, Minnesota, but Geauga Lake had several during its existence. Towering behind it was the Ferris wheel, manufactured by the Eli Bridge Company of Jacksonville, Illinois; Geauga Lake's provided a view down the main midway. (Amusement Park Books Collection.)

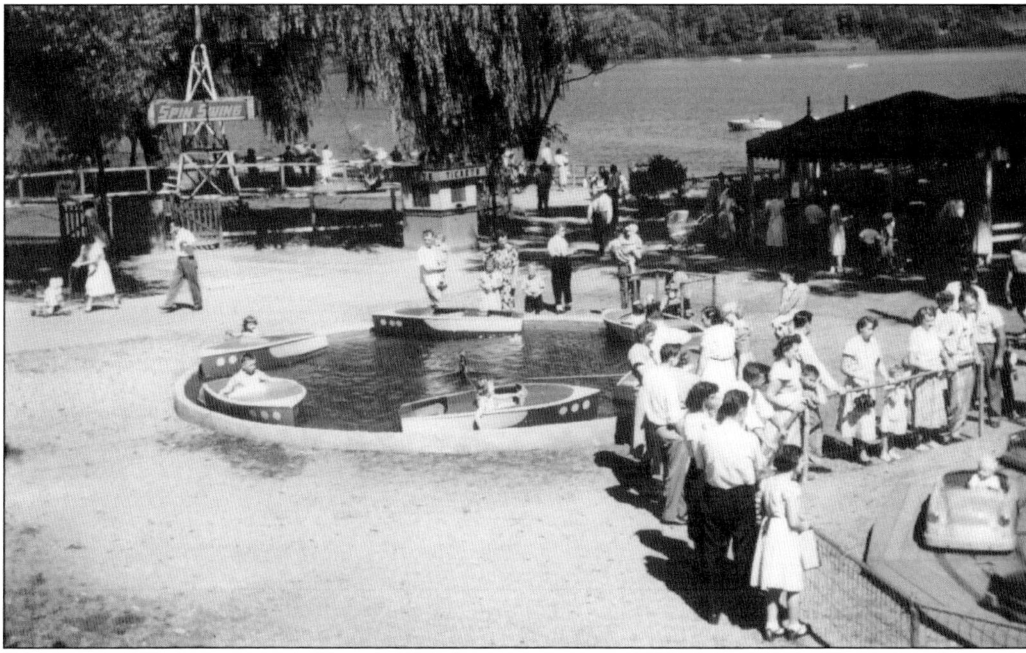

While kiddie rides had been a staple of Geauga Lake since around the 1925 expansion, the small children's area grew in the 1950s as the postwar baby boom increased the number of young visitors, and manufacturers responded with a wide selection of scaled-down rides. Included were the kiddie boat and turnpike rides, both manufactured by the Allan Herschell Company of Tonawanda, New York. (Amusement Park Books Collection.)

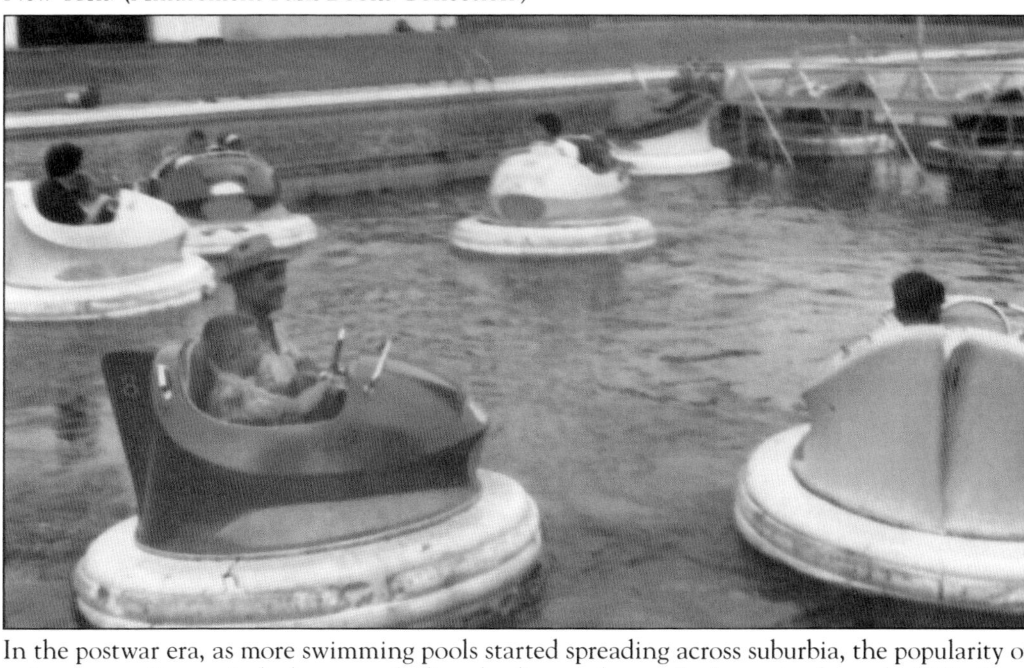

In the postwar era, as more swimming pools started spreading across suburbia, the popularity of swimming at Geauga Lake began to decline, leading to the pool's closure in the early 1960s. For a brief period, the pool was used as a pond for bumper boats, which provided a water-based version of the popular bumper car ride. (Amusement Park Books Collection.)

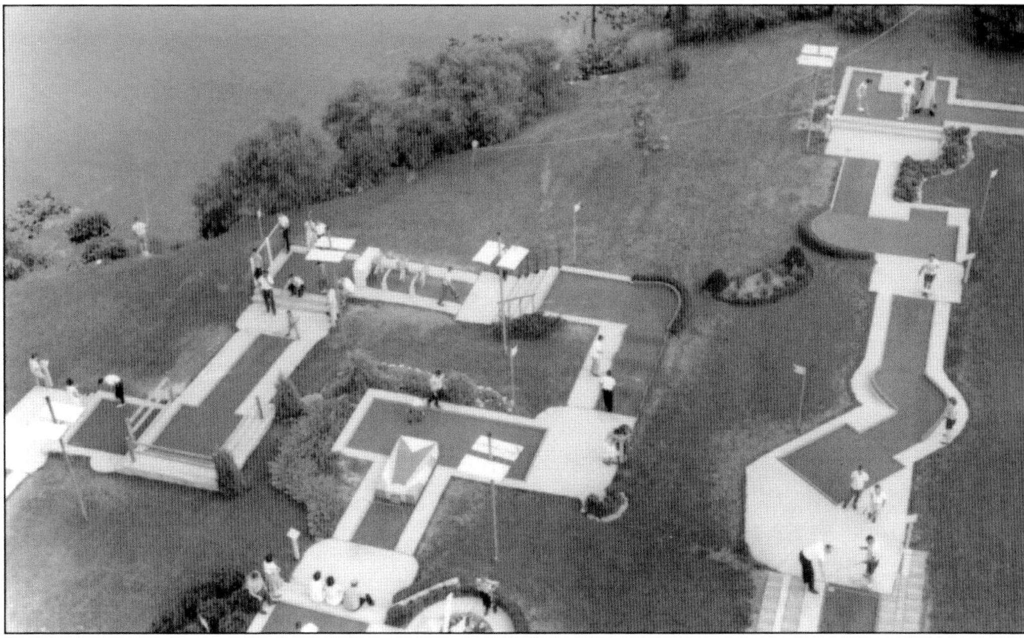

In 1960, the park undertook one of the final expansions of the pre-Funtime era: a $30,000 miniature golf course was constructed along the shore of the lake. To celebrate the opening, the park held a season-long tournament whose winner received a trip to the Miss America pageant in Atlantic City, New Jersey. It was replaced by a new course in 1975. (Amusement Park Books Collection.)

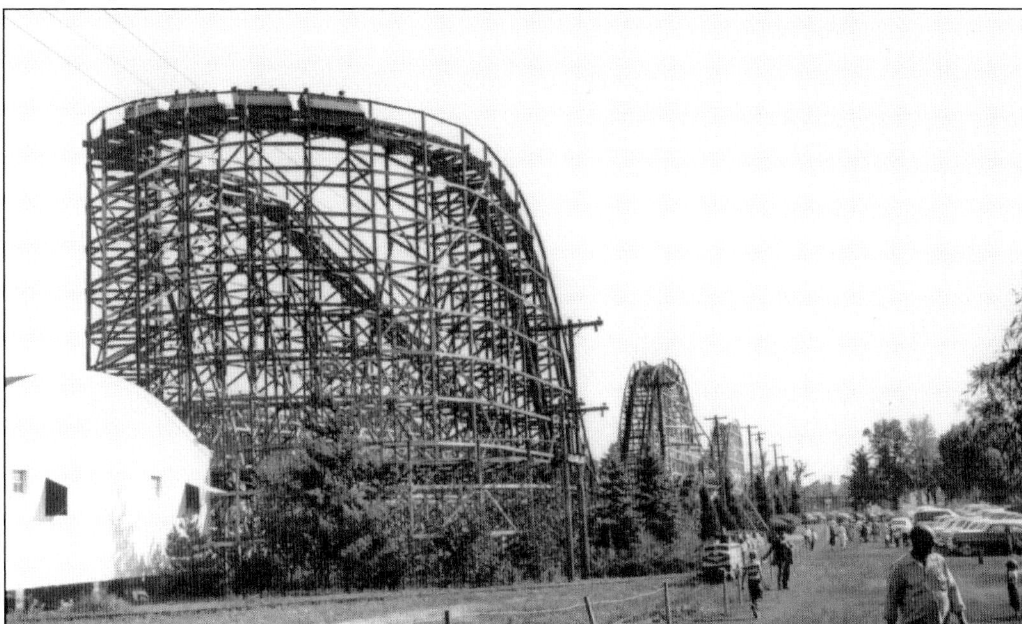

Despite the changes in the park, the roller coaster, renamed the Clipper in 1947, remained its signature ride, defining the park's front boundary. But by the 1960s, Geauga Lake was starting to struggle, facing many of the same issues as its peers—old infrastructure, tired attractions, aging owners, no apparent heirs, and competition from other regional amusement parks. (Amusement Park Books Collection.)

Two

A New Era Dawns 1969–1976

In 1968, at Ohio's Cedar Point, manager of general services Gaspar Lococo and director of marketing Earl Gascoigne were sitting in a staff meeting when they noticed that their chairman gruffly discarded a note, saying, "I'm tired of other people always wanting me to buy their junk." Curious at his outburst, the pair fished the piece of paper out of the trash and found out what junk he was talking about—Geauga Lake was for sale.

Lococo and Gascoigne had both been part of the transformation of Cedar Point from a rundown amusement park into one of the Midwest's leading destinations and were anxious to strike out on their own. The pair met with the Schreyer family, who had taken over the park following the death of William Kuhlman in 1944, and were given 18 months to raise the funds to purchase the operation. With no heirs, the Schreyers were ready to retire.

Knowing that they would not be able to come up with the money on their own, Lococo and Gascoigne teamed up with investment bank the Ohio Company to sell stock to raise the $1 million needed to buy the park along with a secondary offering to raise money for improvements. By fall 1968, the deal came together, and they brought in Cedar Point's manager of operations, M.P. Jacobson, and auditor Dale Van Voorhis to round out the executive team.

The park they purchased was desperately in need of an update. There had been few new attractions added in recent years, the old wooden buildings were worn out, and the walkways consisted of gravel. Attendance had fallen to 250,000 from more than a million in the 1950s, and revenue was just $795,000.

To turn things around, the new management team developed a 10-year master plan and announced a five-year, $5 million improvement program that would double the size of the amusement park, add a hotel, and build a sky ride across the lake to a new oceanarium developed by SeaWorld, Inc. The new company was called Funtime, Inc., and a new era began for Geauga Lake.

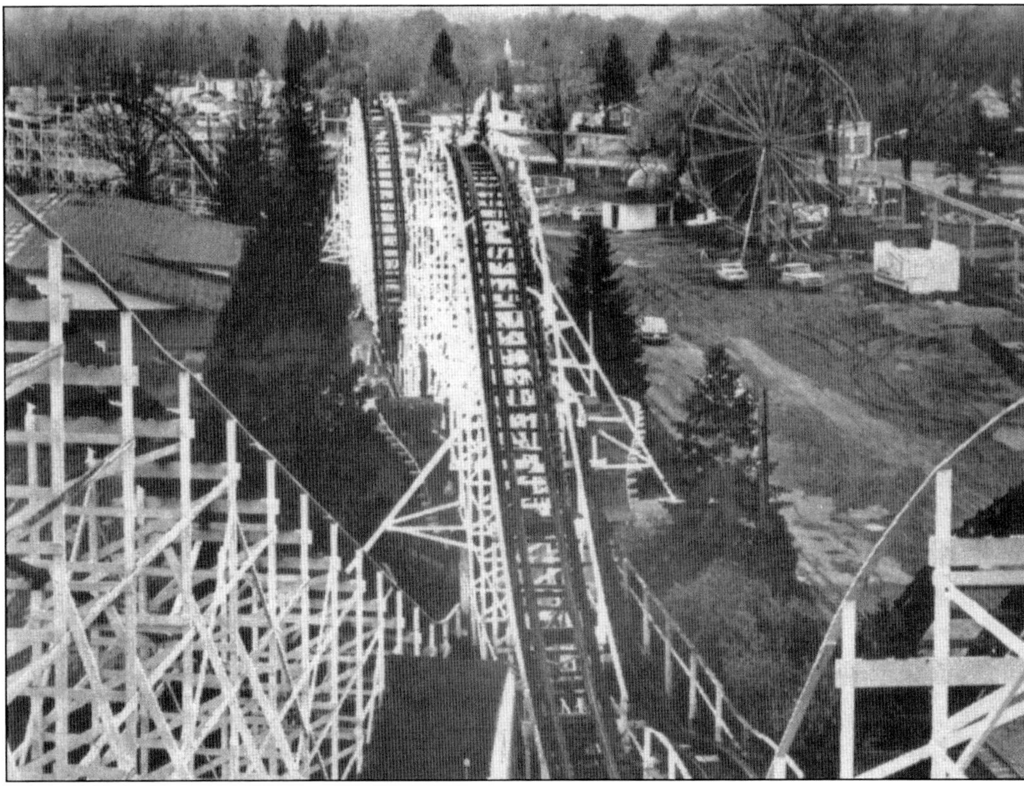

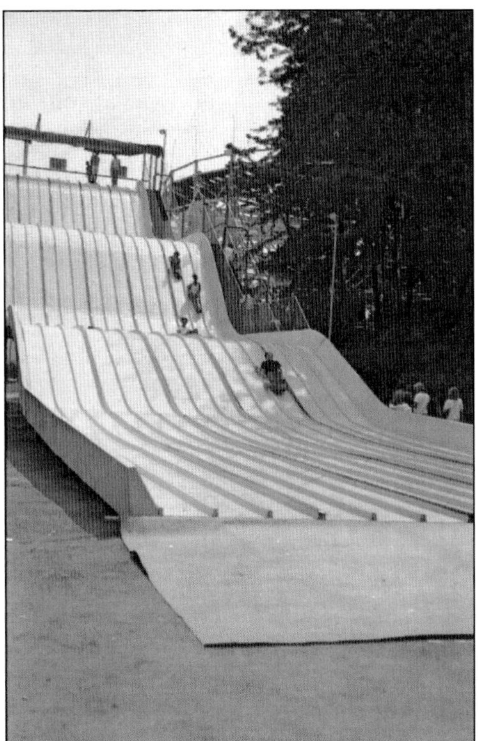

Funtime quickly went to work revitalizing the park, announcing plans to spend at least $1 million annually on improvements. This photograph shows construction well under way to expand the park's boundaries beyond the Clipper for the 1969 season, including a Ferris wheel and a new kiddieland behind it. (Amusement Park Books Collection.)

The giant slide was one of the other new attractions in 1969. Reflecting a popular trend of the era, where giant slides were erected across the country, Geauga Lake featured one of the larger models, with 15 fiberglass lanes. The slide was located near the Big Dipper's turnaround until it was repurposed as a waterslide following the 1982 season. (Jim Futrell collection.)

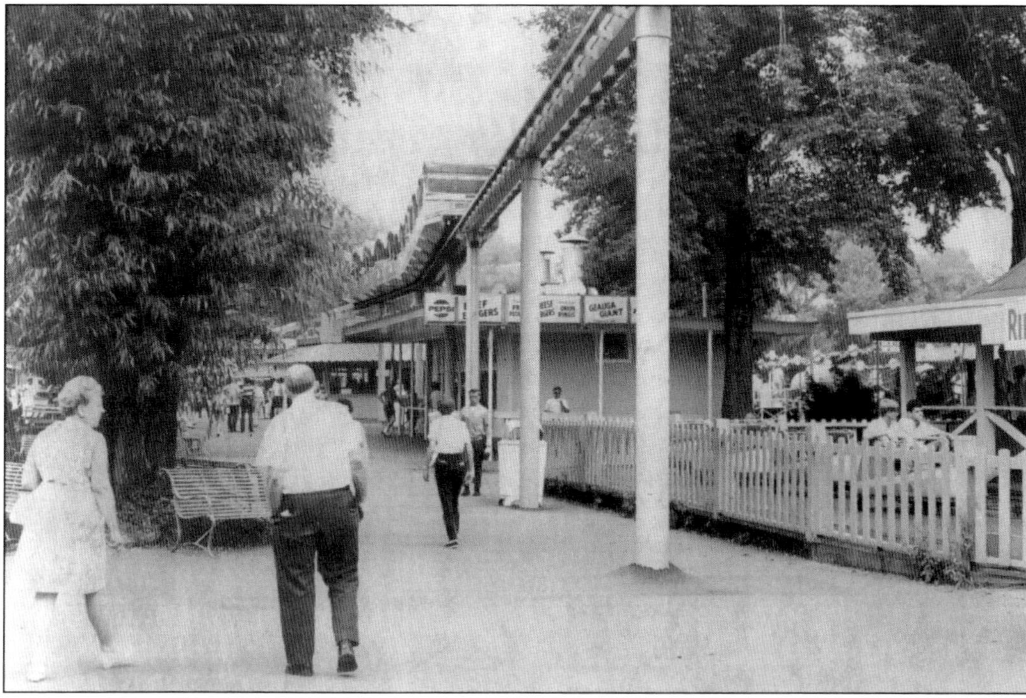

Funtime knew that it had to make a statement, demonstrating that the park was intending to compete in the modern era. As a result, a new monorail ride anchored the improvement program. The ride was built by Universal Design, a company formed in New Jersey in the 1960s to manufacture scaled-down theme park–style attractions for smaller amusement parks. The $500,000 ride featured 2,500 feet of track and completely circled the park, providing a bird's-eye view of its transformation. The station was located in a portion of the former parking lot, and for the first time since 1925, gave the park a new front entrance—underneath the monorail's loading station. (Both, Amusement Park Books Collection.)

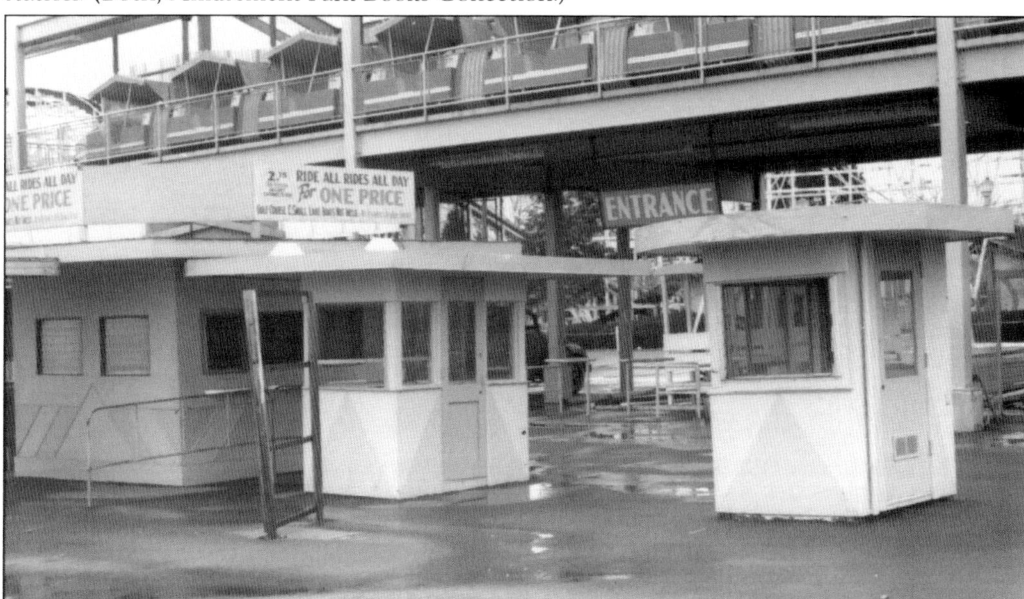

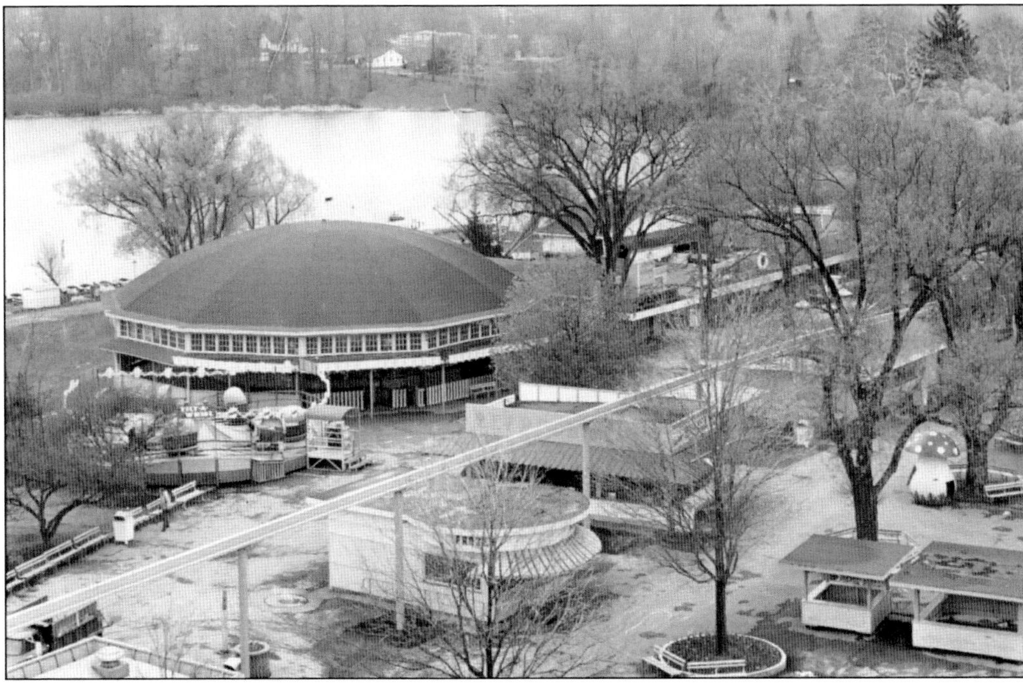

This photograph, taken from the top of the Clipper, soon to be renamed the Big Dipper, shows the original midway with the new monorail track traveling over many of the older concession stands, providing a leisurely tour of both the original park and the new expansion. (Amusement Park Books Collection.)

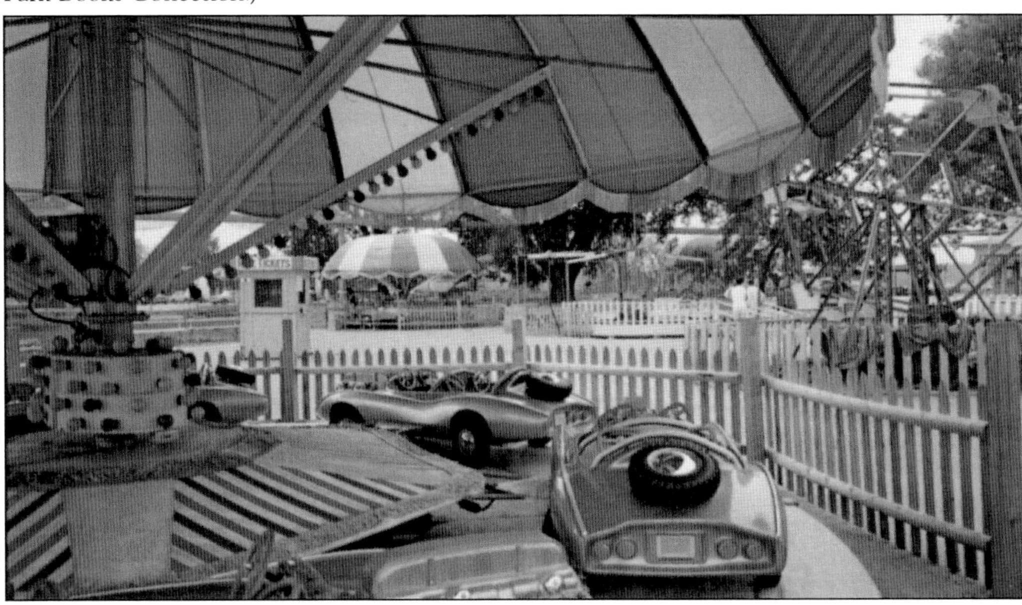

A total of six new rides were added for Funtime's debut season at Geauga Lake. A Trabant spinning ride was imported from Germany, while three new kiddie rides were purchased from Hampton for the new kiddieland. Hampton was one of the largest manufacturers of kiddie rides at the time. Its rides were distinguished by their colorful umbrella canopies, shiny ride cars, and distinctive buzzers. (Jim Futrell collection.)

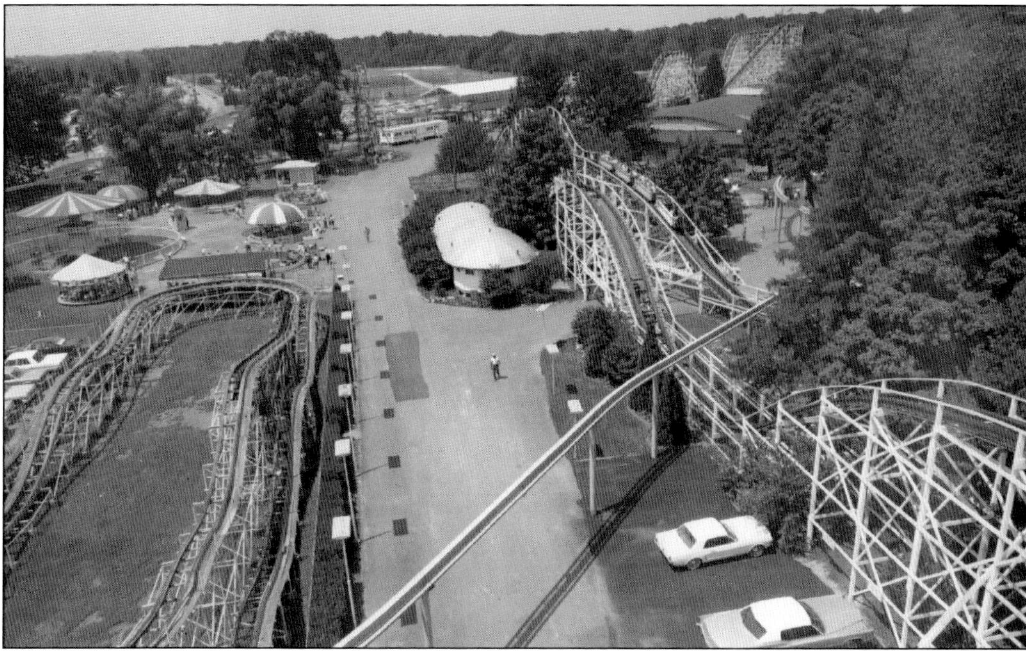

This photograph, taken from Geauga Lake's water tower, shows many of the improvements undertaken in 1969. Just beyond the Little Dipper is the new kiddieland, combining old and new rides. The white-roofed structure in the top center is the loading station for the monorail, with the new park entrance underneath. (Amusement Park Books Collection.)

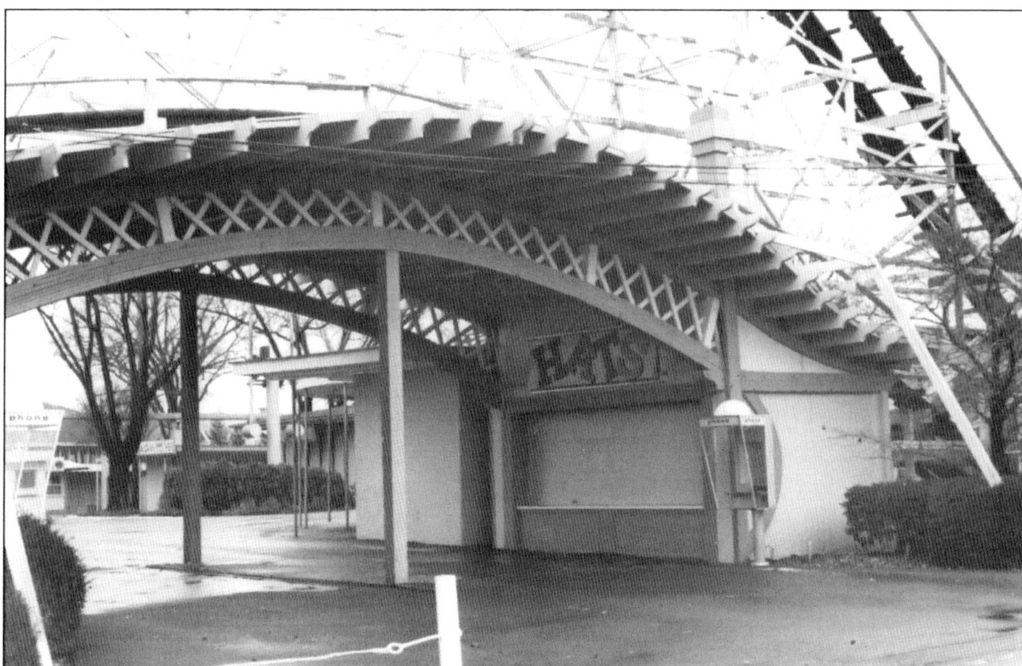

Despite the development of the new front gate, the original 1925 entrance still remained a signature element of the revitalized park, with concession stands at either end of the distinctive arch, including this one selling souvenir hats. (Amusement Park Books Collection.)

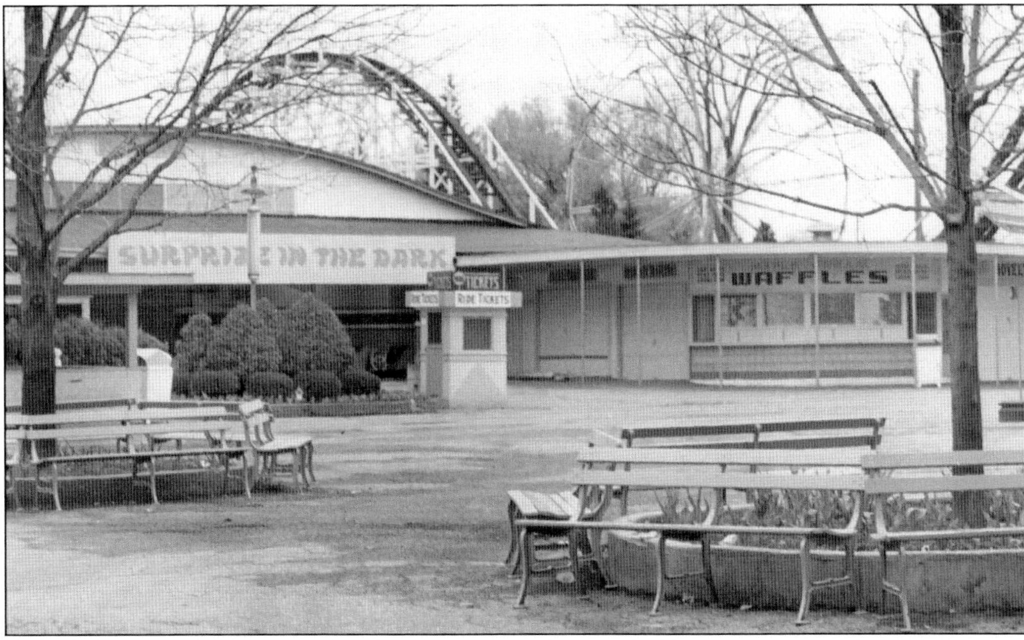

Many of Geauga Lake's older rides remained in service as the park modernized. The Surprise in the Dark was a dark ride built by the Pretzel Amusement Ride Company in 1942 in the recreation arcade. Originally known as the Blackout, it remained in operation until the early 1970s. (Amusement Park Books Collection.)

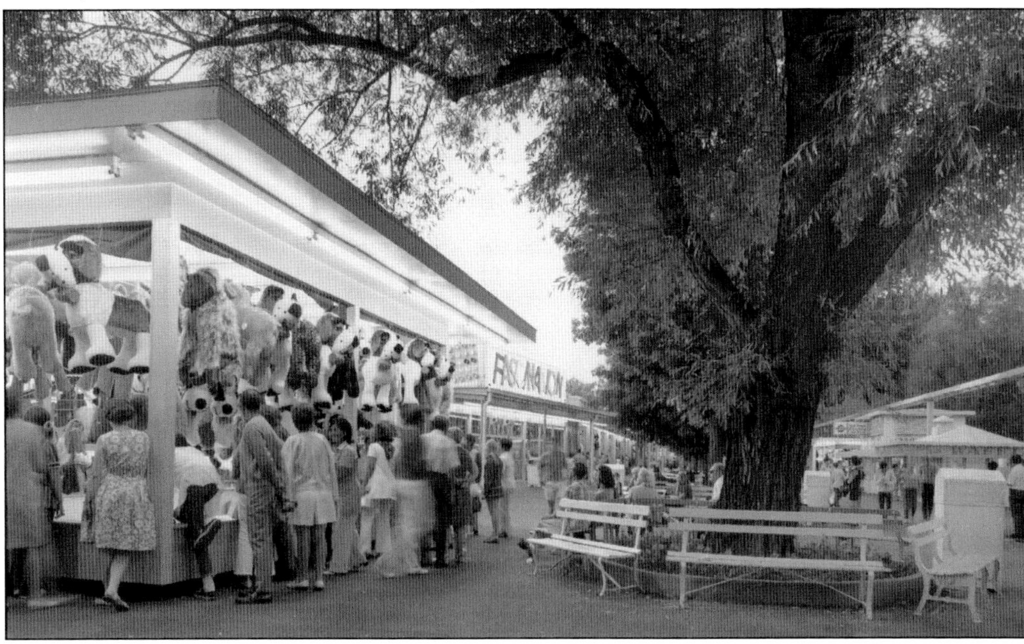

Along with adding new rides, the improvement program included 5,000 gallons of new paint and replacing the aging wooden concession stands with modern metal buildings. This brought a new feel to Geauga Lake's traditional midway area, although the appeal of the games and food stands remained as timeless as ever. The 1969 season was a success, with revenue growing by 36 percent and attendance nearly doubling. (Amusement Park Books Collection.)

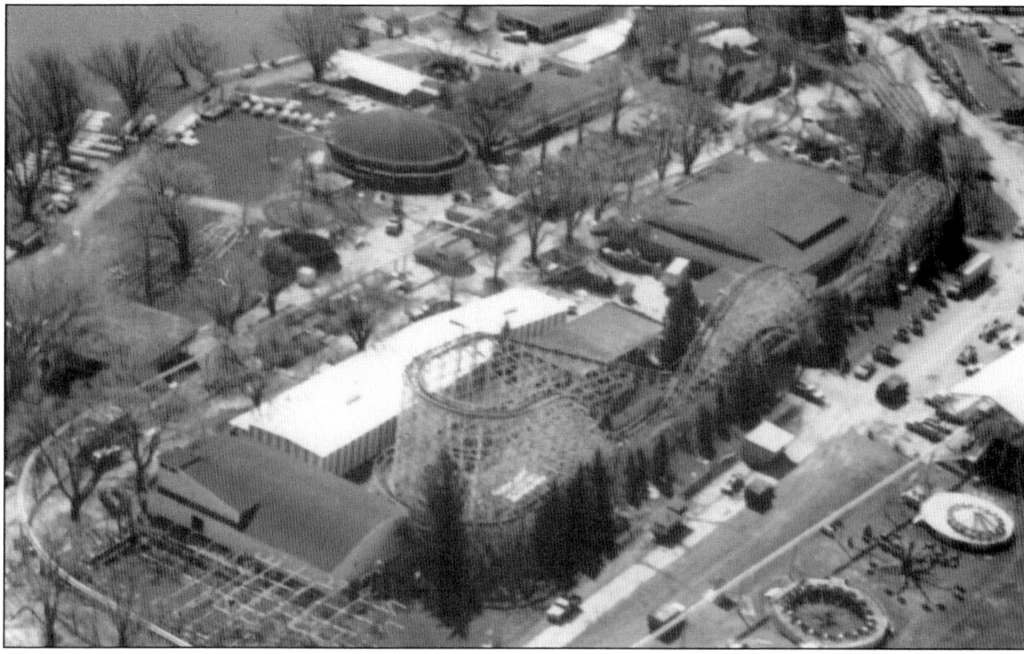

This aerial view, most likely taken in 1970, shows how the revitalized park was changing. The new monorail ride is a prominent feature, while an assortment of new rides line a new midway area in front of the Big Dipper in what was a parking area. Older attractions like the Wild Mouse and fun house on the left would both soon be replaced. (Amusement Park Books Collection.)

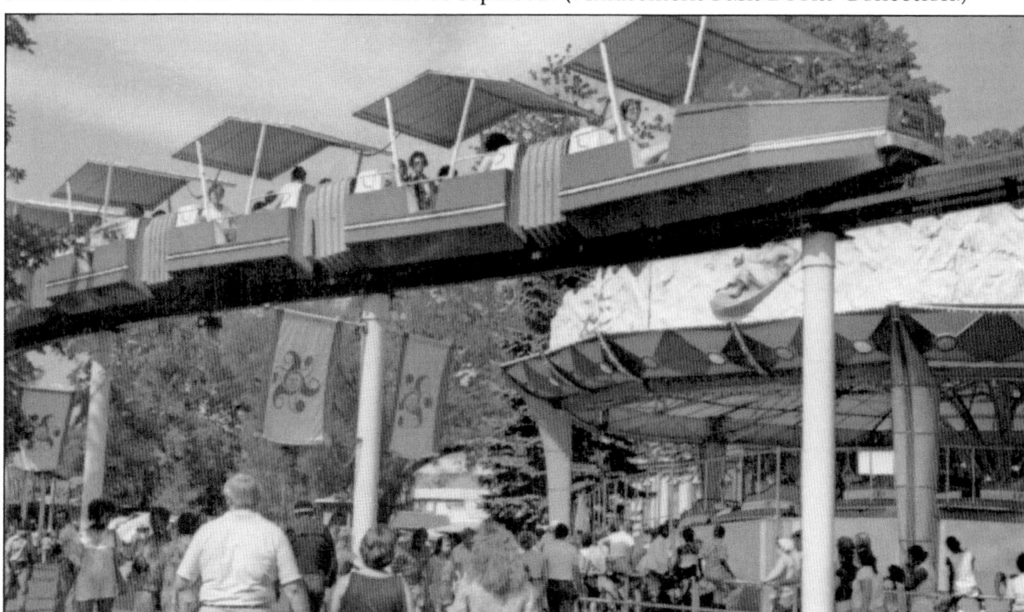

Funtime spent another $1 million in improvements for the 1970 season, adding the Wharf restaurant, a new Dodgem building, and a "funway" with several new rides, including the Spider, Flying Coaster, and Himalaya, shown above behind the monorail. The Himalaya, like many of the rides added during this time, were imported from Europe, which at the time had a reputation for providing the newest and flashiest rides. (Jim Futrell collection.)

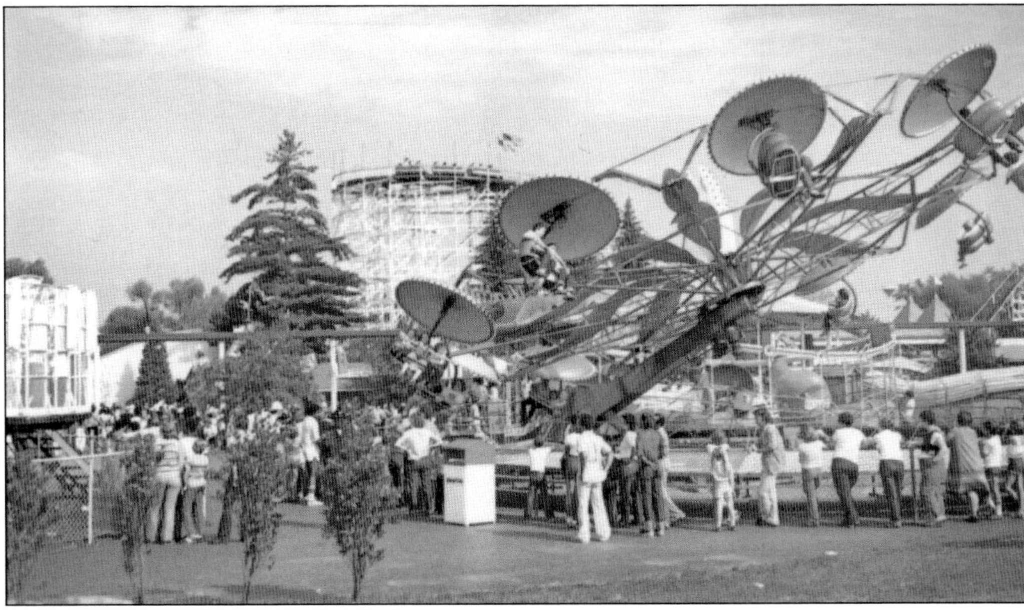

In 1971, another $1 million in improvements saw five rides making their debuts. Included were the Sky Ride, Round Up, and Paratrooper, seen here, along with two kiddie rides. Revenue had now tripled, and attendance doubled since 1968. In July of that year, a new $1.75-million stock offering was announced to cover improvements in the coming years. (Jim Futrell collection.)

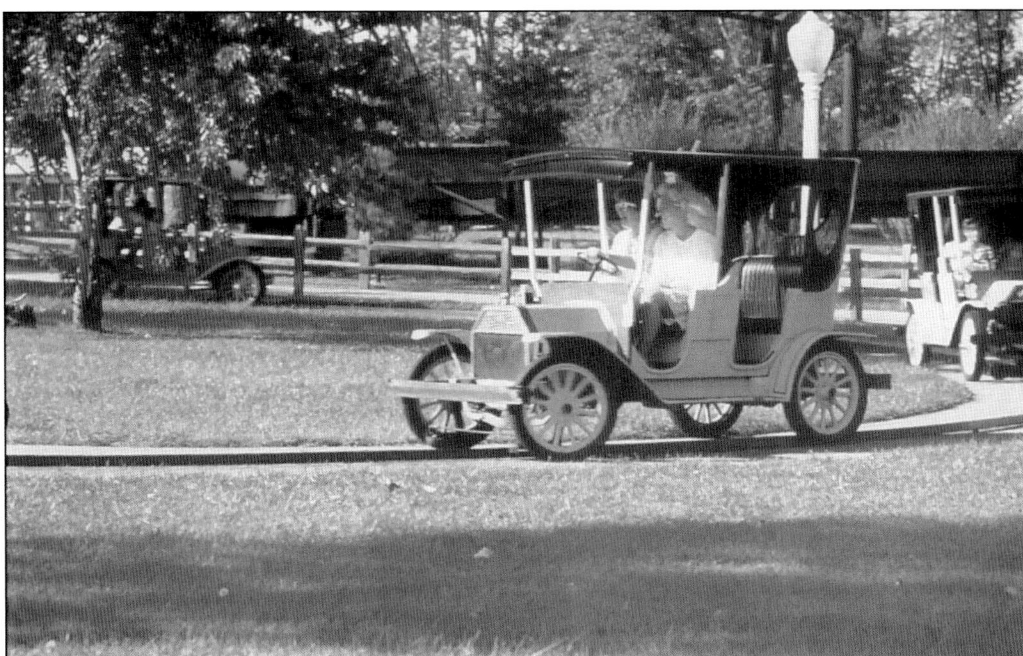

Geauga Lake made a major commitment in 1972, investing $1.5 million in improvements. One of the anchors was the Merry Old-Mobiles, scale replicas of 1911 Cadillacs that guests could drive along a winding roadway. Powered by a 7.5 horsepower gasoline engine, the $180,000 ride was made by Arrow Dynamics, one of the leading ride manufacturers of the era. (Jim Futrell collection.)

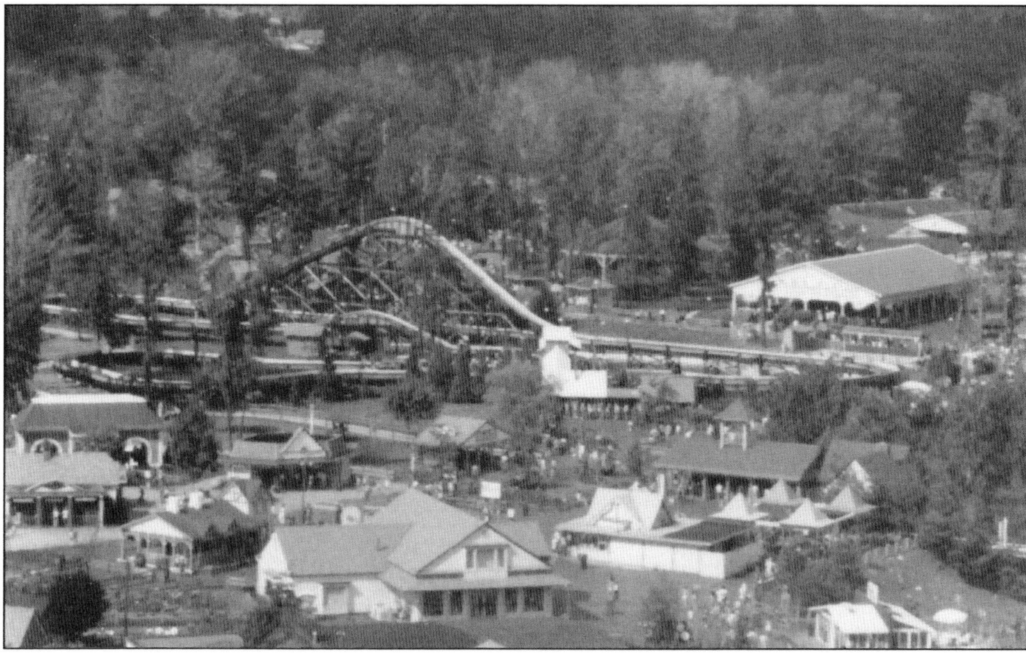

Anchoring the expansion was the Gold Rush, a 2,600-foot-long log flume manufactured by the Japanese firm Sansei. Sansei was a popular supplier of log flume rides in the early 1970s and sold several throughout the country. The most popular part of the $750,000 ride was a 40-foot-tall hill that culminated in a cooling splashdown. Both the Gold Rush and Merry Old-Mobiles were erected in a previously unused wooded area that was initially named Forest Funland. (Above, Dave Hahner collection; right, Jim Futrell collection.)

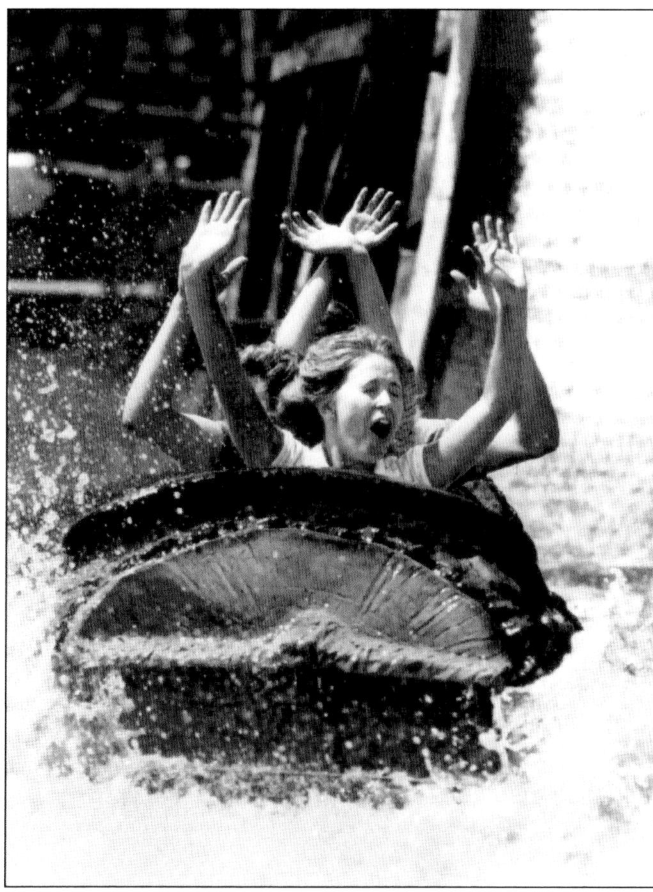

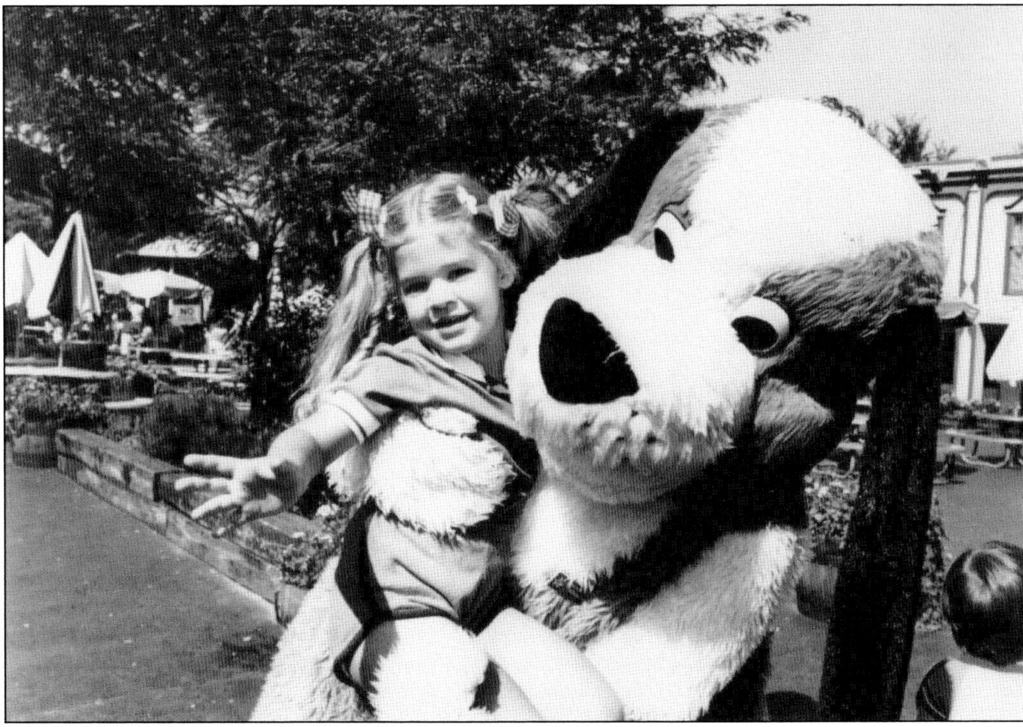

With parks around the country introducing costumed mascots, Geauga Lake added its own in 1972 with the creation of the legendary Geauga Dog. For much of the Funtime years, Geauga Dog delighted visitors young and old. (Jim Futrell collection.)

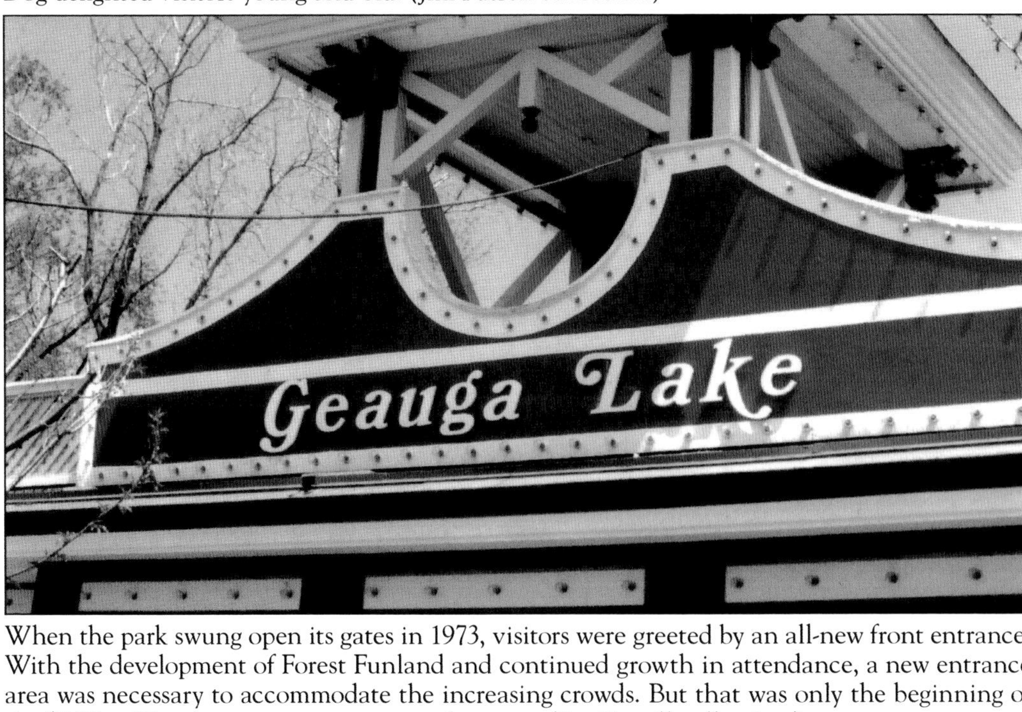

When the park swung open its gates in 1973, visitors were greeted by an all-new front entrance. With the development of Forest Funland and continued growth in attendance, a new entrance area was necessary to accommodate the increasing crowds. But that was only the beginning of the $1.25-million improvement program that year. (Jim Futrell collection.)

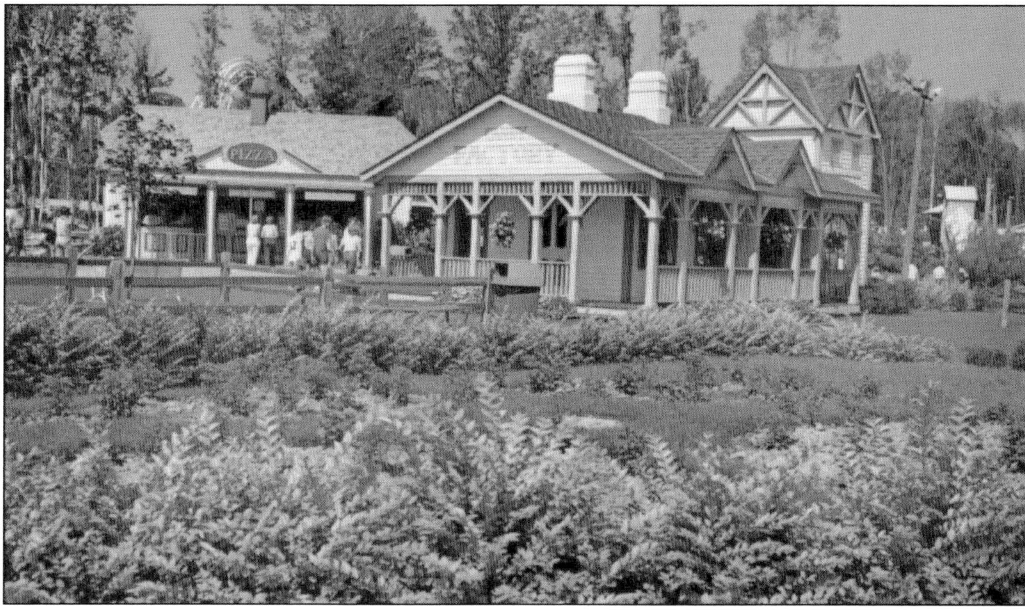

The new front gate was just part of a two-year project to develop a new, beautifully landscaped entrance area right inside the gate to link the older area of the park with the newly developed Forest Funland. In 1972, a gift shop and shooting gallery were built. The 1973 expansion complemented them with a pizza parlor and candy factory. Other projects that year included a new kiddie Dodgem ride and the refurbishment of the carousel, which included stripping off up to 18 coats of paint on the wooden horses and rewiring the electric lights. (Both, Jim Futrell collection.)

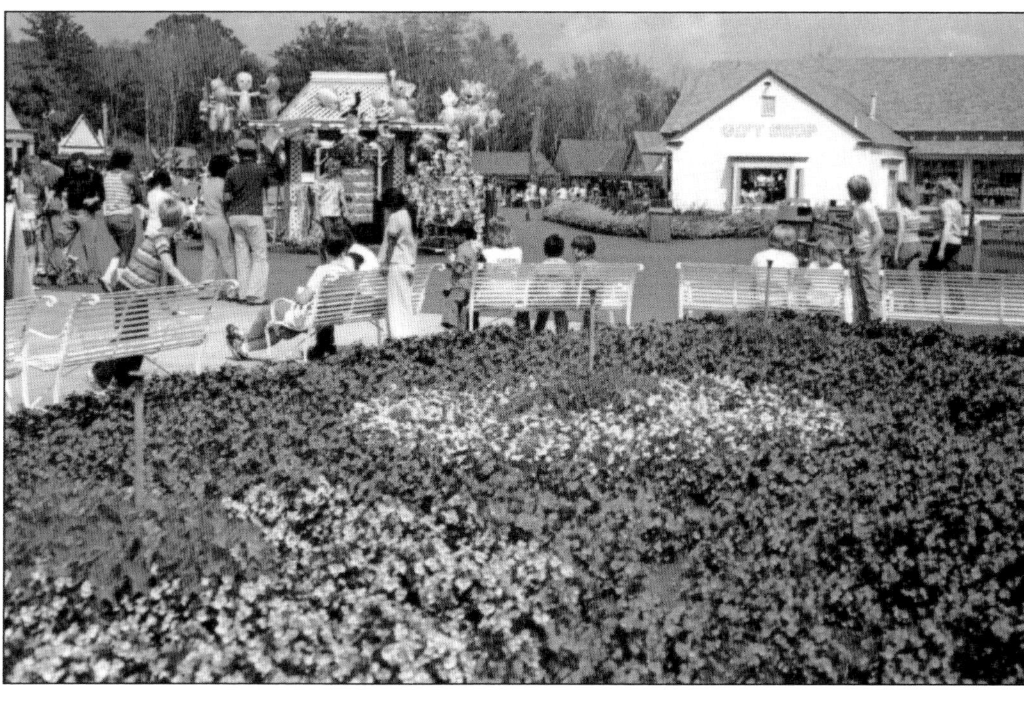

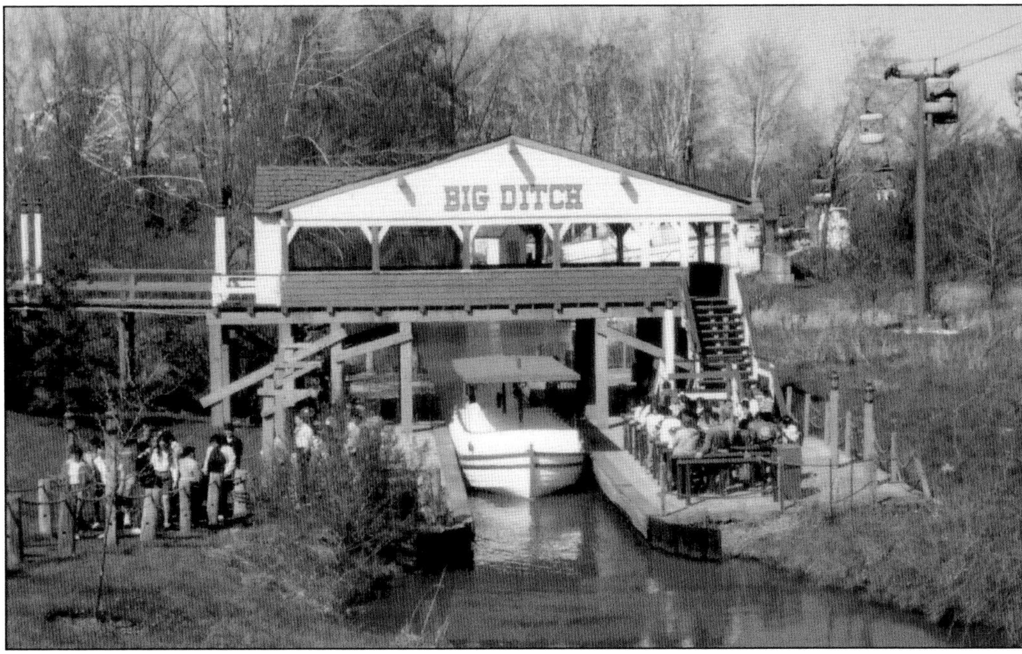

The major addition for 1973 was the $400,000 Big Ditch, a recreation of an 1839 canal boat through the wilds of old Ohio. Geauga Lake's answer to Disney's Jungle Cruise, the ride started out as a cruise on the lake that then entered a canal where scenes from Ohio's early days were displayed, including woodland life, a work camp, a farm, and a battle between villagers and gamblers culminating in a riverboat explosion. The above photograph also provides a glimpse of the Sky Ride, which opened in 1971. (Both, Jim Futrell collection.)

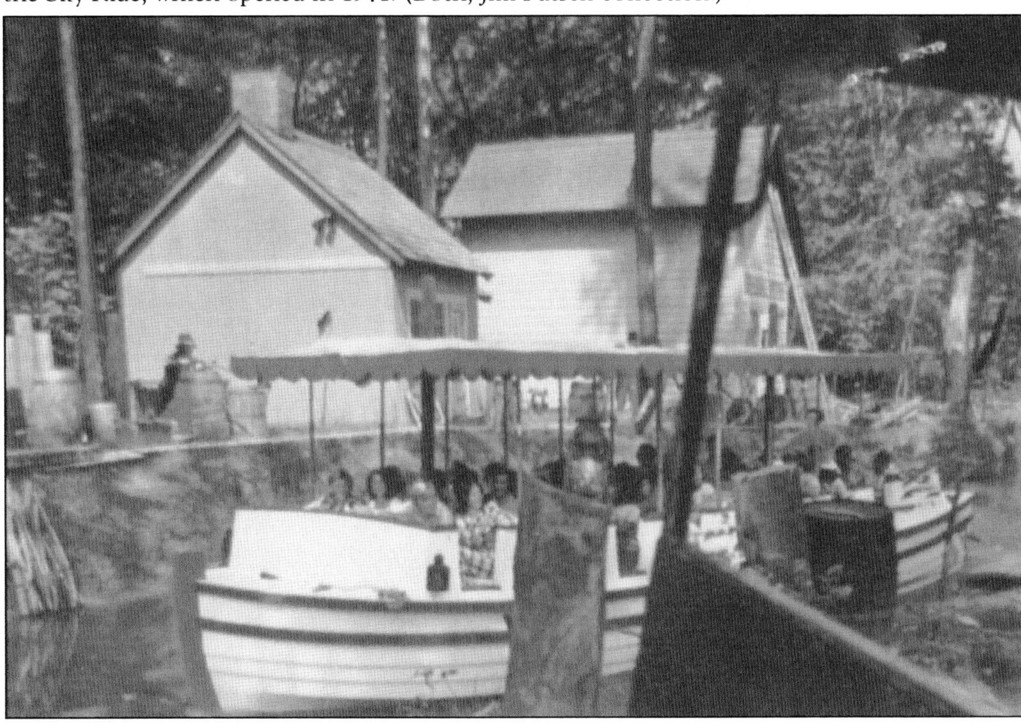

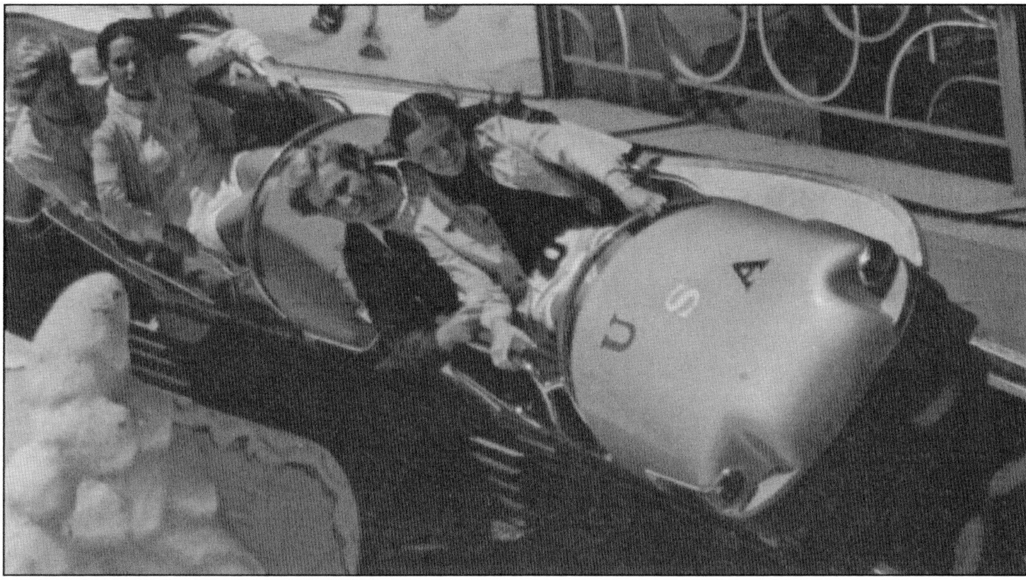

In addition to adding high-profile themed attractions such as the Big Ditch, Funtime continued to import a number of spinning rides from Europe. The $100,000 Bayern Kurve was one such attraction. Invented in 1965 by the legendary German ride engineer Anton Schwarzkopf, the ride featured 16 bobsled-themed cars that traveled at 40 miles per hour around a circular, single-hilled track. (Jim Futrell collection.)

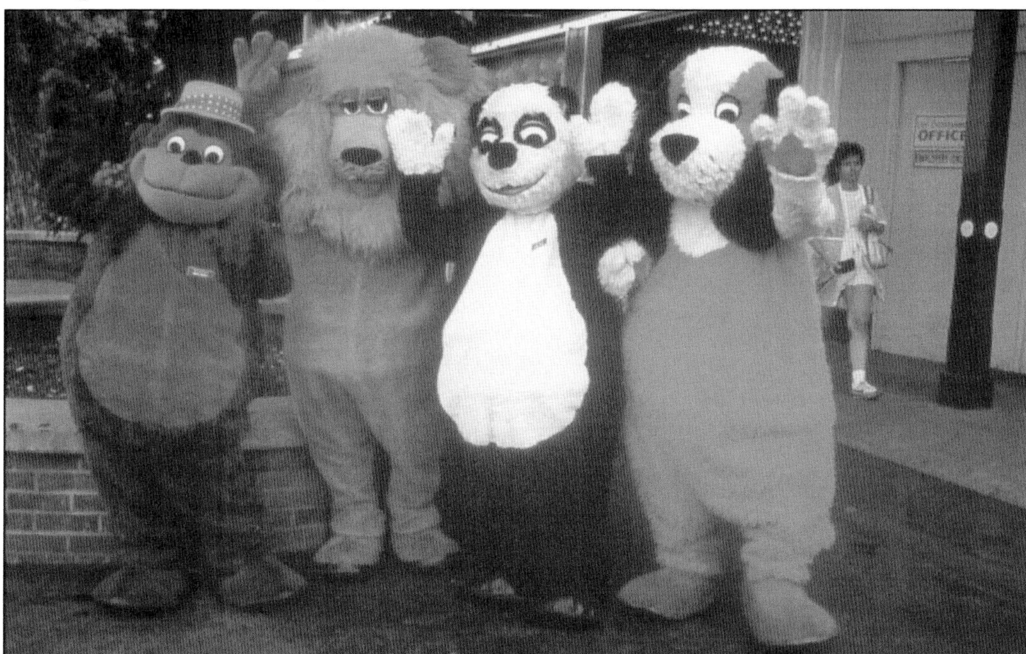

Geauga Dog found it increasingly hard to greet the growing crowds. As a result, three new friends were added in 1973—Gunky Monkey, Dandy Lion, and Peter Panda. Named the Fun Bunch, the characters were a fixture in the 1970s and pressed into service in 1975 when the park first introduced live entertainment in the new Gold Rush Theater, starring in the show *Happy Birthday USA*. (Jim Futrell collection.)

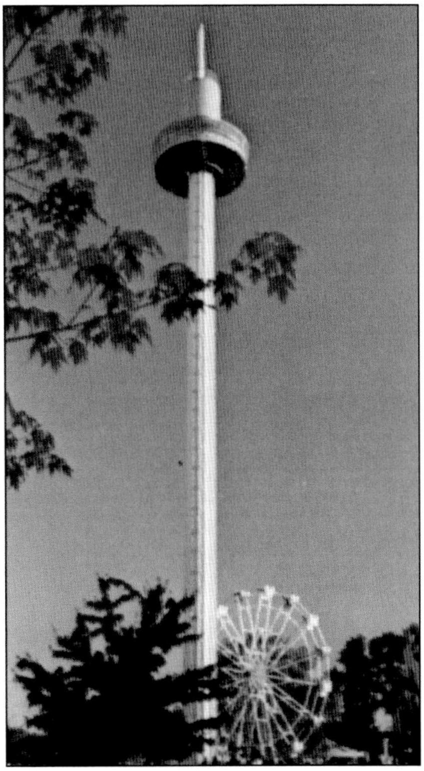

With attendance and revenue reaching new heights, the park decided to shoot for the stars in 1974, with the tallest attraction in its history. The $550,000 Skyscraper was a 200-foot-tall observation tower on which passengers traveled to the top in a 50-person circular cabin. European ride manufacturer Intamin AG built the ride. Other improvements included a new Tilt-A-Whirl ride. (Jim Futrell collection.)

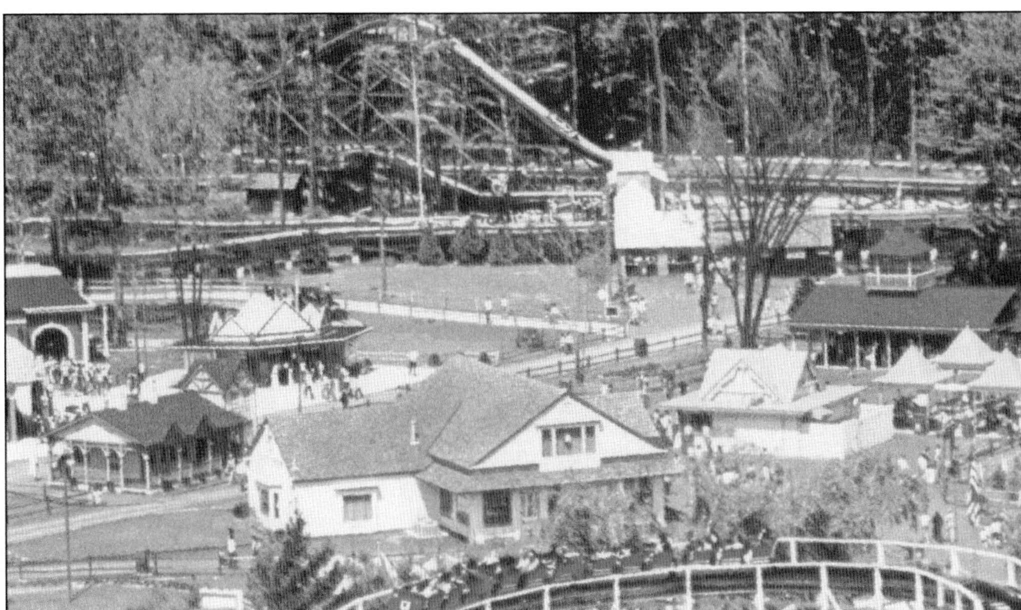

This photograph taken from the Skyscraper highlights much of Geauga Lake's growth in the early 1970s. Beyond the high turn of the Big Dipper is the newly constructed entrance mall with its various concession buildings. On the far left is the station for the Merry Old-Mobiles, while the Gold Rush dominates the background. In just five short years, the park had a completely different personality. (Jim Futrell collection.)

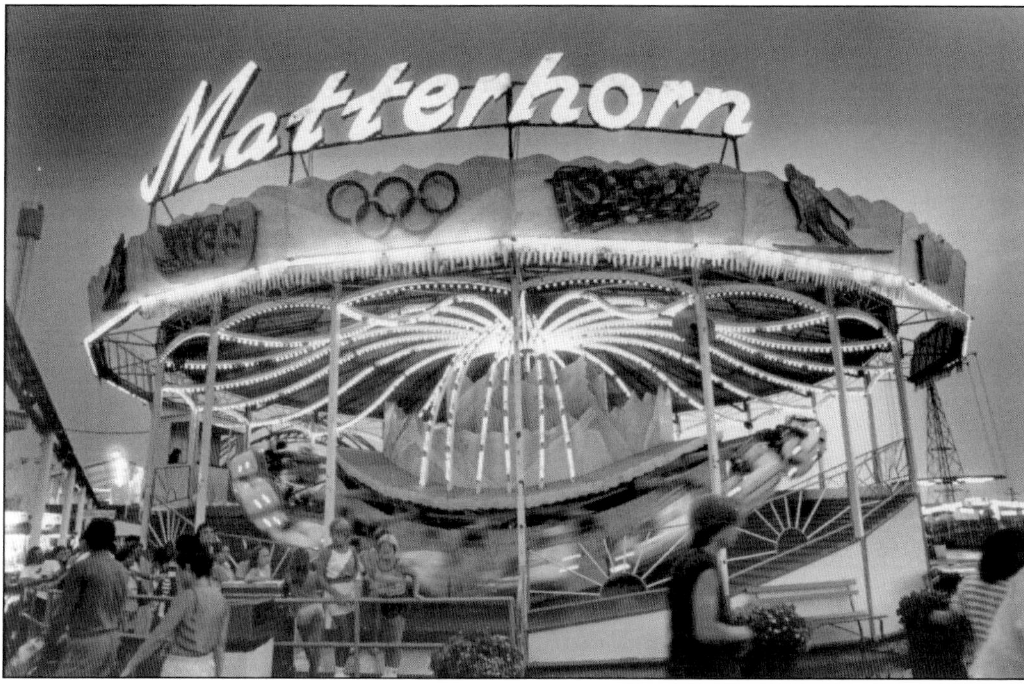

In 1975 and 1976, a total of $3 million was spent on improvements—adding six new rides, most of which were flashy new ones imported from Europe, including the Calypso, Himalaya, Super Cat, and Matterhorn. Made by the German manufacturer Mack, the Matterhorn operated at the park until 2007 and in later years was also known as the Yukon Yahoo and Hay Baler. (Jim Futrell collection.)

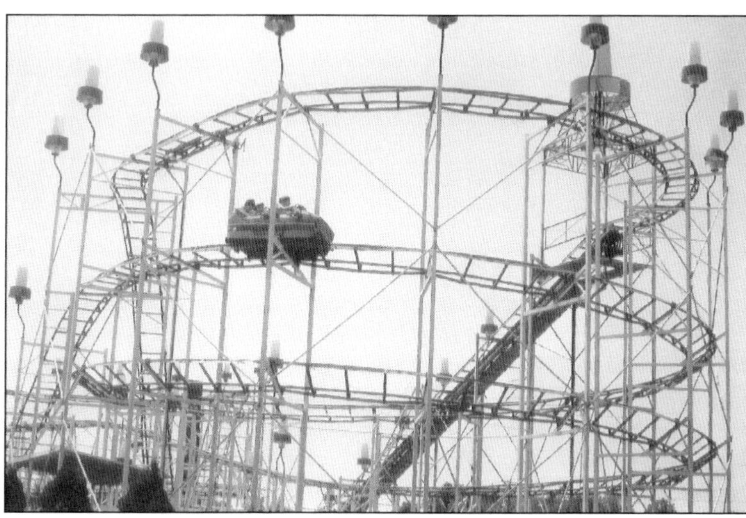

By the mid-1970s, the Little Dipper was aging, and Funtime replaced it with the Cyclone in 1976. Built by the Italian firm Pinfari, the Cyclone stood nearly 40 feet tall and featured 1,400 feet of track. Costing $275,000, it represented the most expensive of the three rides added that year. (Michael Horwood collection.)

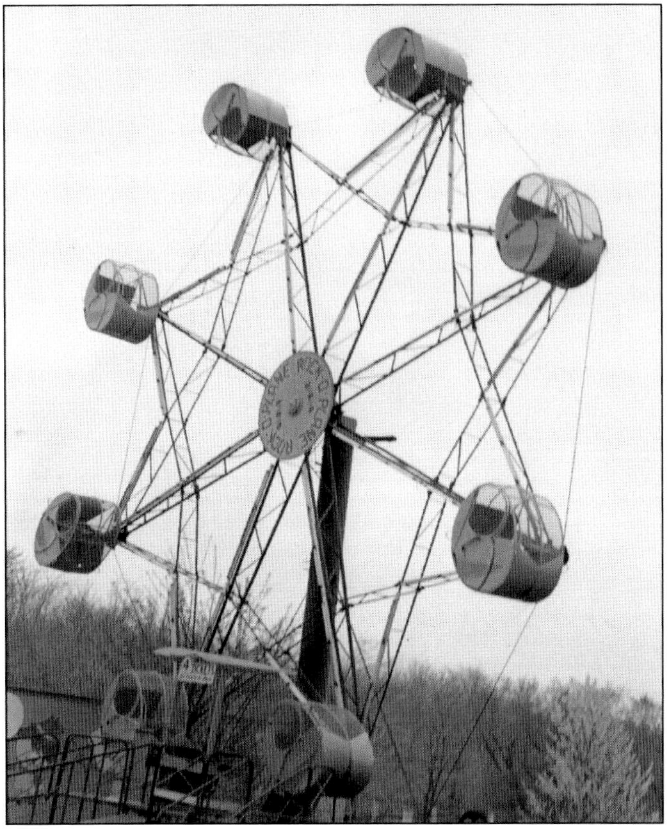

While the new attractions gained most of the attention, Geauga Lake also made it a point to keep a number of its older attractions to maintain that nostalgic atmosphere. One such ride was the Rock-O-Plane. Made by Eyerly Aircraft, the ride was installed in 1953 and allowed riders to control the motion of their individual cars. (Amusement Park Books Collection.)

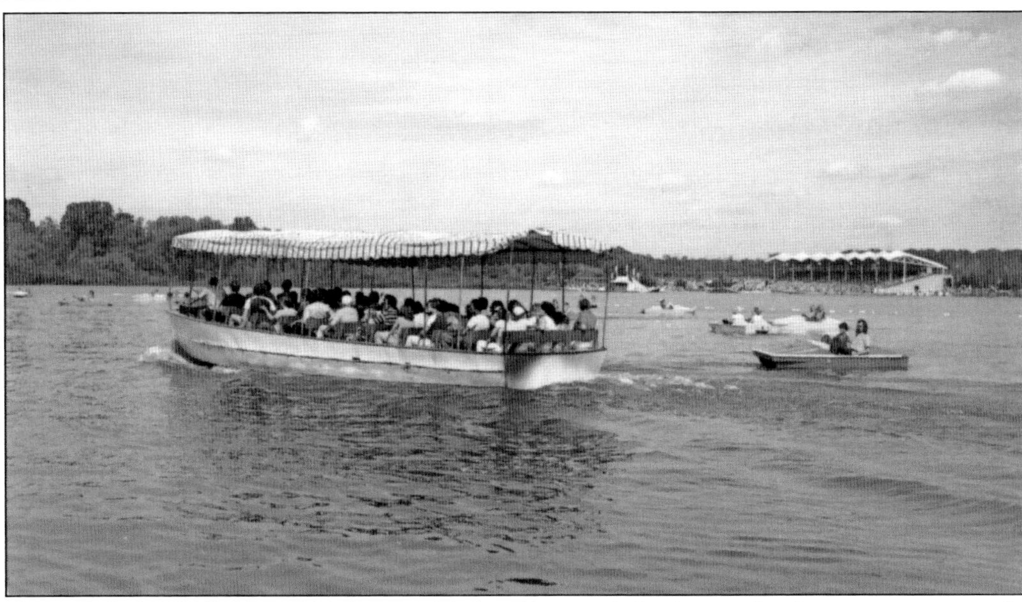

Despite all the flashy new rides being added to Geauga Lake during the first seven years under Funtime's ownership, the timeless appeal of the lake still drew crowds. The *Geauga Queen* provided a relaxing ride on the waters, while those desiring a little more action could pilot their own paddleboats, which replaced the U Drive-em boats in the early 1970s. (Jim Futrell collection.)

Three

Getting Loopy 1977–1982

By the time the nation celebrated its bicentennial in 1976, Funtime had transformed Geauga Lake, spending over $9 million to develop a thriving, modern amusement park. Revenues exceeded $6.5 million, and attendance approached 800,000. But Funtime knew that it could not rest on its laurels. Competition in the area was just too aggressive.

By this time, a roller coaster arms race had taken root in America as new theme parks were building larger and more advanced rides, complete with high speeds, 100-foot drops, and loops. Geauga Lake knew it had to stake a claim as a roller coaster destination, but also knew that it could not put all its eggs in one basket by building one mega ride.

As a result, using the creativity that defined the Funtime era, the company decided to add not one, but two roller coasters. Kicking it off in 1977 was the Double Loop, the first roller coaster to feature two vertical loops. That was followed in 1978 by the Corkscrew, which featured two corkscrew inversions. This made Geauga Lake the first amusement park in the world with two looping roller coasters and the only place on the planet where people could be flipped upside down four times.

The Double Loop continued the development of the former Forest Funland area, which had now taken on a Western theme and would soon become home to several new and relocated rides, including the Enterprise, carousel, Scrambler, and Dodgem. This increased the developed acreage of the revitalized park to 120 acres, triple the size of the park in 1969.

Funtime knew it had a successful formula and sought to roll it out at other locations. In 1975, it looked at acquiring Familyland in the Wisconsin Dells and later that year optioned 185 acres outside Ann Arbor, Michigan, for potential development of a new park. While these tentative ventures did not work out, in 1982, the company succeeded in acquiring an interest in Darien Lake, then a large campground in upstate New York. As with Geauga Lake, Funtime launched a multiyear expansion that turned it into the largest theme park in the state.

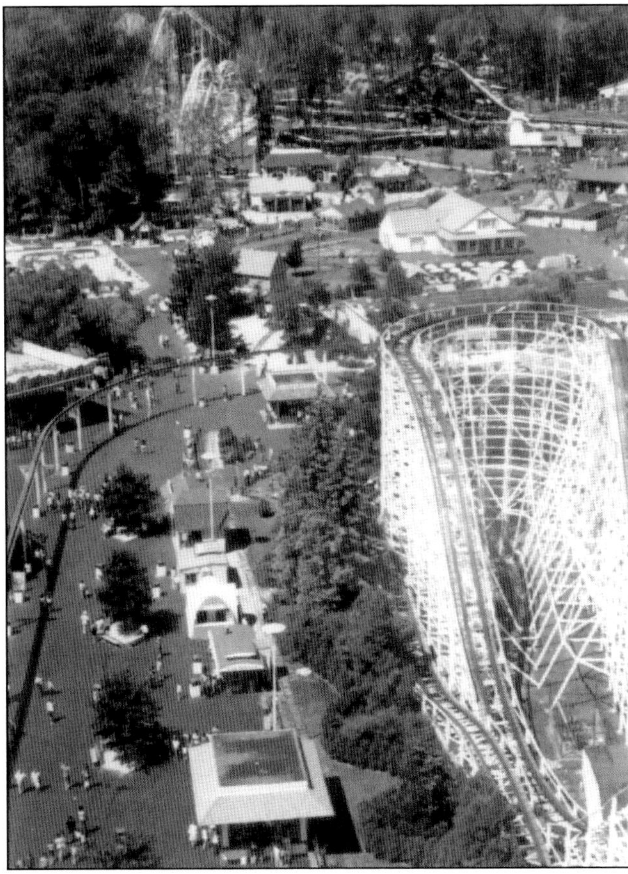

This view, taken from the Skyscraper in the late 1970s, provides a good look at where most of the growth occurred over the first decade of Funtime ownership. The midway in the foreground was home to many of the new attractions added in the early 1970s, with the new entrance area located beyond that. In the background are the Gold Rush flume and the anchor attraction for the $2 million expansion in 1977, the largest in park history—the Double Loop roller coaster (below). (Both, Jim Futrell collection.)

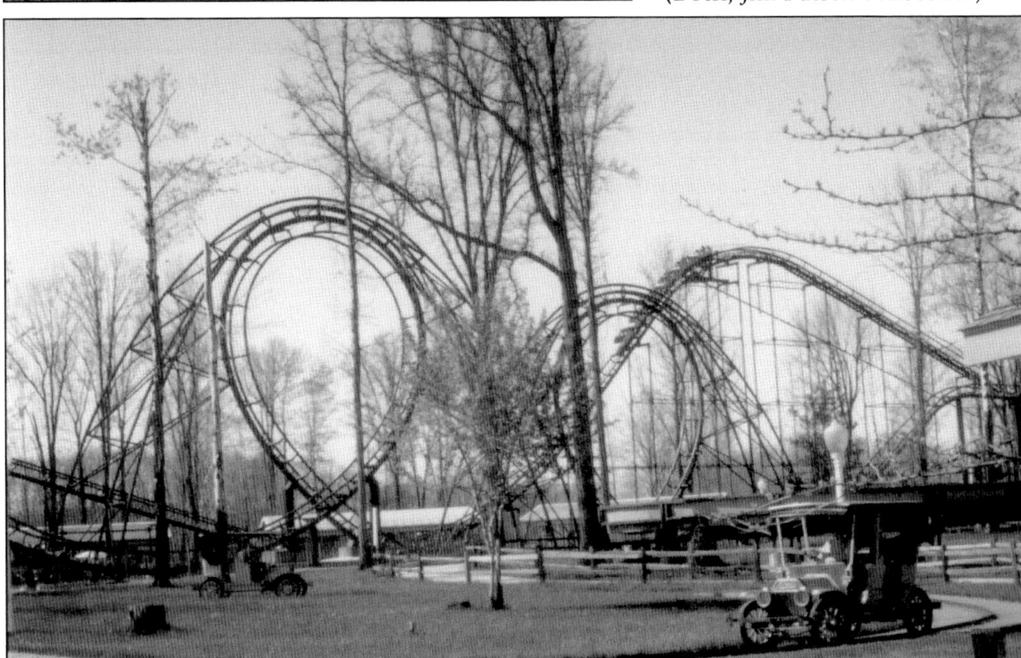

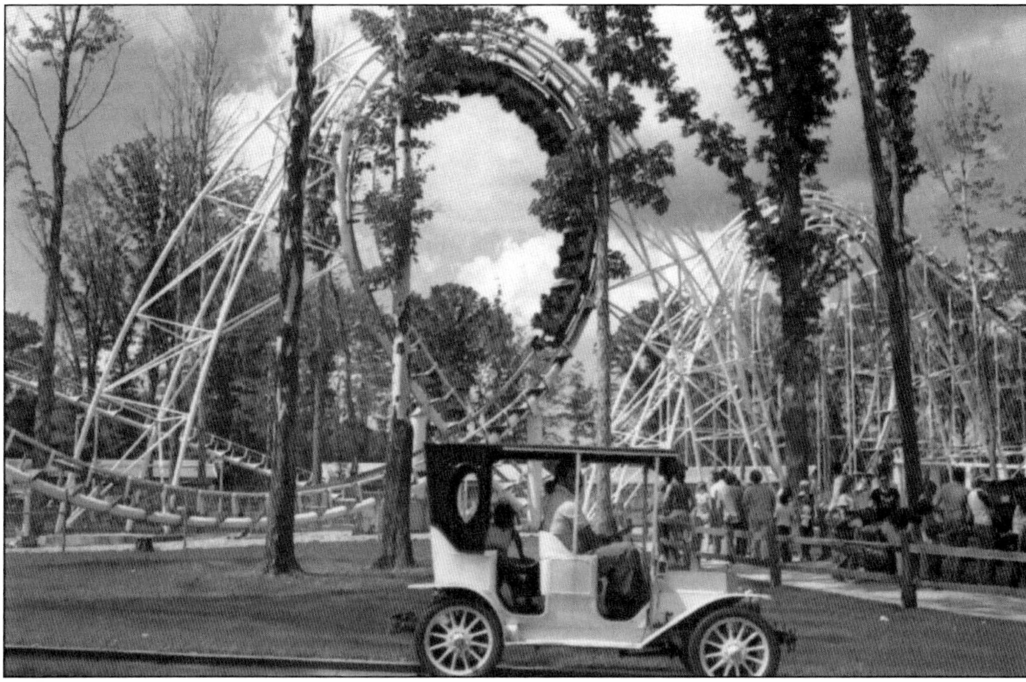

The Double Loop was built at a cost of $1.35 million. Manufactured by Arrow Dynamics, which was one of the pioneers in the development of looping roller coasters in the 1970s, the ride featured 1,800 feet of track along with a 90-foot drop, a helix, and two vertical loops standing 55 and 50 feet tall. It was the first roller coaster developed with two vertical loops and immediately put Geauga Lake on the map for roller coaster enthusiasts. Until 2007, it was a favorite landmark, interacting with the Merry Old-Mobiles and Gold Rush. (Both, Jim Futrell collection.)

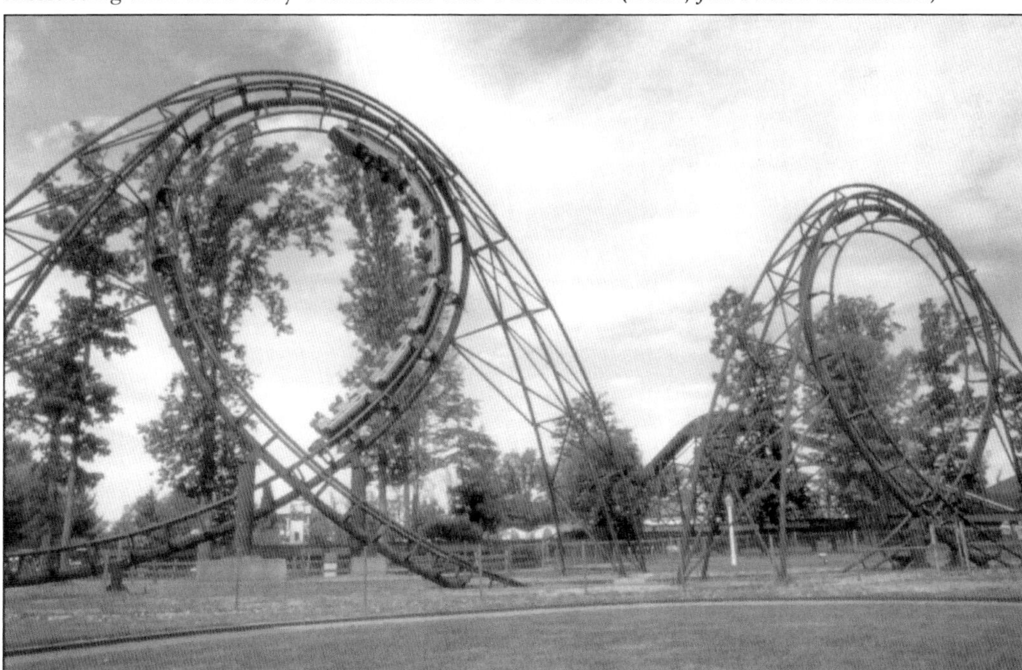

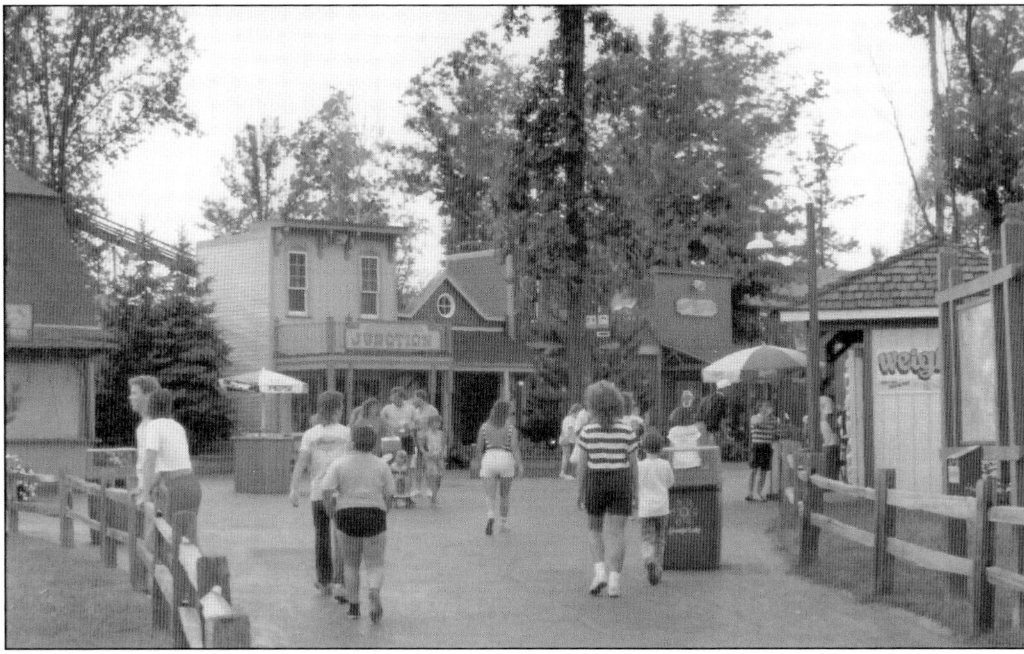

The Double Loop anchored a newly developed Western Village area in the former Forest Funland that included a snack stand, candy store, gift shop, pottery shop, and sketch stand. The park's existing Fly-O-Plane and Scrambler were also relocated into the new area. (Joel Styer collection.)

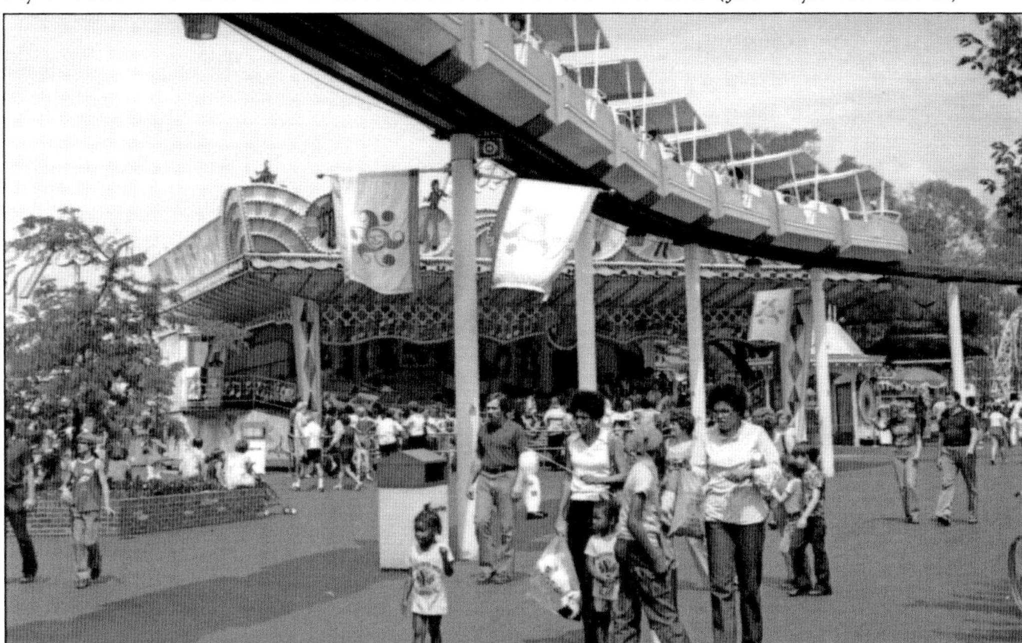

Geauga Lake also undertook several other improvements in the older part of the park. The Music Express, seen behind the monorail, was a $125,000 high-speed spinning ride known for its flashing lights and loud music. Meanwhile, the fun house was converted into the $125,000 Palace Theater, an 800-seat live-entertainment venue, and the parking lot was expanded. (Jim Futrell collection.)

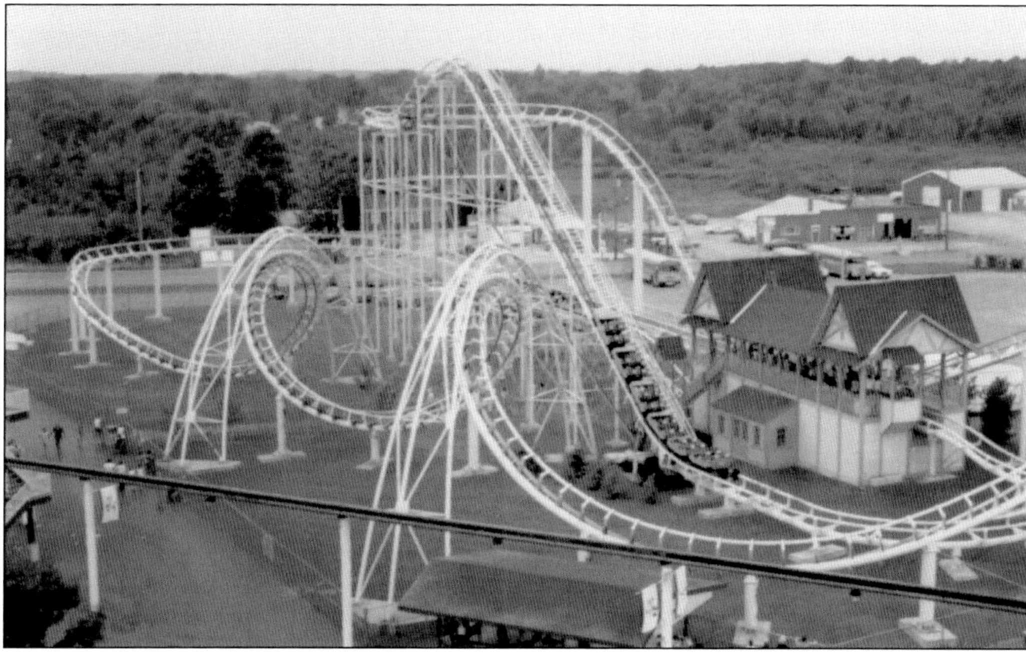

The Double Loop was a huge hit, with attendance increasing by more than 117,000 and revenue jumping 36 percent. To follow up, the park added the Corkscrew in 1978. Occupying a portion of the former parking lot, the Corkscrew stood 70 feet tall with 1,250 feet of track and two corkscrew inversions. Geauga Lake placed one of the first orders for a Corkscrew in 1975, shortly after Arrow Dynamics introduced the ride, but installation was delayed by financing issues. (Above, Augie Geist collection; below, Jim Futrell collection.)

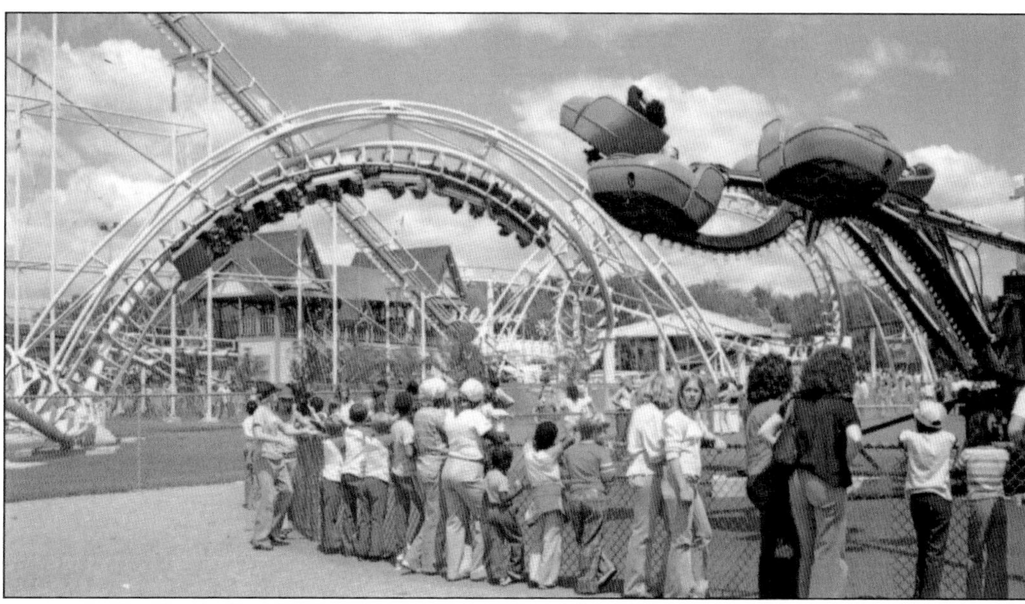

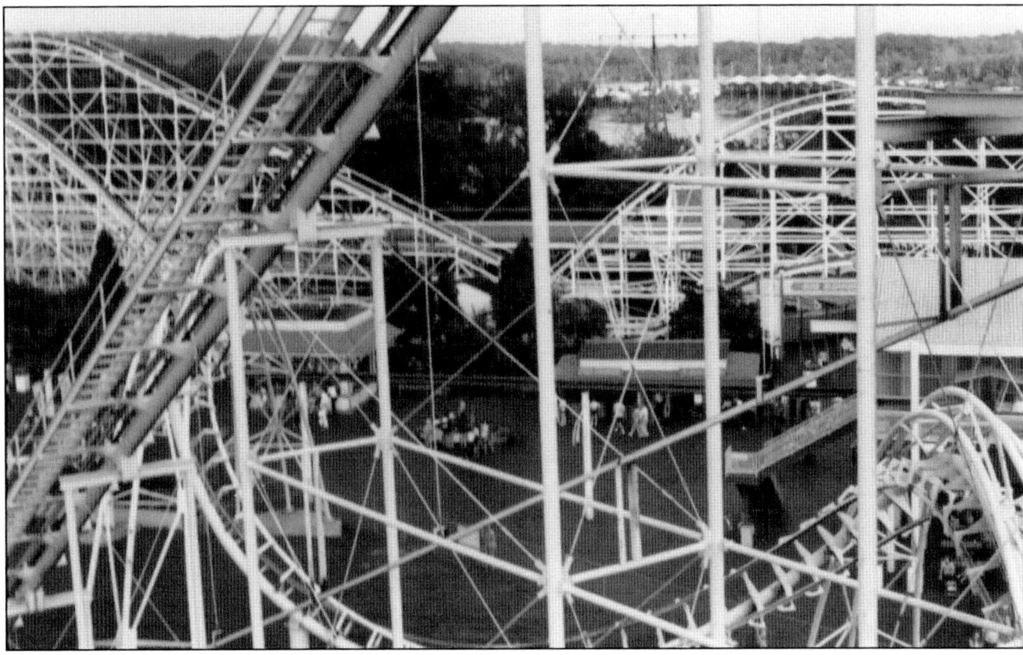

The Corkscrew had an immediate impact on Geauga Lake's skyline. This photograph shows a veritable jumble of tracks that includes the new Corkscrew in the foreground with the Big Dipper rising behind it. In the distance are the Rocket Ship tower and the stadiums of SeaWorld. (Augie Geist collection.)

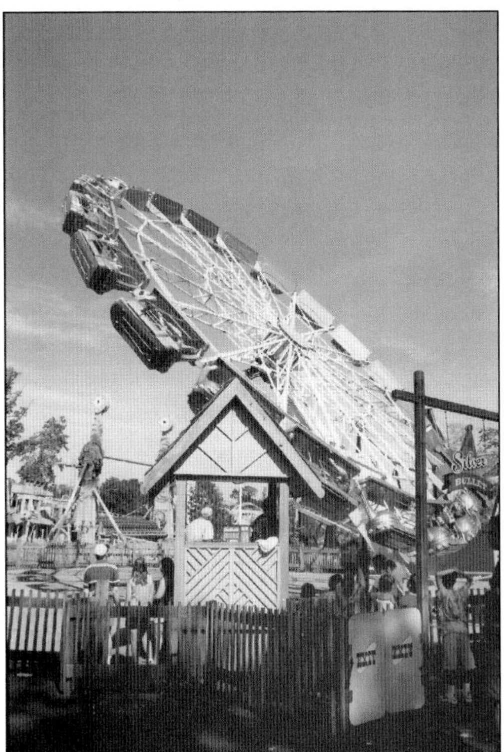

Development of the Western area continued in 1979 with the addition of the Enterprise, manufactured by Huss, a German ride-builder. The $450,000 attraction started at ground level and then moved into a vertical position, while spinning and flipping riders upside down. Later known as the Silver Bullet, it was removed in 2003. A new 4,000-square-foot Dodgem building also opened next to the Enterprise in 1979. (Joel Styer collection.)

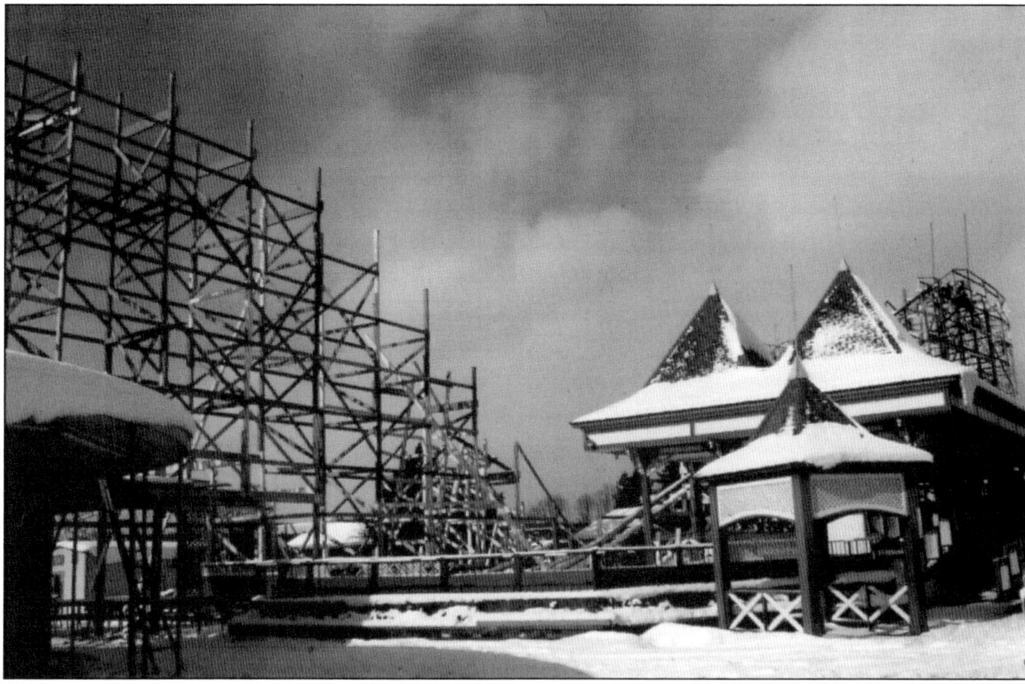

After spending more than a decade focusing its resources on adding new rides and attractions, Geauga Lake's $1.5-million improvement program for 1980 focused on preserving its most iconic attraction. For many years, Funtime knew that the Big Dipper provided a ride that was a little too jarring for its family-oriented crowd. As a result, in the winter of 1979 the park undertook a reconstruction of the vintage ride that saw 90 percent of the wood, 29,000 feet in all, replaced. (Both, Lee O. Bush collection.)

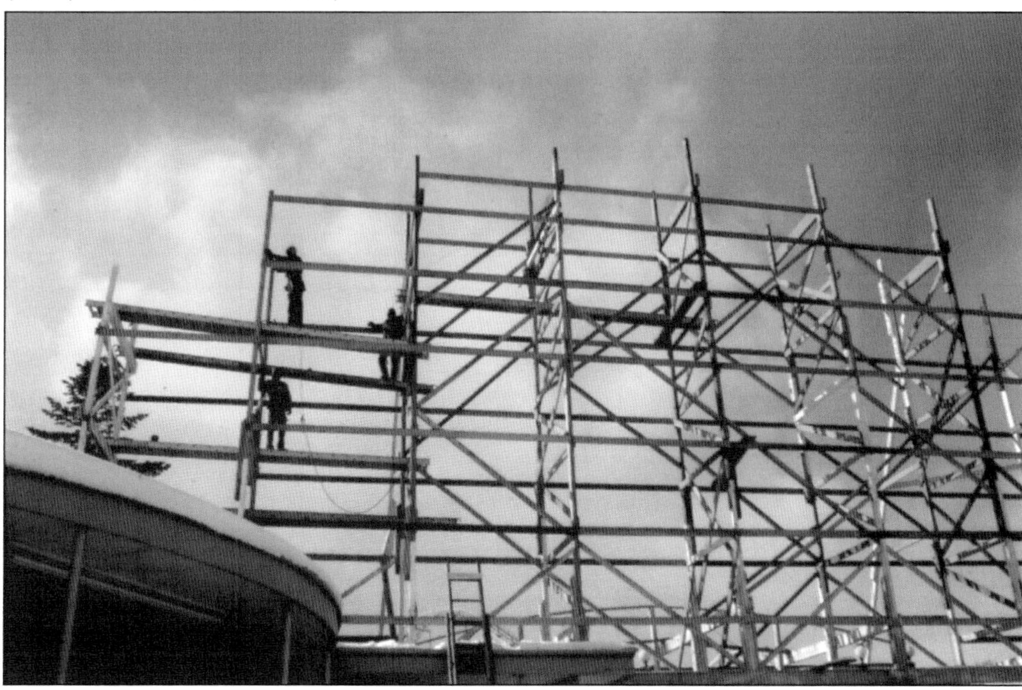

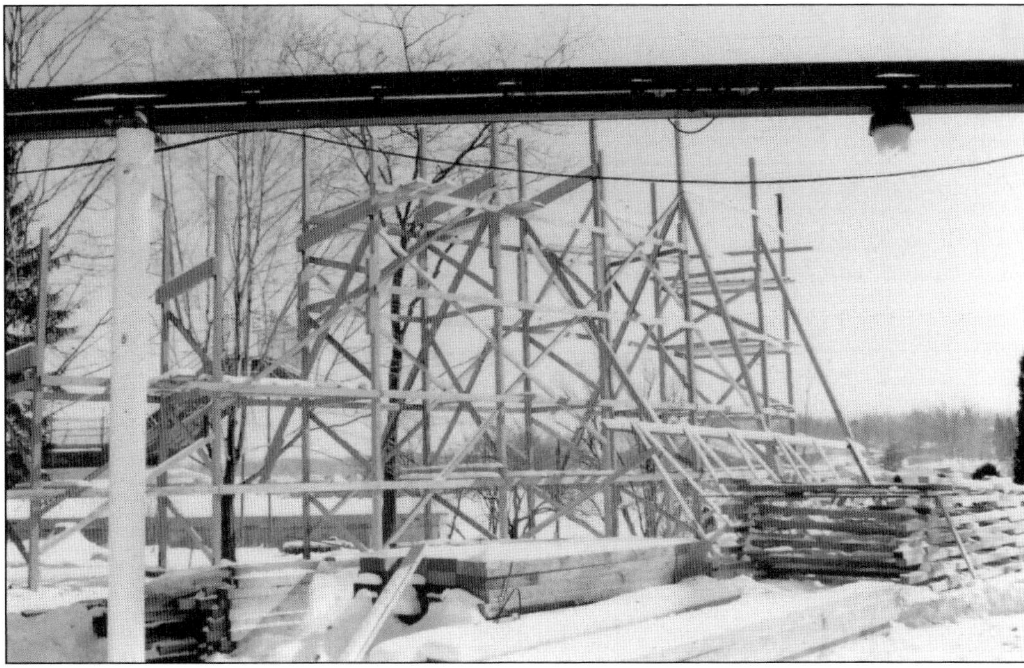

At a cost of $800,000, the entire structure after the first hill was taken down to the ground, the footers replaced, and a new support structure built. All-new track was then installed, and the entire structure was covered in 500 gallons of a special paint that allowed the wood to breathe. Some structural modifications were made, including shortening the first hill slightly, increasing the angle of descent on the first drop, and eliminating the double dip. While the Big Dipper received the bulk of the attention for the 1980 season, the park also added the Cinema 180, a $150,000 domed structure showing movies on a wraparound screen. (Both, Lee O. Bush collection.)

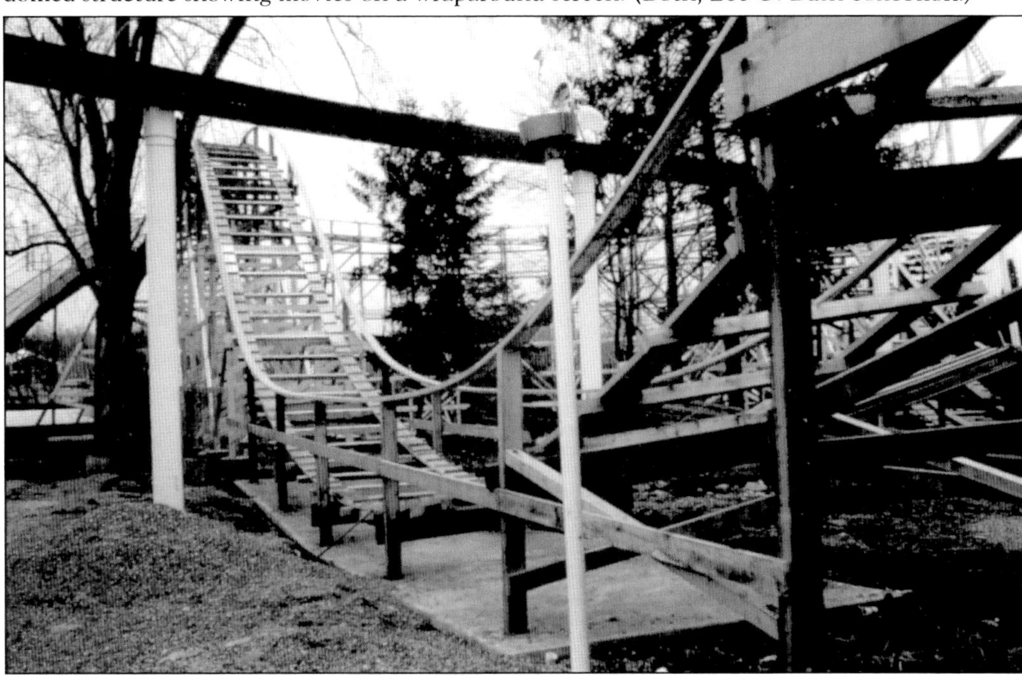

A look at the park from the south end to the northwest around 1979 shows the Cyclone on the left with the monorail, Big Dipper, Ferris wheel, Skyscraper, and Corkscrew in the background. Following the 1980 season, the Cyclone was sold to Holiday World in Santa Claus, Indiana. (Jim Futrell collection.)

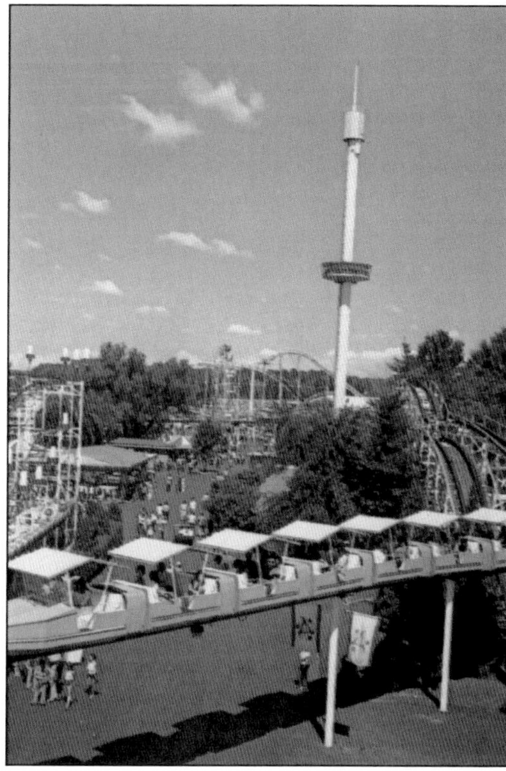

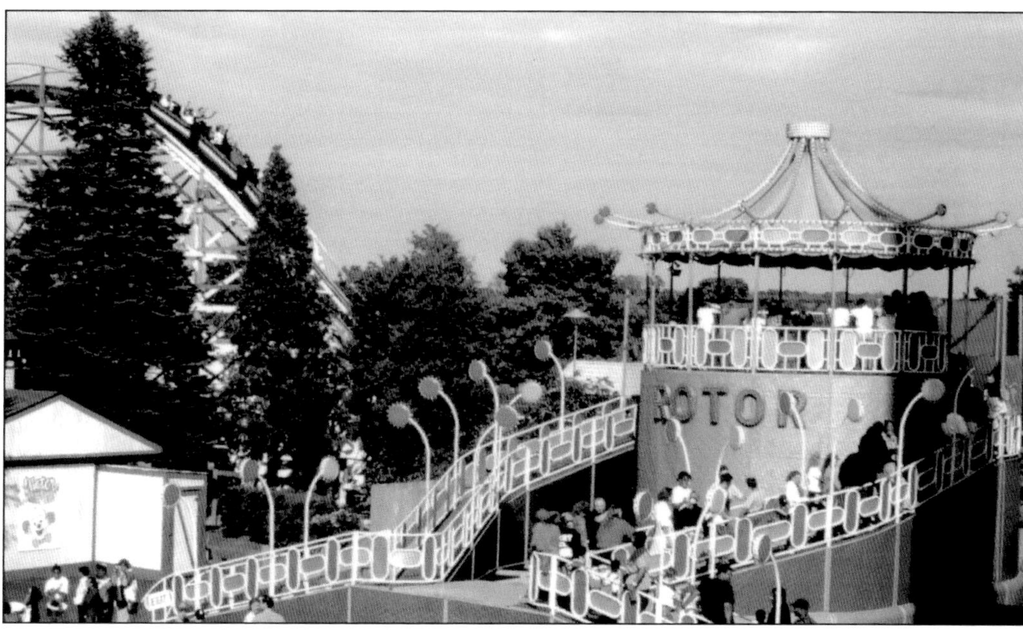

In 1981, Geauga Lake purchased three new rides from Chance Rides of Wichita, Kansas, as part of $1.25 million in improvements. A new Trabant replaced the model installed in 1969. Others included the Yo-Yo, a swing ride, and the Rotor, which allowed riders to defy gravity. In addition, the kiddieland received $100,000 in improvements, including a new kiddie Ferris wheel. (Jim Futrell collection.)

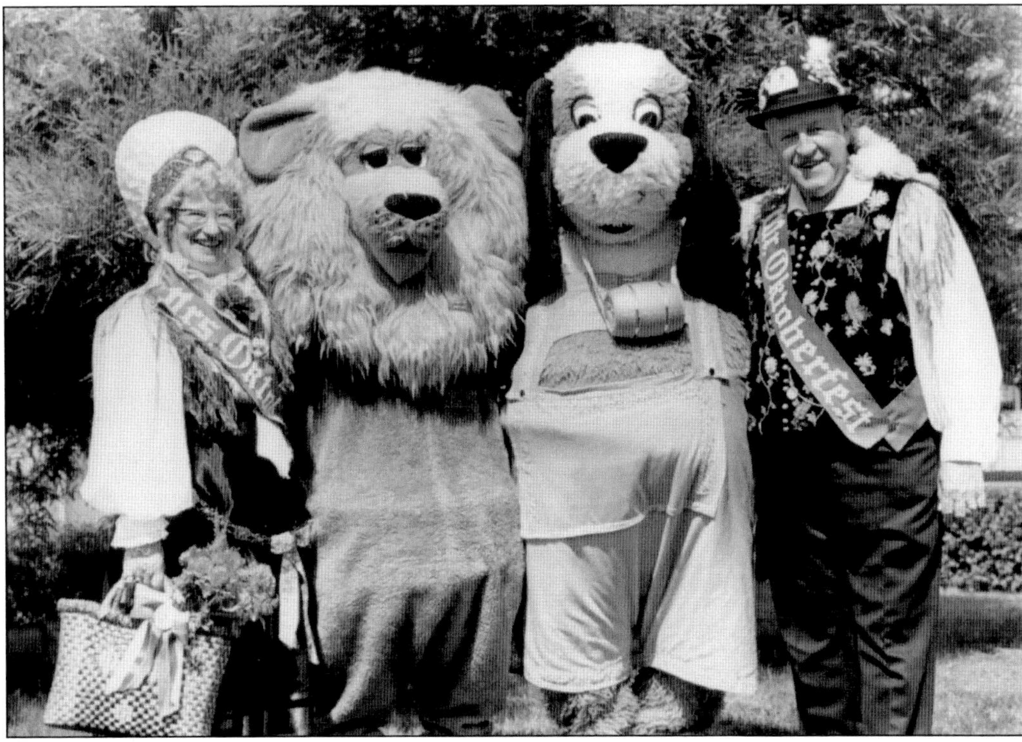

Geauga Lake was one of the pioneers in fall special events, when it decided to extend its season past Labor Day for the first time in 1981 with its Old World Oktoberfest. The idea for Geauga Lake's Oktoberfest was inspired by a trip to Oktoberfest in Germany by one of Funtime's executives. For one weekend, the park was transformed. Festivities kicked off each day with a traditional keg-tapping ceremony, and multiple entertainment areas offered everything from polka music and ethnic entertainment to oldies performances. (Both, Jim Futrell collection.)

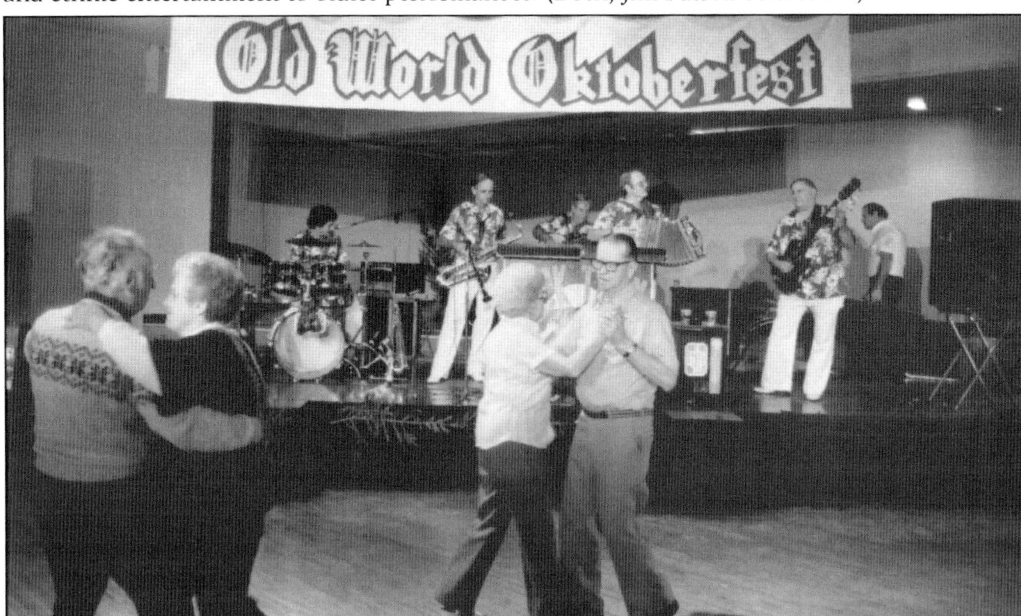

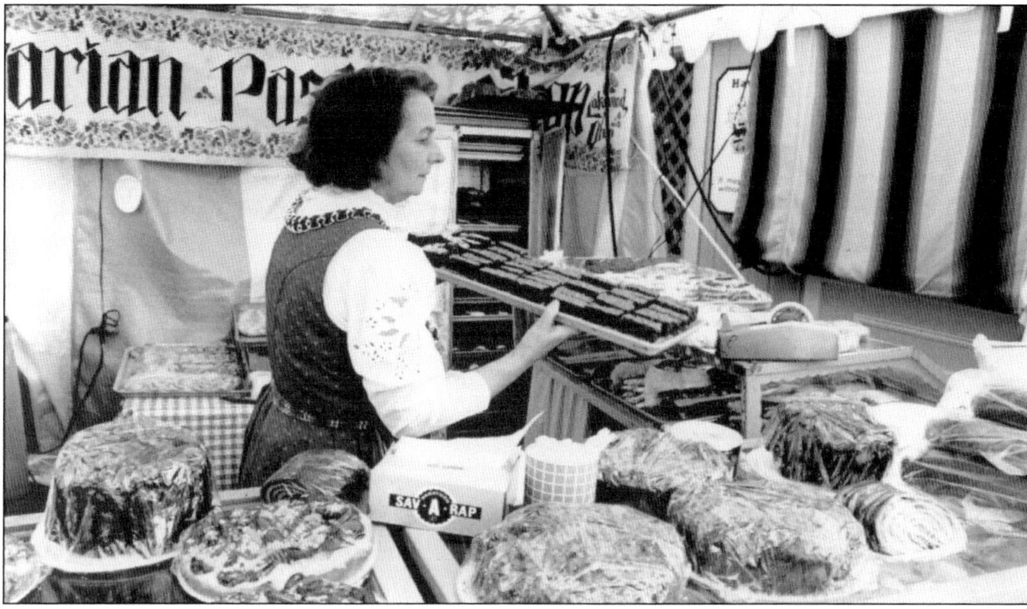

Many people came to Oktoberfest for the dozens of food vendors set up throughout the grounds. Options ranged from German specialties such as sausage and pastries to other offerings from around the world. Additional activities included contests such as mug sliding and wine stomping. The Oktoberfest soon became a beloved September tradition in northeastern Ohio. Ironically, the park's last operating weekend was the 2007 Oktoberfest. (Jim Futrell collection.)

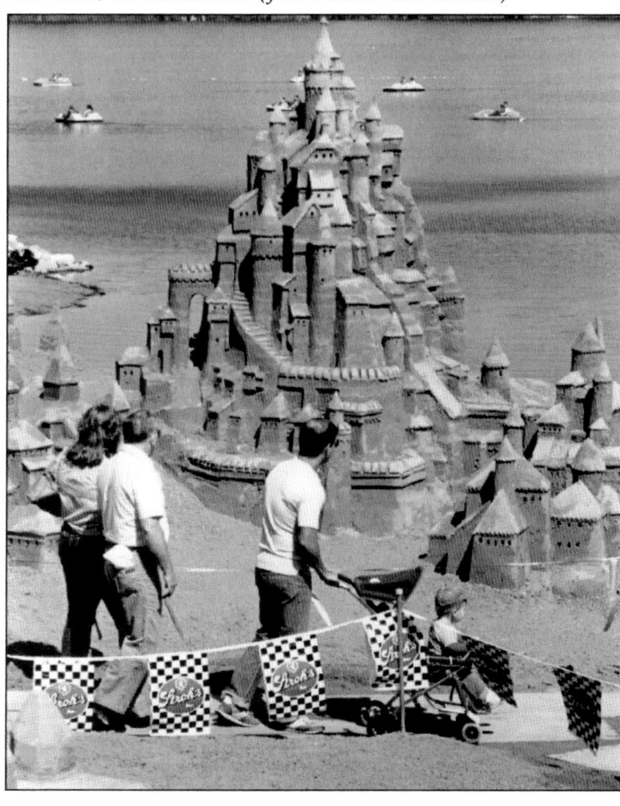

Throughout its existence, Oktoberfest brought in other special demonstrations. In the mid-1980s, Sand Sculptures USA came to Oktoberfest to erect enormous sand castles made of up to 200 tons of sand standing up to 16 feet tall along the lakeshore. While Geauga Lake's Oktoberfest is now but a memory, fall events at amusement parks around the world are now commonplace. (Jim Futrell collection.)

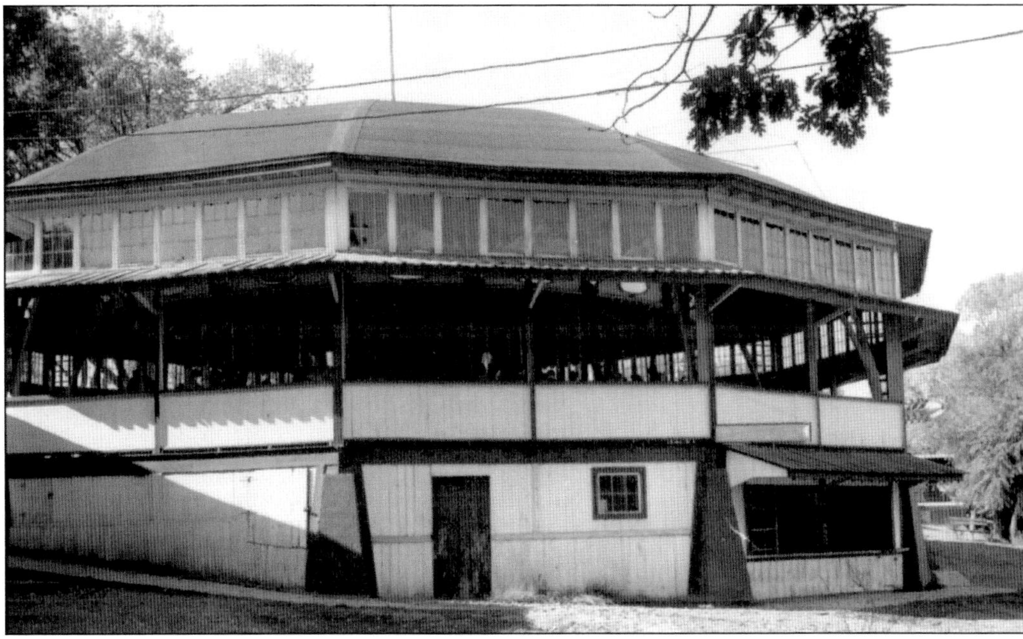

As the park was preparing for the 1982 season, it was discovered that the old carousel building was severely deteriorated. Dating back to the 1925 expansion, the structure took advantage of the slope from the midway to the lakeshore to offer a concession stand for many years on the lower level underneath the carousel. It was decided that the building could not be repaired and had to be demolished. (Amusement Park Books Collection.)

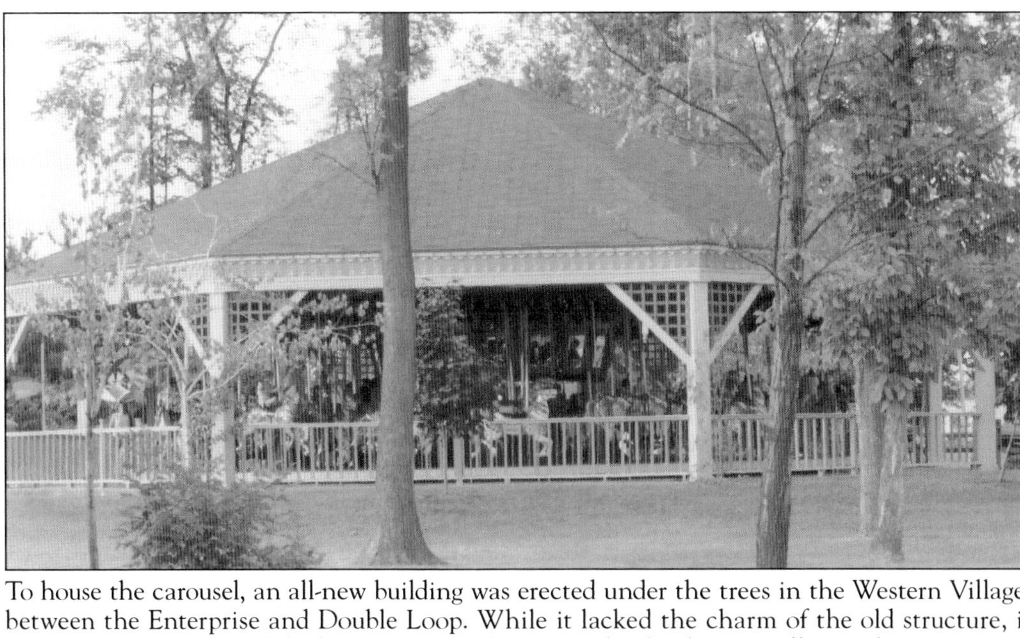

To house the carousel, an all-new building was erected under the trees in the Western Village, between the Enterprise and Double Loop. While it lacked the charm of the old structure, it provided a better view of the historic carousel to passersby. (Joel Styer collection.)

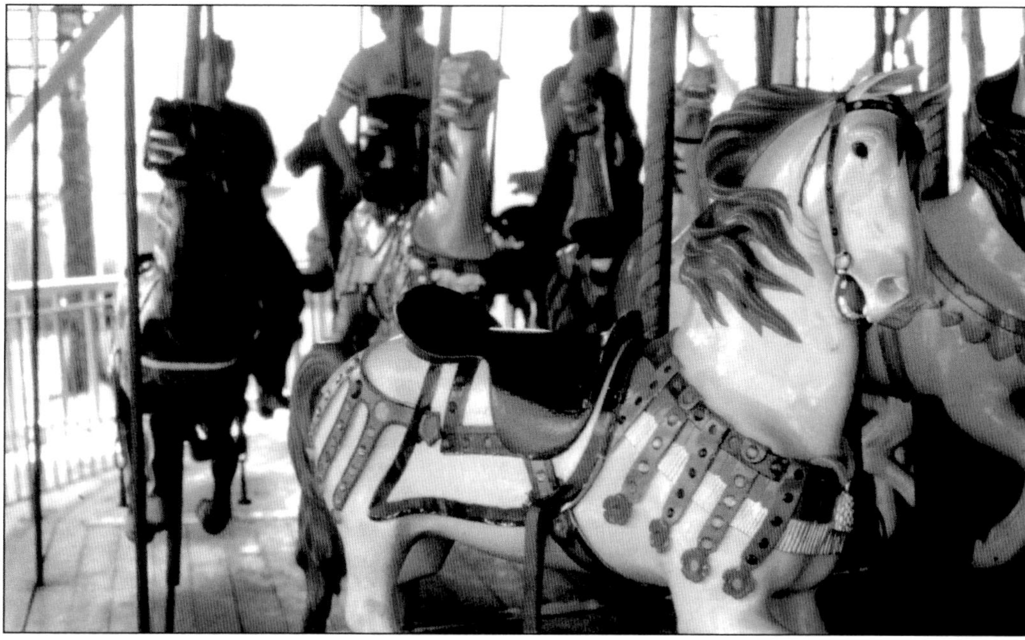

The carousel continued to be a beloved attraction in its new home and remained one of the finest examples of carousel art. With 64 hand-carved horses arranged in four rows, the ride had a unique feature in that the horses would swing outward as the carousel picked up speed. Over the years, the ride underwent several restorations and renovations, in 1973, 1986, and 1994. (Jim Futrell collection.)

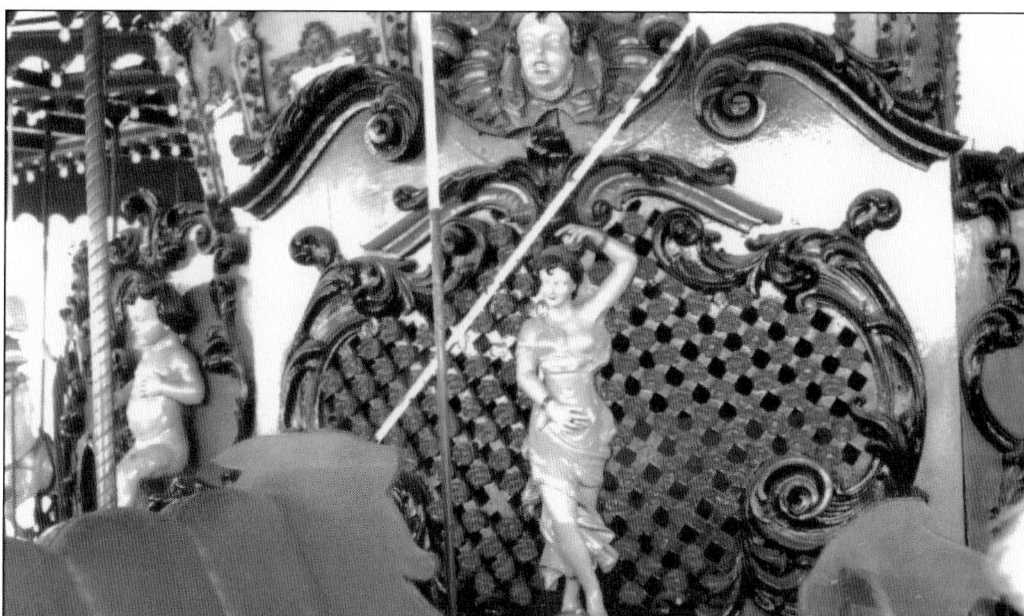

While the carousel originally had a band organ to provide music when it was acquired in 1937, it was being stored for the winter in the old roller rink when it was destroyed in the 1952 fire. For decades, the hand-carved band organ cabinet with its beautiful roses remained silent. (Jim Futrell collection.)

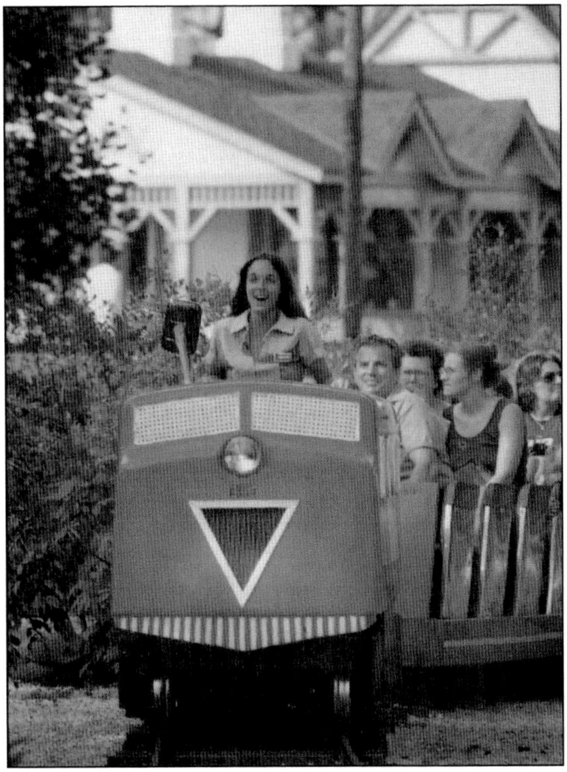

As Geauga Lake continued to grow, some attractions hauled their last riders. Since the 1925 expansion, a miniature railroad chugged along the base of the Big Dipper. This version, added in 1953, witnessed the park's transformation, but in 1981, the aging ride was retired. After that time, the only train rides could be found in the kiddieland. (Jim Futrell collection.)

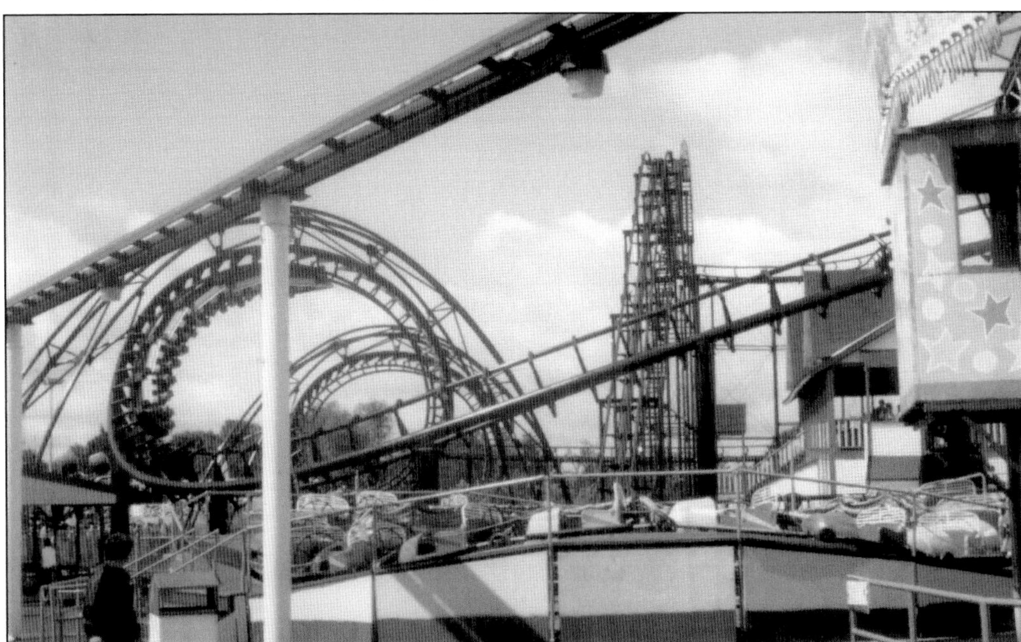

The Caterpillar was another classic ride that operated at Geauga Lake. Manufactured by the Allan Herschell Company of New York, the ride was highlighted by a canopy that covered the cars. In its later years, it was dwarfed by the Corkscrew before carrying its last riders in 1982. (Jim Futrell collection.)

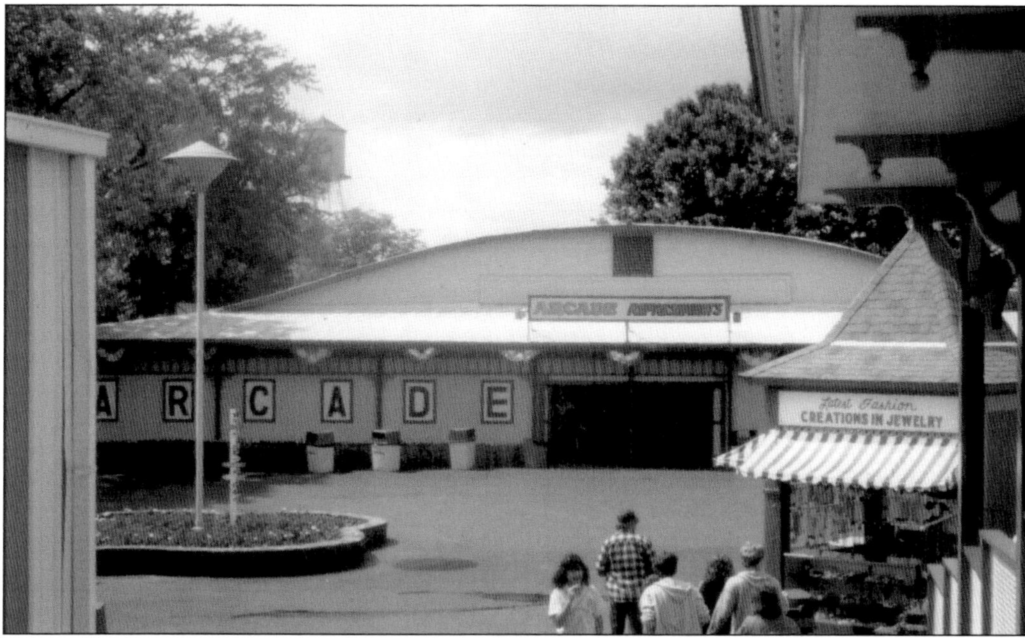

By the beginning of the 1980s, Funtime, Inc. had spent nearly $16 million expanding and renovating Geauga Lake. While it was very much a modern amusement park, a number of the park's original features remained. The recreation arcade, which was a fixture in the 1925 expansion, continued being used as an arcade and games location. (Jim Futrell collection.)

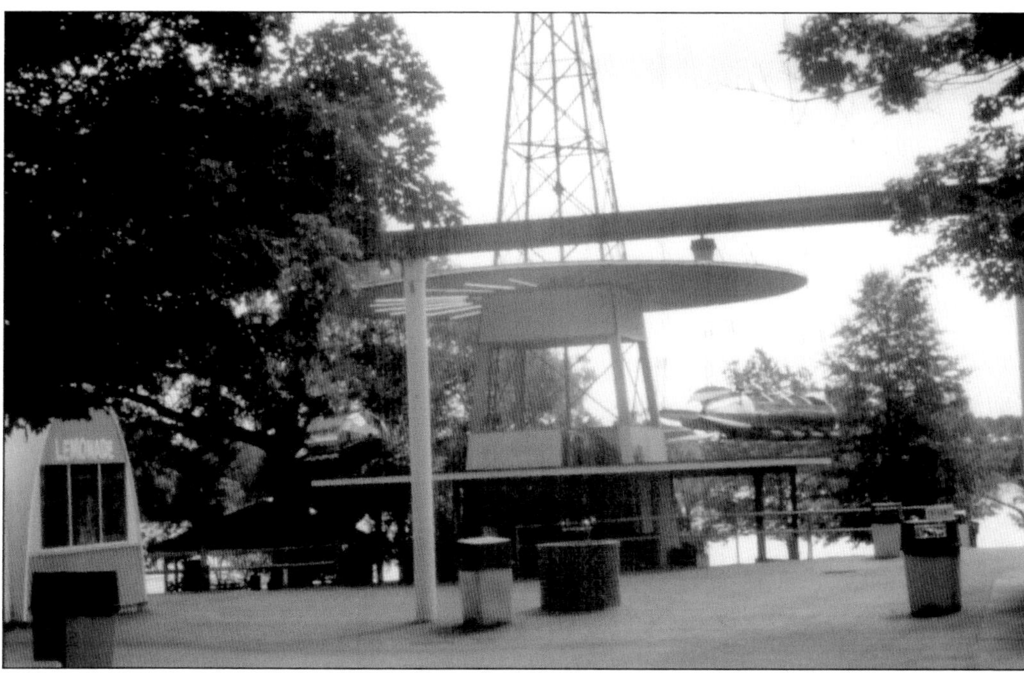

Along the lakeshore, the aerial swing remained in operation, providing the same opportunity to soar above the treetops that visitors had in 1925. However, by the 1980s, as with the stainless-steel rockets, the ride was much more about nostalgia than thrills. (Jim Futrell collection.)

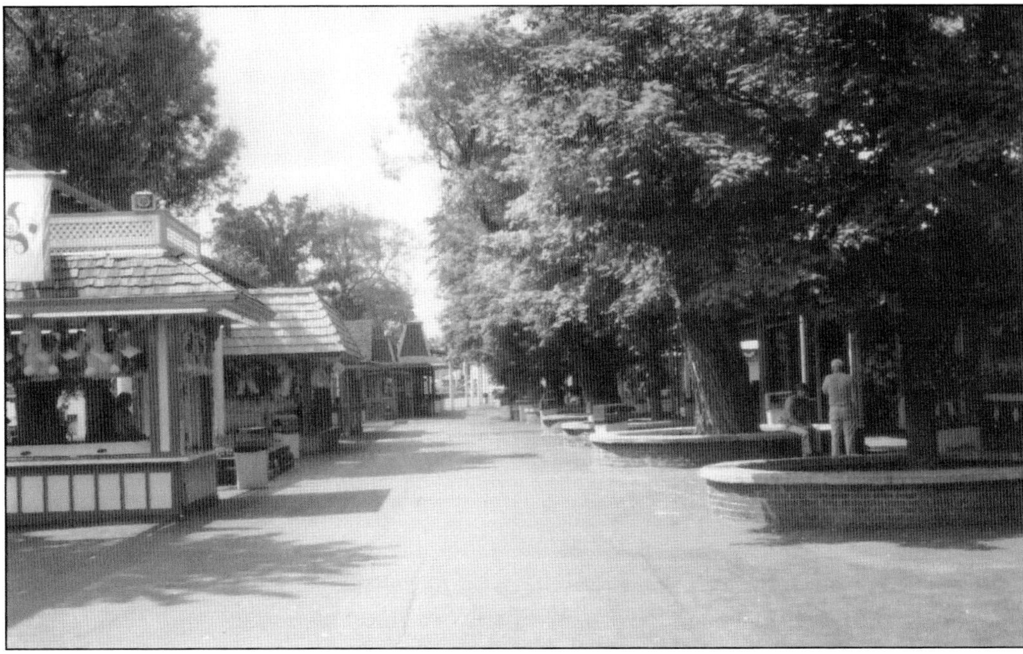

By the early 1980s, the midway built during the 1925 expansion was a much different place. While it still maintained its nostalgic atmosphere, the buildings had been modernized, the walkways paved, and the trees were much bigger, providing welcome shade on a hot summer day. (Jim Futrell collection.)

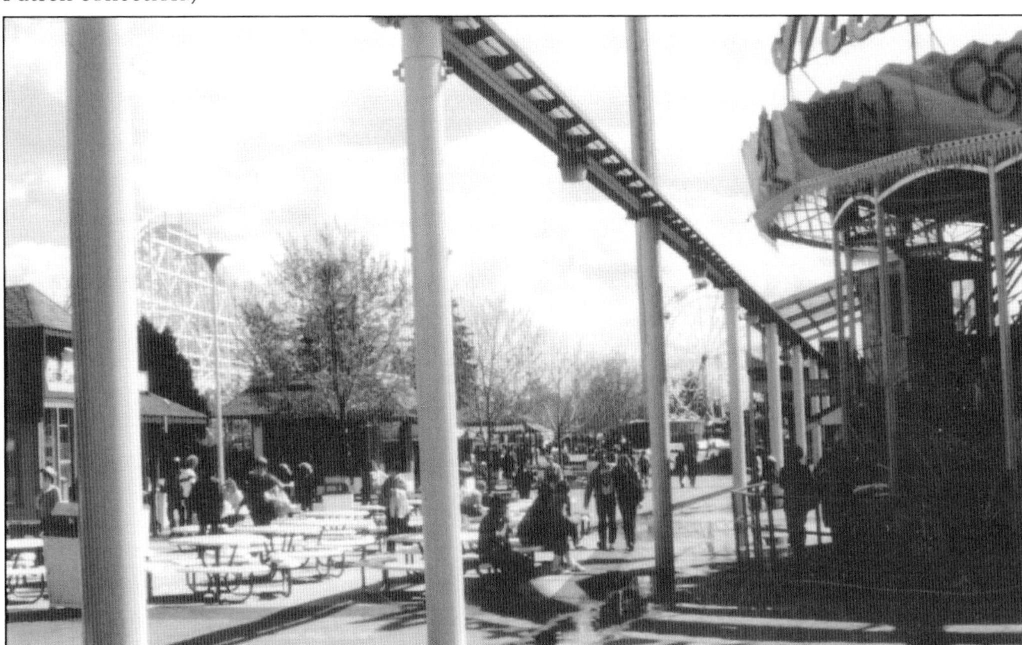

A quiet day on the midway at Geauga Lake illustrates some of the challenges the park was facing in the early 1980s. The industrial economy of the park's trade area was struggling in the wake of plant closures. With half of Geauga Lake's business coming from group picnics, attendance was starting to decrease, falling from a record 909,000 in 1980 to 785,000 in 1982. (Jim Futrell collection.)

Four

Making a Splash 1983–1987

As Geauga Lake entered the 1980s, the park was still defined by its selection of roller coasters and wide array of traditional amusement park rides. In fact, with more than 50 rides in operation, Geauga Lake had one of the largest collections in the country.

But while Geauga Lake had undergone a remarkable transformation, it was struggling. The region's industrial economy was in a tailspin, impacting business. In 1979, Geauga Lake experienced its first decrease in attendance since Funtime purchased the facility. By 1982, attendance had fallen to 785,000, fourteen percent below the record high in 1980.

To compound the challenge, the industry in which it competed was again changing. The roller coaster arms race was largely over by the early 1980s, and park operators were turning to other new ways to attract customers, including simulators and water-based attractions.

Water-based attractions such as waterslides and wave pools had started spreading around the country in the late 1960s. In 1978, Wet 'n Wild, considered to be the first full-scale water park, opened in Florida. Meanwhile, many amusement parks started to add waterslides to their attractions lineups. But these waterslides were limited in scope and required a separate admission.

In these attractions, Geauga Lake saw an opportunity to reignite its business, stand out in the marketplace, and do something truly innovative. The result was Boardwalk Shores, a full-scale water park developed on the shore of the lake. But what was truly groundbreaking was that Boardwalk Shores was fully integrated into the rest of Geauga Lake and included in the same admission price. It was the first time that an amusement park and water park had been integrated into one attraction.

Not only did the industry pay attention, with the concept soon spreading throughout the country, but so did the marketplace, with attendance jumping to record levels. The next few years were marked by continued growth in water attractions, with Funtime exporting the concept to Columbus, Ohio, where it transformed the tired Zoo Amusement Park into Wyandot Lake, a combined water and amusement park in 1984.

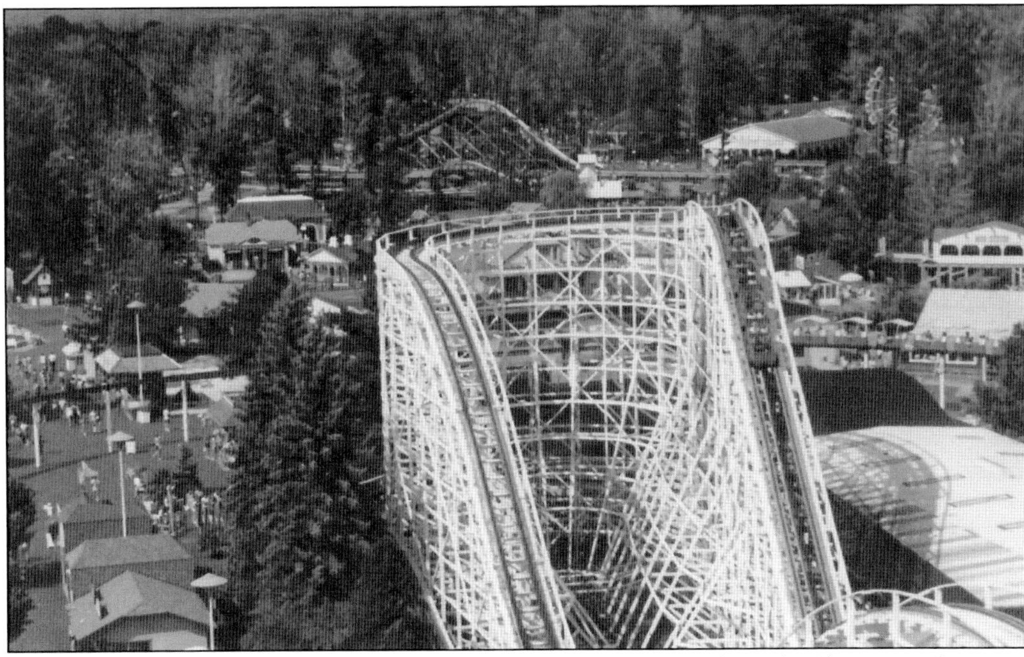

This 1983 view looking toward the Western Village area of the park from the Skyscraper showcases the lift hill and first drop of the Big Dipper. In the distance, one can see the Gold Rush log flume, Enterprise, and Big Ditch loading dock, with the monorail gliding nearby. Geauga Lake had become a well-rounded, modern amusement park under Funtime's control. (Dave Hahner collection.)

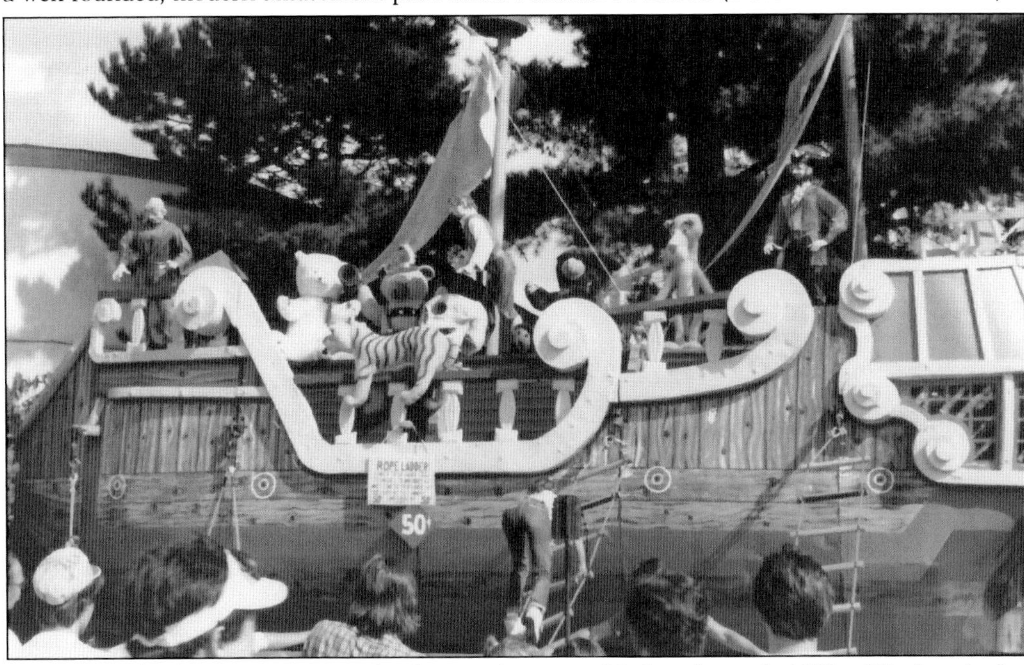

The ladder climb game was a popular feature that was added in the early 1980s. Climbers had to reach the top of a rope ladder and ring the bell to be a winner, a task much harder than it looks. What set Geauga Lake's version apart from other parks was the elaborate pirate ship theme, making a great spot for photo opportunities. (Dave Hahner collection.)

In winter of 1982, Geauga Lake made an announcement that would change the entire amusement industry. The park would spend $1.5 million to add a full-scale water park that would be integrated with the amusement park, all for one admission. Never before attempted, the project dubbed Boardwalk Shores would transform an underutilized section of the park. (Jim Futrell collection.)

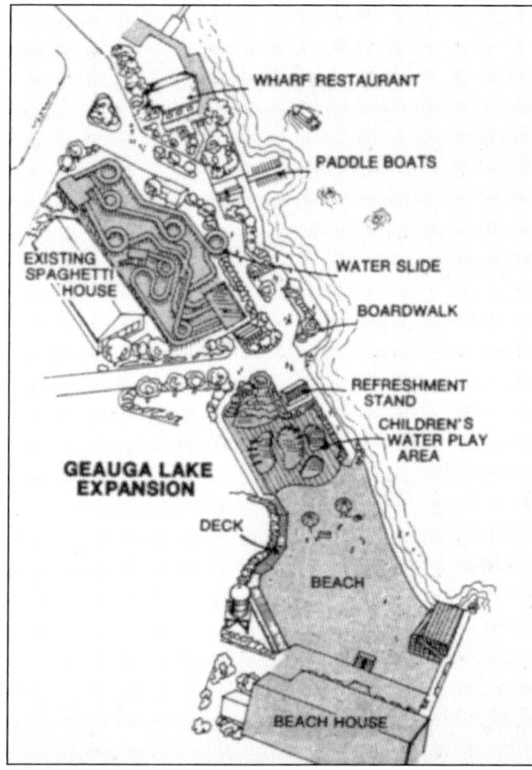

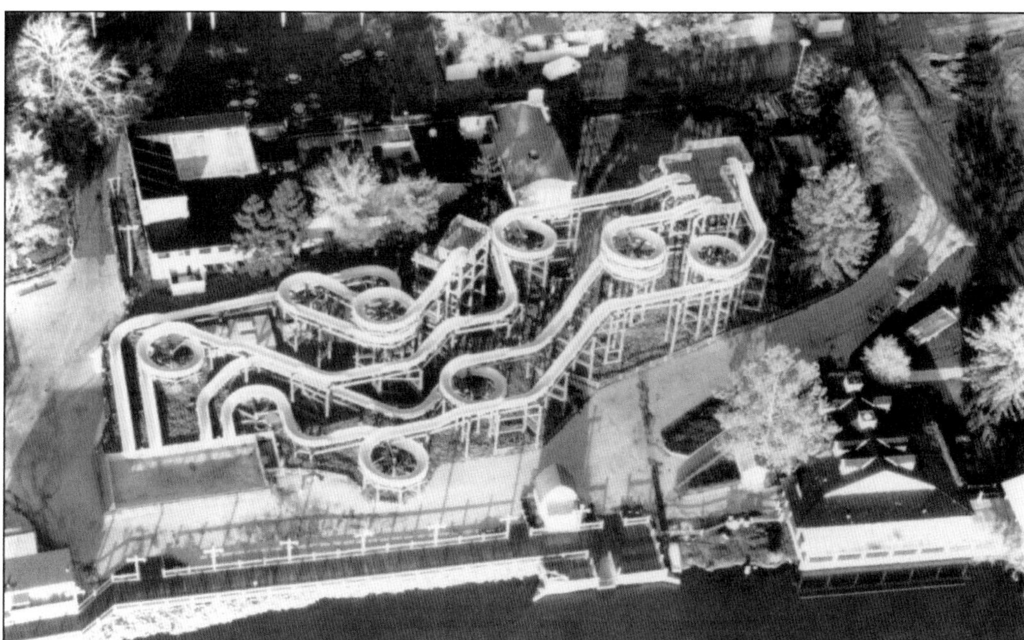

The largest part of Boardwalk Shores would be the addition of Neptune's Falls, featuring four twisting, interlocking body slides overlooking the shoreline of Geauga Lake. The expansion would also include a refurbished Wharf restaurant located along the lakefront, while a portion of the 1941 ballroom was converted into a bathhouse for the new area. (Jim Futrell collection.)

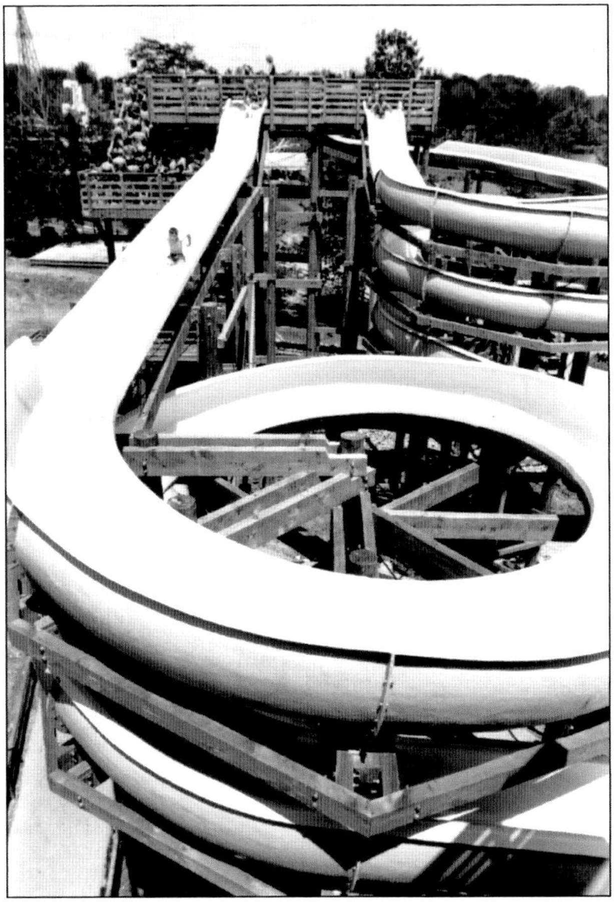

Neptune's Falls was an immediate hit with visitors to Geauga Lake. Long lines were not uncommon for the four twisting body slides, especially on hot summer days. The slides varied in length and twisting elements, but all ended in a shallow splash pool along the boardwalk. The entire first phase of the Boardwalk Shores project utilized most of the lakeside property from the ballroom to where the carousel used to be located. The nearby giant slide that once was located along the lakefront would be shortened in height and repositioned to become a wet slide into the lake. It would be removed after the 1985 season to extend the 300-by-60-foot sandy beachfront near the ballroom. (Both, Jim Futrell collection.)

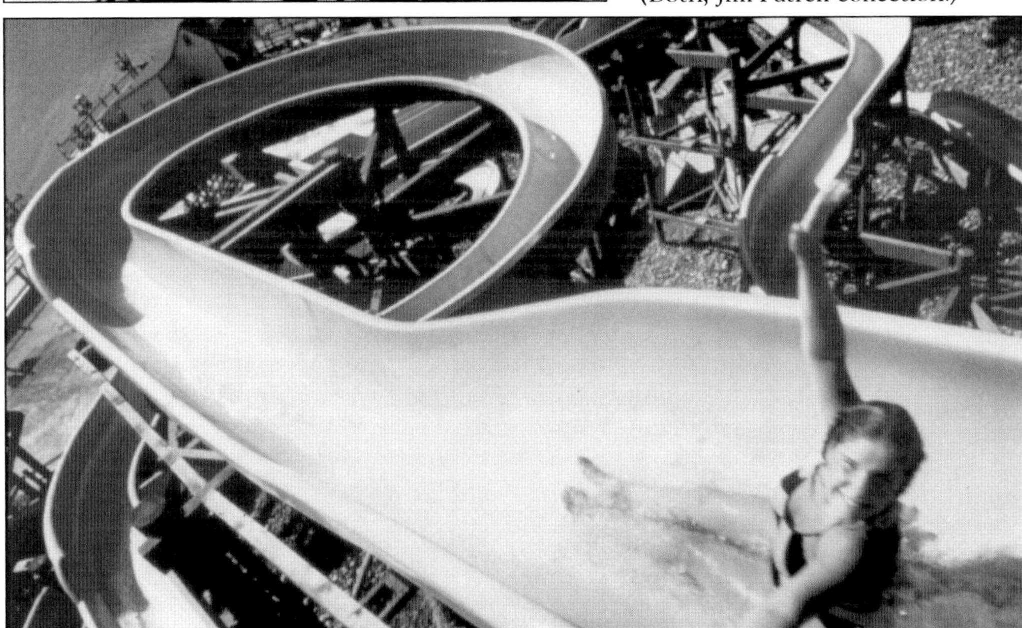

Another water park attraction added to Boardwalk Shores during the first phase was the Undertow. This unusual attraction featured two 30-foot-high slides near the Big Dipper's back turn. Daring passengers would ride a small plastic sled down the steep chutes and skim across the water of a small pool like a stone being skipped along the water. The repurposed giant slide can be seen in the background. (Jim Futrell collection.)

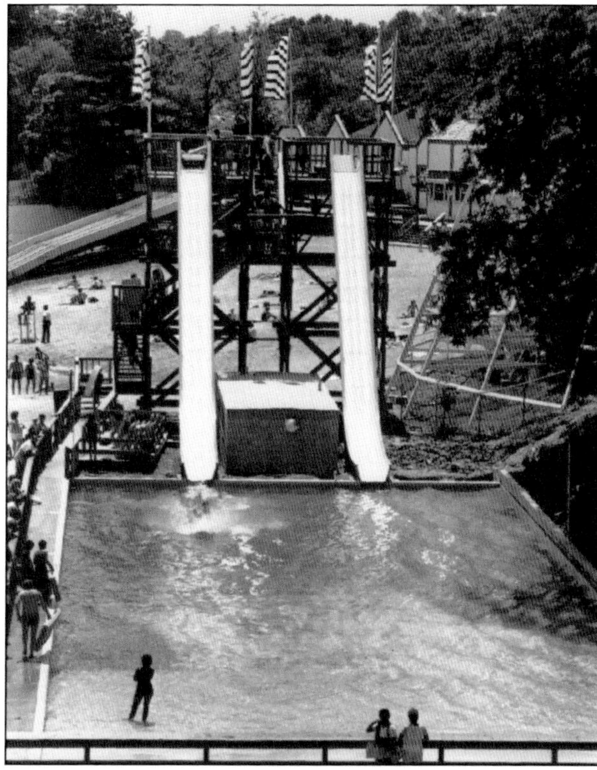

The location of Boardwalk Shores was ideal. Not only did it give public beach access for the first time in years from within the park, but it also offered a picturesque seaside feel to the entire water park complex. But, probably most important, the twisting waterslides of Neptune's Falls were quite visible from across the lake at neighboring SeaWorld. (Dave Hahner collection.)

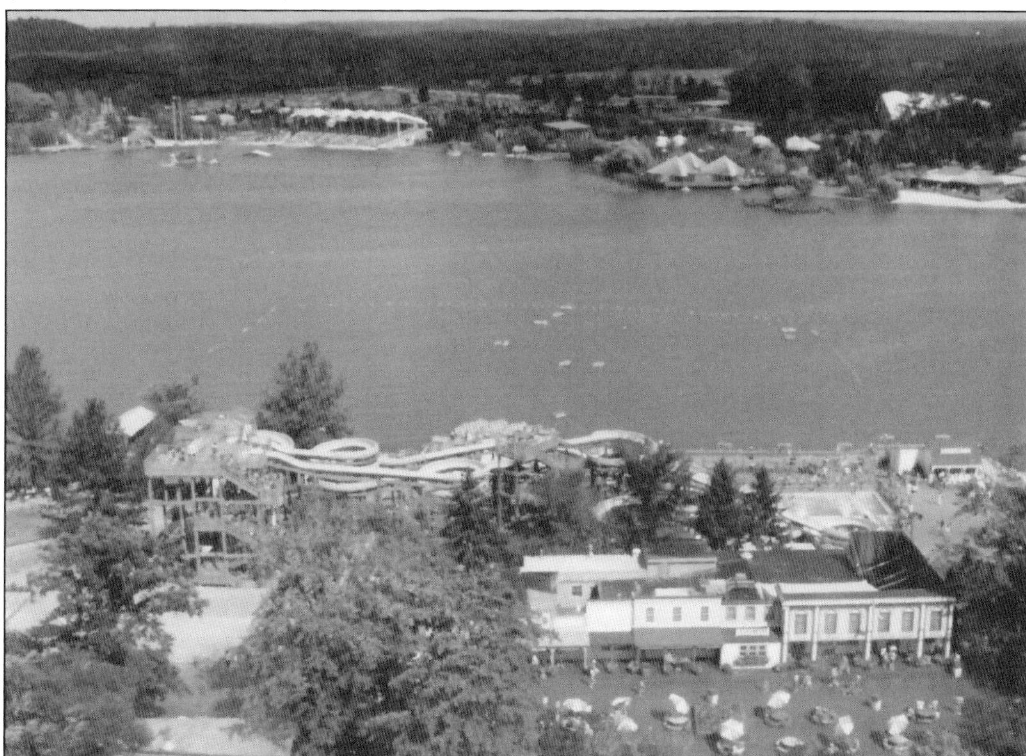

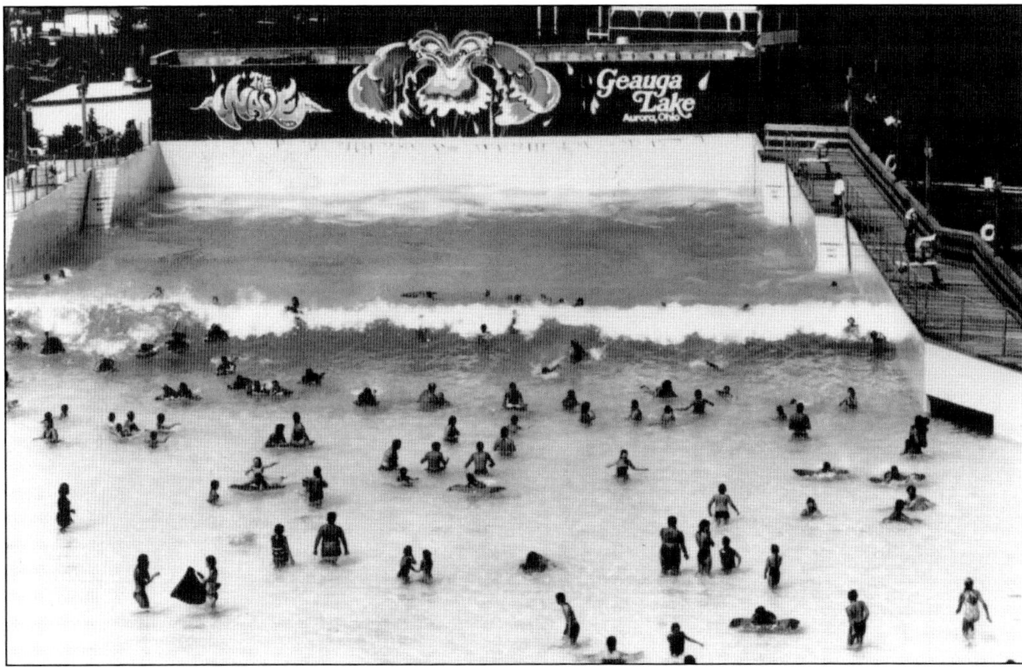

The success of Boardwalk Shores was nothing short of phenomenal. Attendance jumped 14 percent, from 785,000 in 1982 to 915,000 in 1983, as a result of the water park. In 1984, phase two of Boardwalk Shores would be enormous, with the addition of the Wave, the largest wave pool built east of the Rocky Mountains. The mammoth 57,000-square-foot concrete ocean held 1.78 million gallons of water and cost $2 million to construct. Unlike most of today's wave pools with periods of constant wave action, the Wave was a tsunami-style wave pool, with one large, crashing wave sent about every 45 seconds to two minutes. (Both, Jim Futrell collection.)

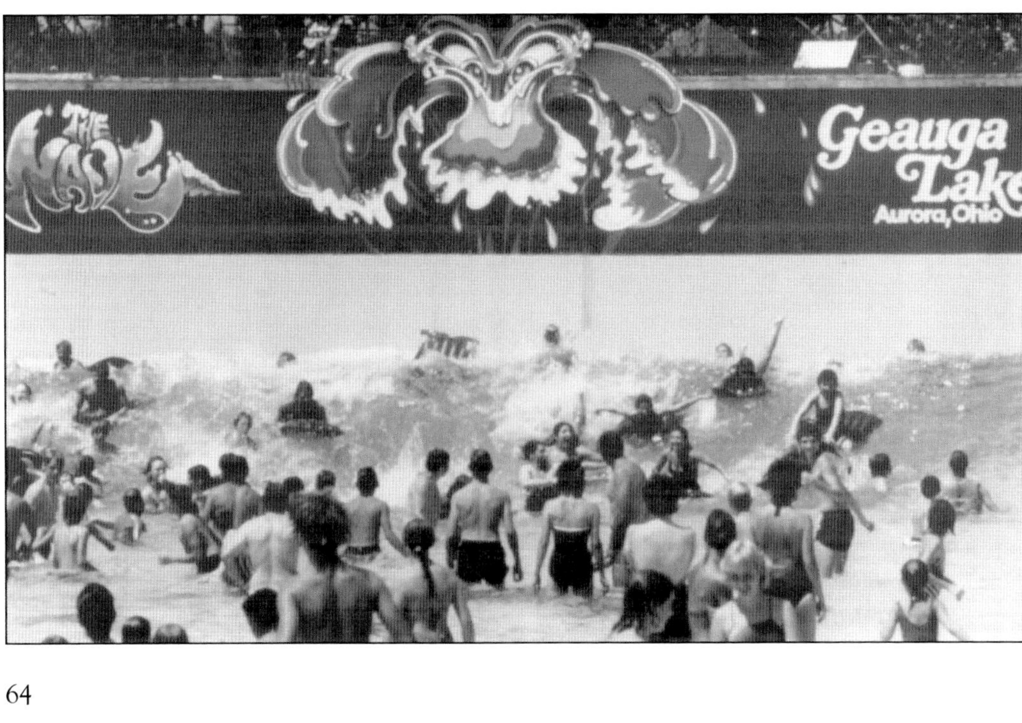

Each of the Wave's four-to-six-foot-high crashing waves traveled about 16 miles per hour and carried over 240,000 gallons of water with every blast, knocking over or carrying along all in its wake. The Wave was an instant hit with park guests, increasing the attendance for the park to 960,000 in 1984, which was once again a new park record under Funtime. (Jim Futrell collection.)

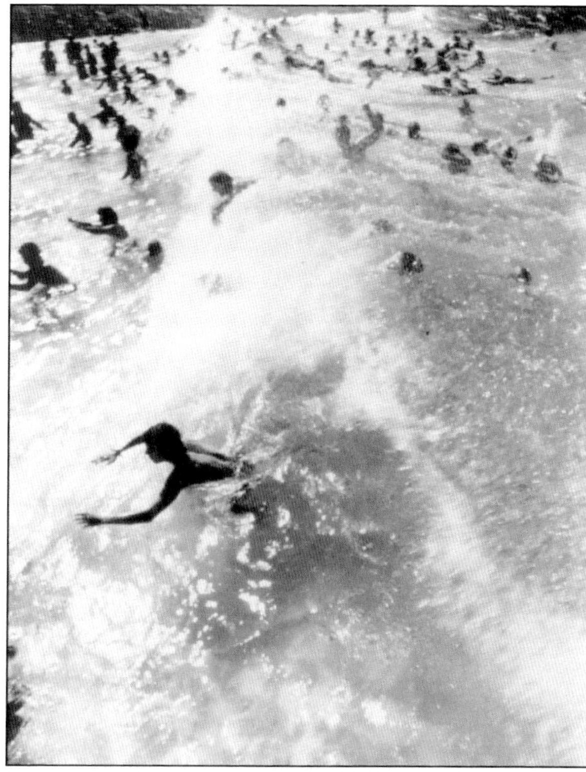

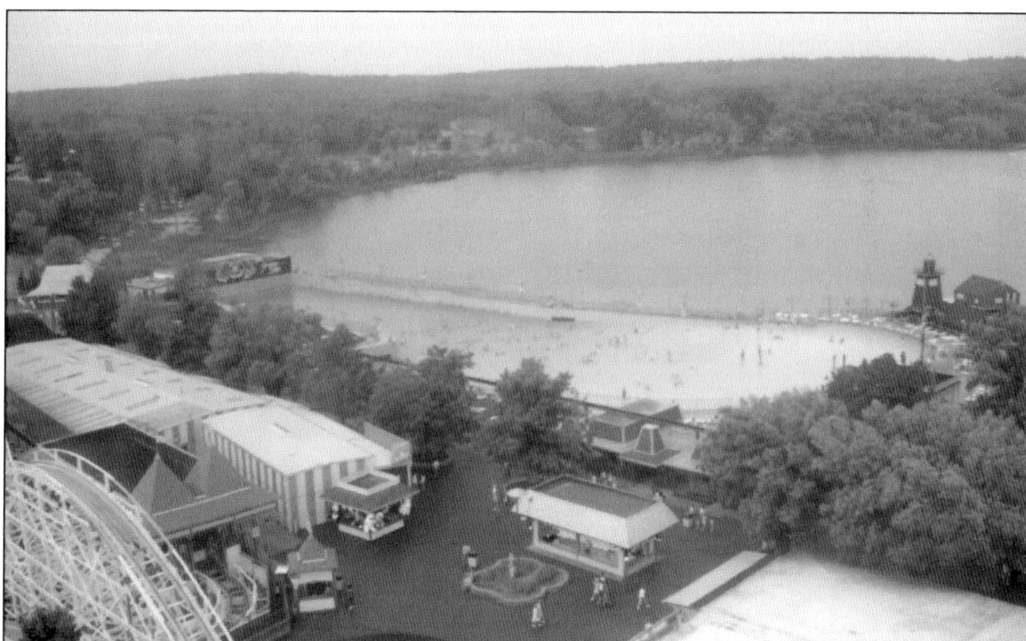

The enormity of the Wave's pool can be seen in this 1988 aerial view from the Skyscraper tower. The length of the pool reached over 400 feet, with the force of the wave literally carrying swimmers almost the entire distance. The addition of the Wave along the lakefront necessitated the redevelopment of the nearby midway. (Dave Hahner collection.)

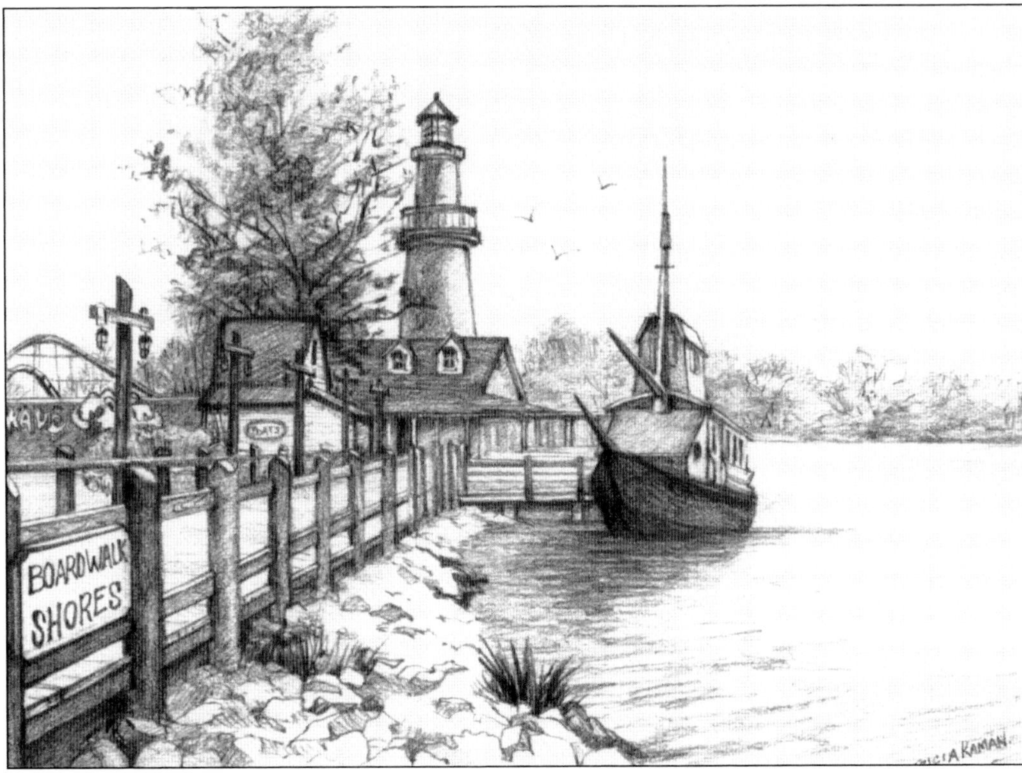

In 1985, a more modest upgrade to the Boardwalk Shores area would occur. This pre-production artwork depicts a new lighthouse and boat dock that would be added along the lakefront near the Wave, featuring shops and an old boat converted into a raw bar. Also added that year was a new restaurant called the Funtime Sail Co., which was located near the Big Dipper's back turn. (Jim Futrell collection.)

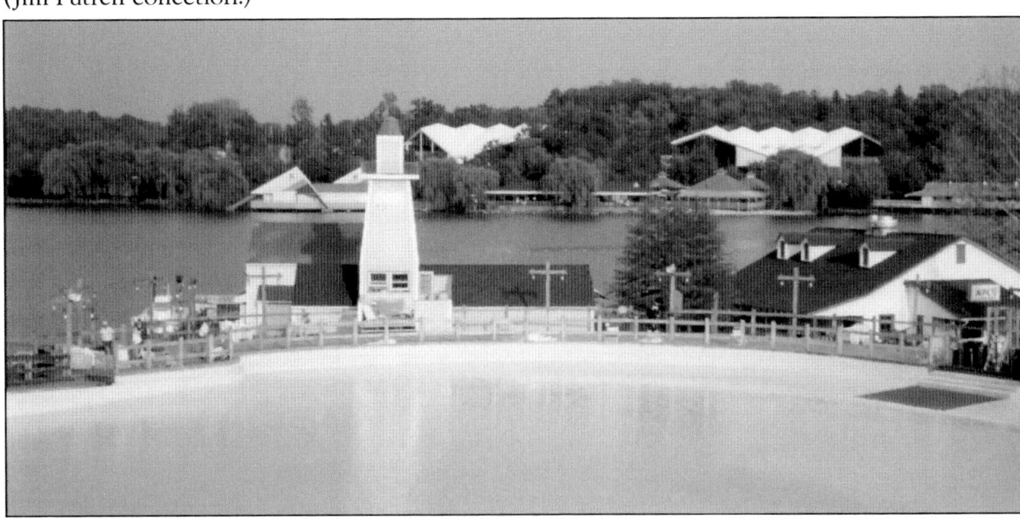

The lighthouse, as seen in later years in this image, would be home to a new lake cruise. The long-running Big Ditch boat ride would close in 1984, but the boats would be reused for the cruise through the lake, giving great views of both Geauga Lake amusement park and neighboring SeaWorld. (Dave Hahner collection.)

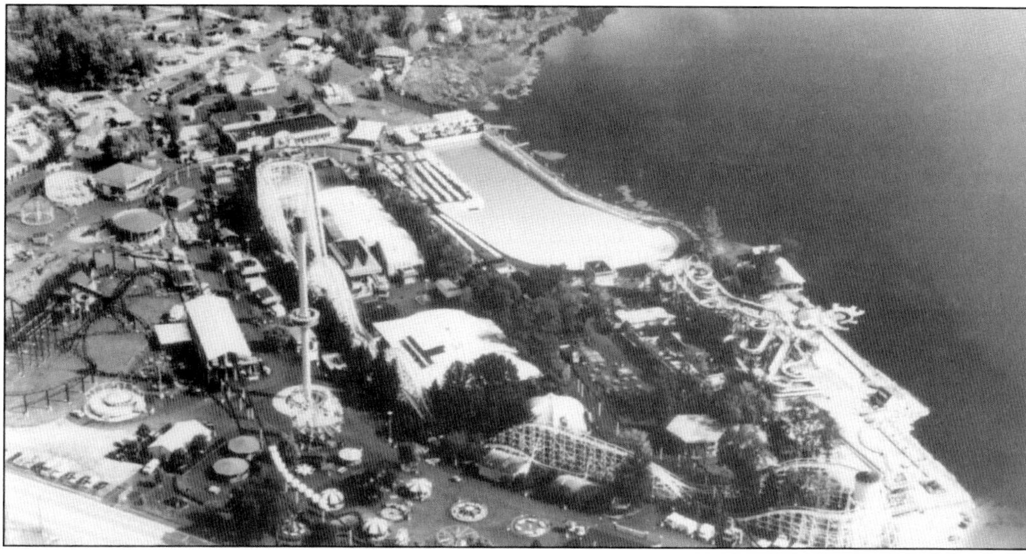

This 1984 aerial view of the park illustrates the impact that the Wave had on the face of Geauga Lake. But something that would foreshadow things to come was happening behind the scenes during the fall of 1985, as Harcourt Brace Jovanovich, owner of SeaWorld, made a bid to buy Geauga Lake and merge it with the marine park. The deal fell through for undisclosed reasons. (Jim Futrell collection.)

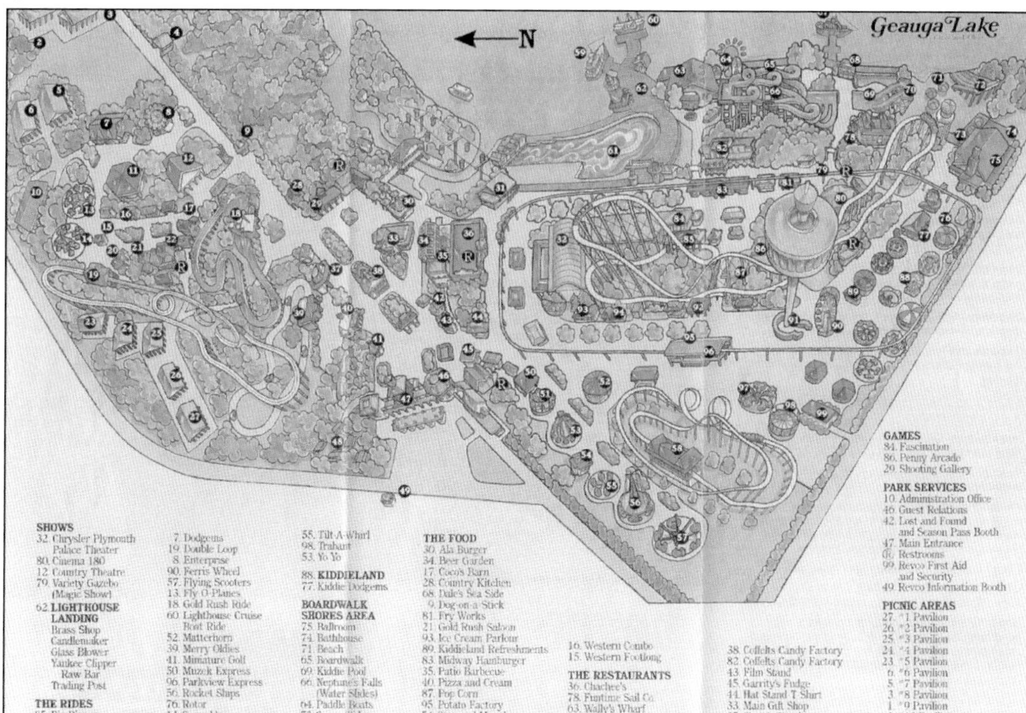

In this 1985 map of Geauga Lake, the scale of the Wave and Boardwalk Shores is evident, as it takes up nearly the entire lakefront property. Also, a new midway was developed near the Corkscrew roller coaster, featuring several old favorites along with some newer rides. (Sam Shurgott collection.)

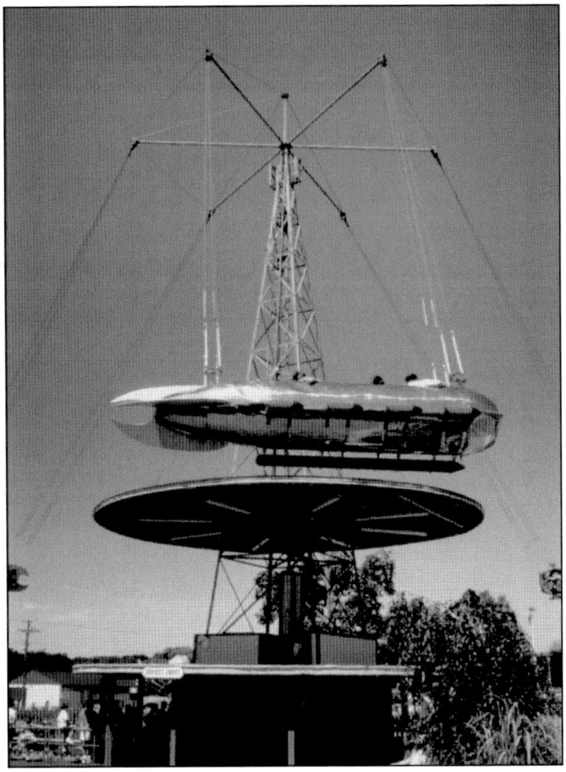

With the addition of the Wave, several longtime attractions that used to be found near the lakefront had to be relocated. The Eyerly Rock-O-Plane was moved to Wyandot Lake in Columbus, Ohio, as part of that park's transformation. But one of the park's oldest attractions, the Harry Traver circle-swing ride known as the Rocket Ships, found a new home in the park. (Jim Futrell collection.)

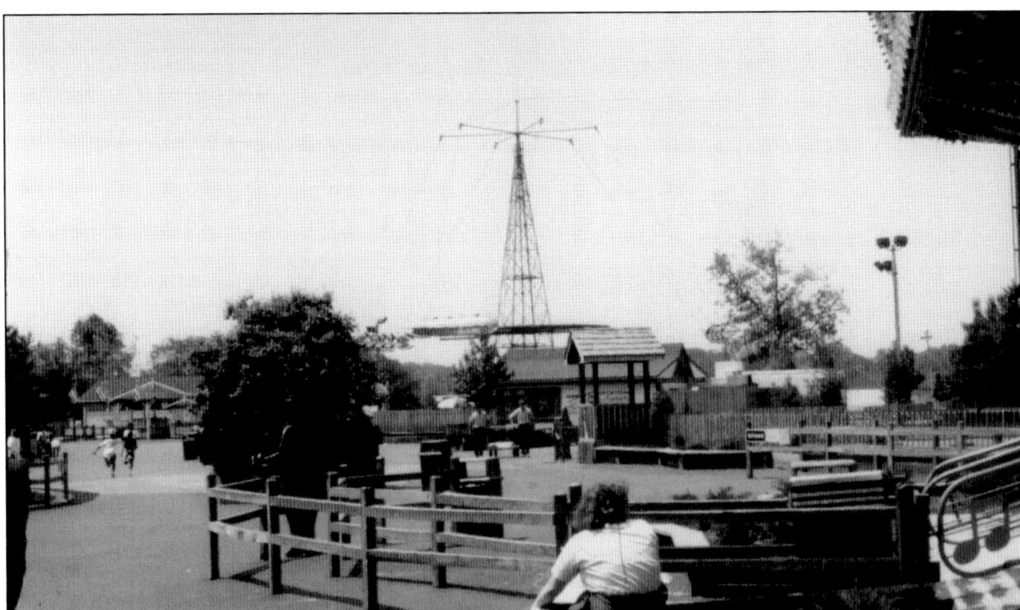

The circle swing was featured in a new midway area next to the Corkscrew that also included the Flying Scooters and Tilt-A-Whirl. A family ride by nature, the Rocket Ships were often a favorite of the young and the young-at-heart. Fortunately, Geauga Lake management realized the importance of the old ride, giving it a new home near the park's Corkscrew roller coaster. (Jim Futrell collection.)

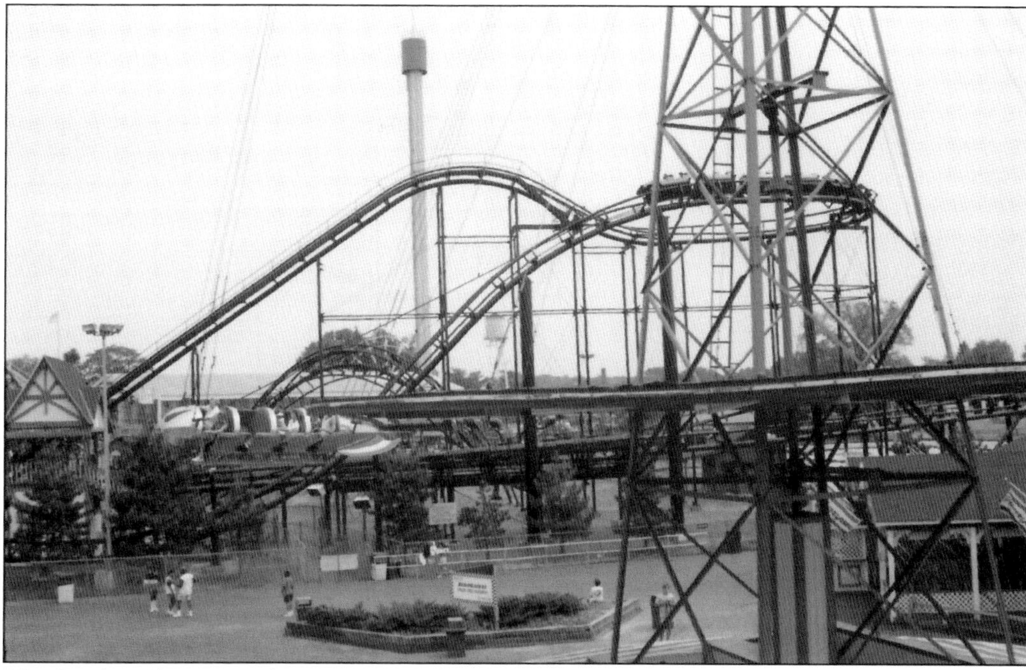

The Rocket Ships' new location near the Corkscrew may not have been quite as scenic as it was near the lake, but it was still a very refreshing ride for those who were not into intense thrills. Unfortunately, the venerable ride would be removed for the 1996 season under the new ownership of Premier Parks. It was the last ride of its kind in operation in the United States. (Dave Hahner collection.)

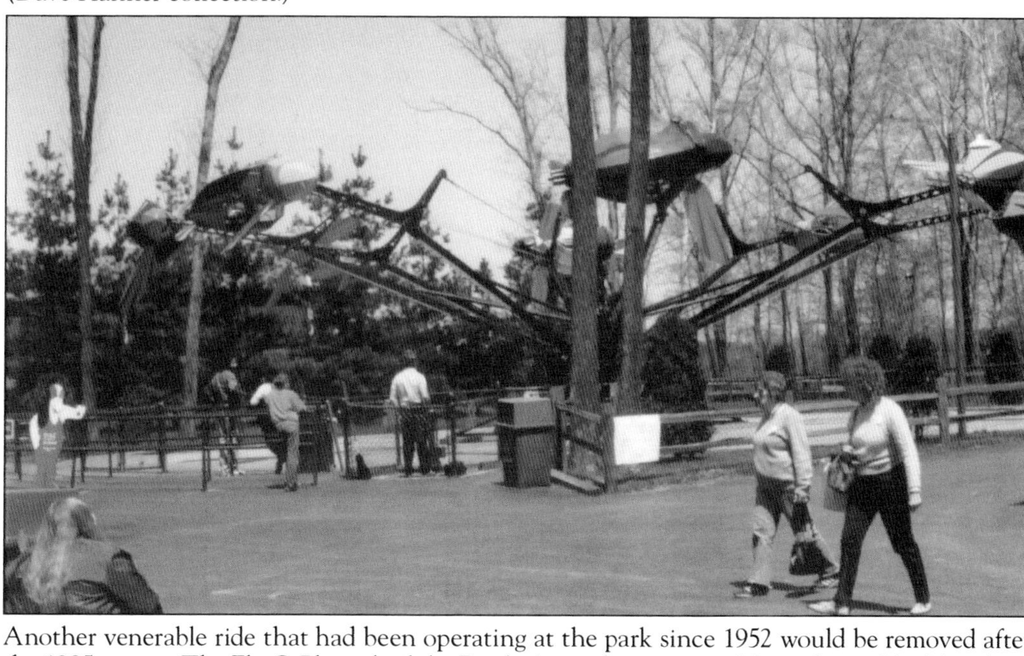

Another venerable ride that had been operating at the park since 1952 would be removed after the 1985 season. The Fly-O-Plane, built by Eyerly Aircraft, was moved from the park's old midway to near the Double Loop roller coaster in 1977, but it would be replaced by the Flying Scooter in 1986. (Jim Futrell collection.)

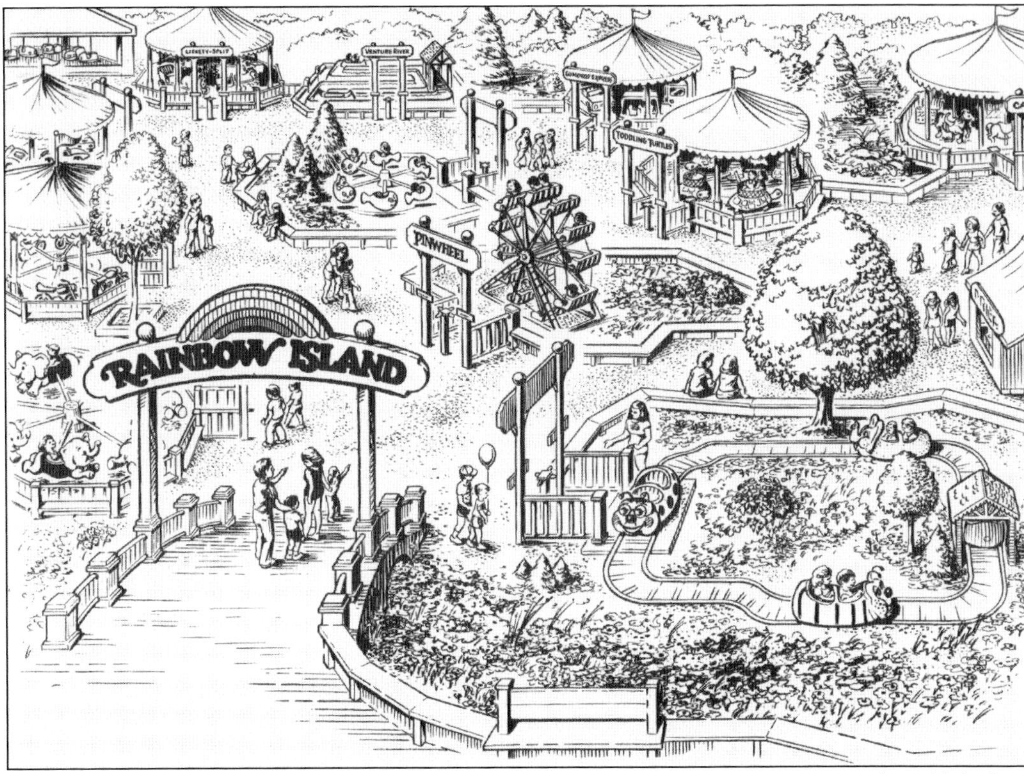

With most of the additions from the last few years being focused on the new water park and lakefront area, attention was turned in 1986 to the enlargement and improvement of the park's kiddieland. Rainbow Island would occupy the same area as the previous children's area, near Highway 43 and the Big Dipper, but would be upgraded with new rides and a new look. (Jim Futrell collection.)

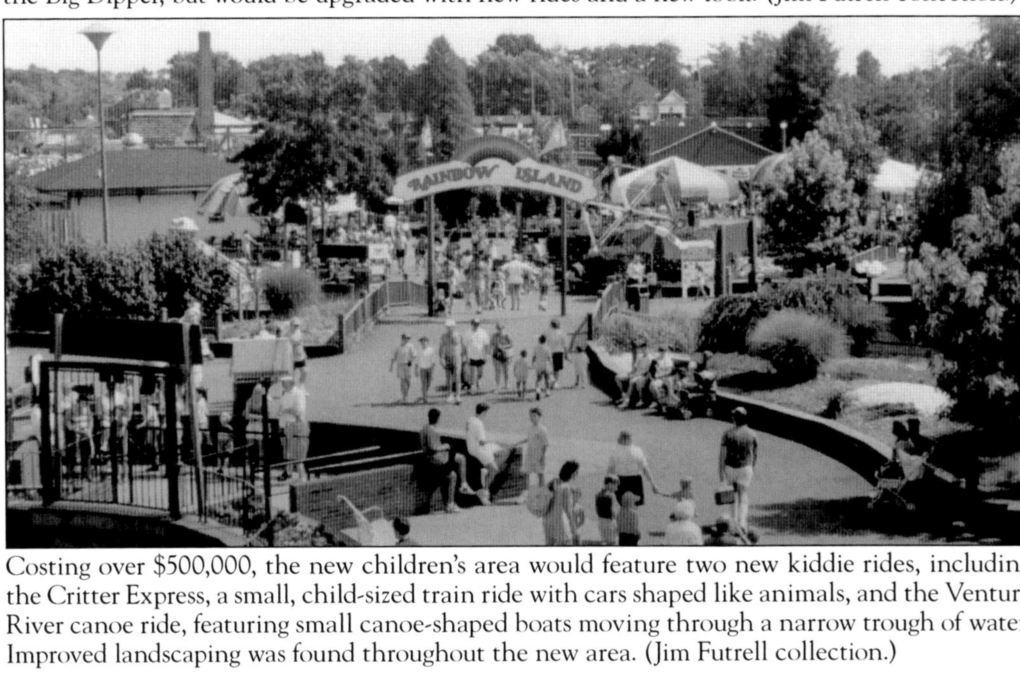

Costing over $500,000, the new children's area would feature two new kiddie rides, including the Critter Express, a small, child-sized train ride with cars shaped like animals, and the Venture River canoe ride, featuring small canoe-shaped boats moving through a narrow trough of water. Improved landscaping was found throughout the new area. (Jim Futrell collection.)

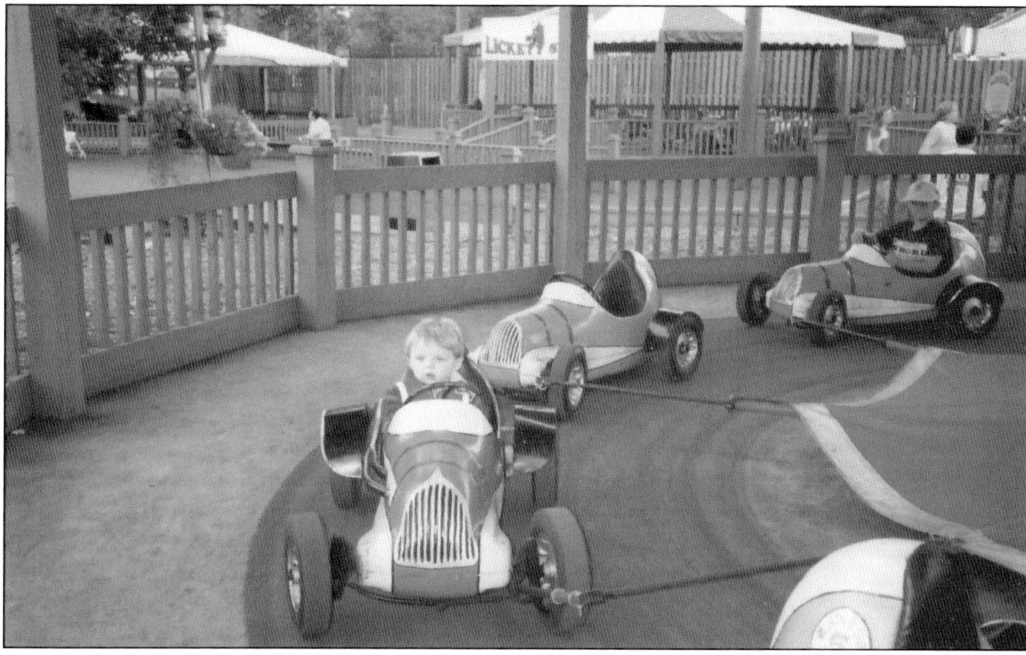

The Midge-O-Racer, one of the older kiddie rides dating back to 1953, was completely refurbished for the Rainbow Island makeover, offering a new generation of children the same fun that their parents and grandparents may have experienced. The vintage look of the race cars remained virtually unchanged from when the ride was first installed. (Dave Hahner collection.)

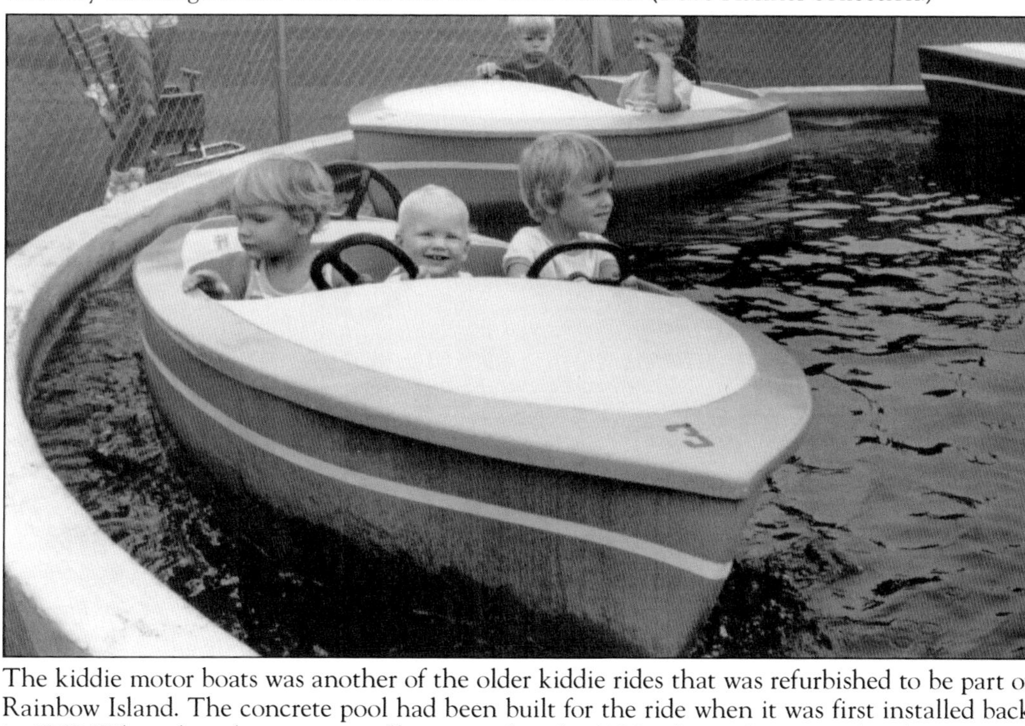

The kiddie motor boats was another of the older kiddie rides that was refurbished to be part of Rainbow Island. The concrete pool had been built for the ride when it was first installed back in 1969. When the ride was eventually removed in the 1990s, the pool remained and was turned into a flower planter. (Jim Futrell collection.)

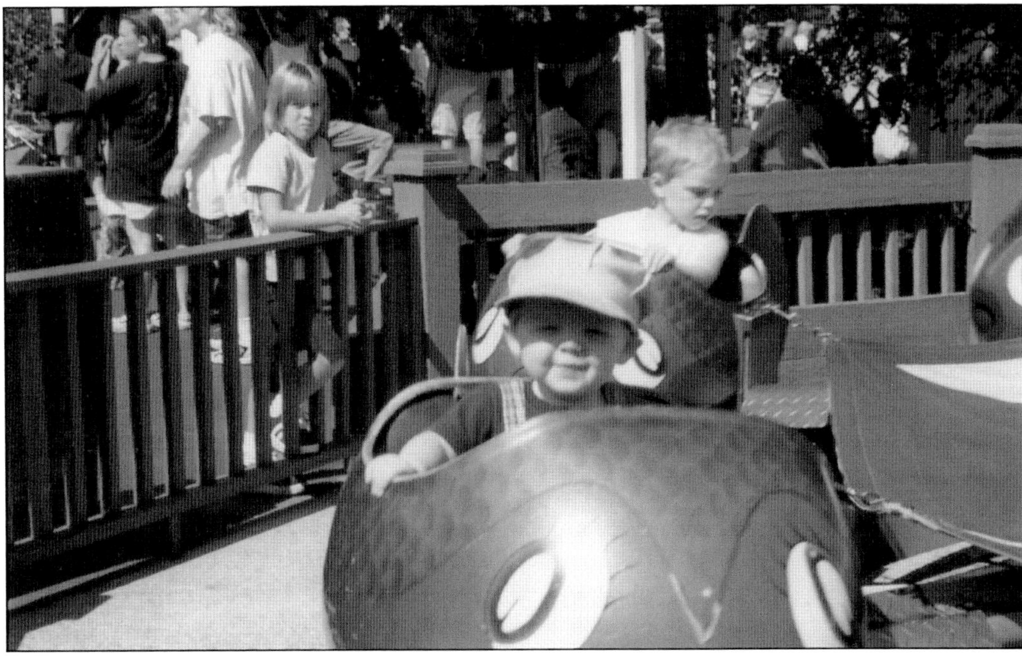

One of the more popular rides found in Rainbow Island was Bulgy the Whale, also called the Guppy. Built by Eyerly Aircraft, it was originally purchased by Geauga Lake in 1953. Children loved to ride these bouncing fish-shaped vehicles along the undulating track. Rainbow Island was a perfect respite for families with small children who were too small for the larger rides. Unfortunately, all of these kiddie rides would be removed after the 1999 season, with many of them dispersed to other Six Flags parks, sold to other amusement parks, or retired to make way for a new wave pool with the expansion of the water park into Hurricane Harbor. Sadly, none were kept at the park for the transformation into Six Flags Ohio in 2000. (Above, Dave Hahner collection; below, Sam Shurgott collection.)

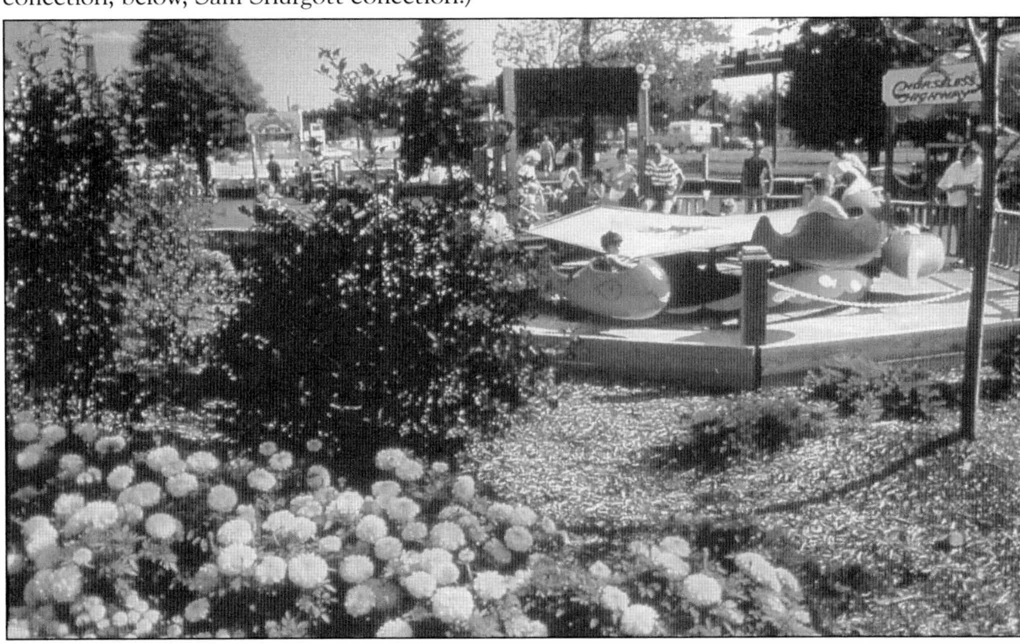

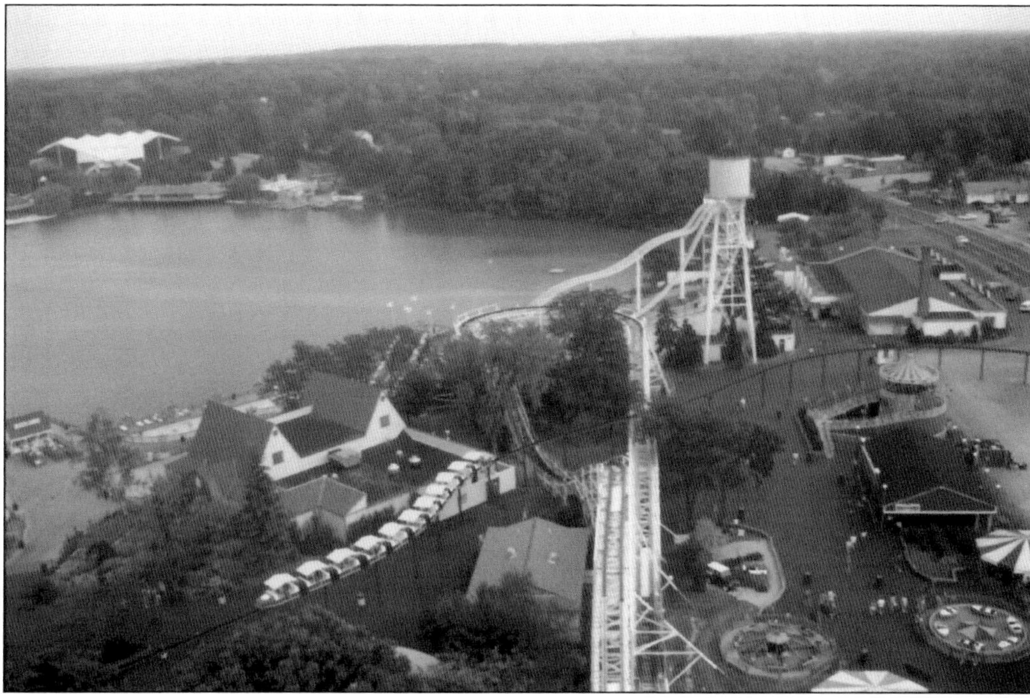

After the successful introduction of Rainbow Island, attention once again returned to the Boardwalk Shores water park in 1987. Where the giant slide once stood along the beach near the old ballroom, a tower with three new waterslides would rise 70 feet above the lakeshore. Dubbed the Stingray, these speed slides would be the tallest and fastest slides at Geauga Lake. Two of the slides consisted of a series of three smaller dips, side-by-side. The third speed slide was a nearly 70-foot plummet at a very steep angle. Many passengers had to work up their nerve before attempting to take the plunge on this slide, often opting for the two racing slides instead. (Both, Dave Hahner collection.)

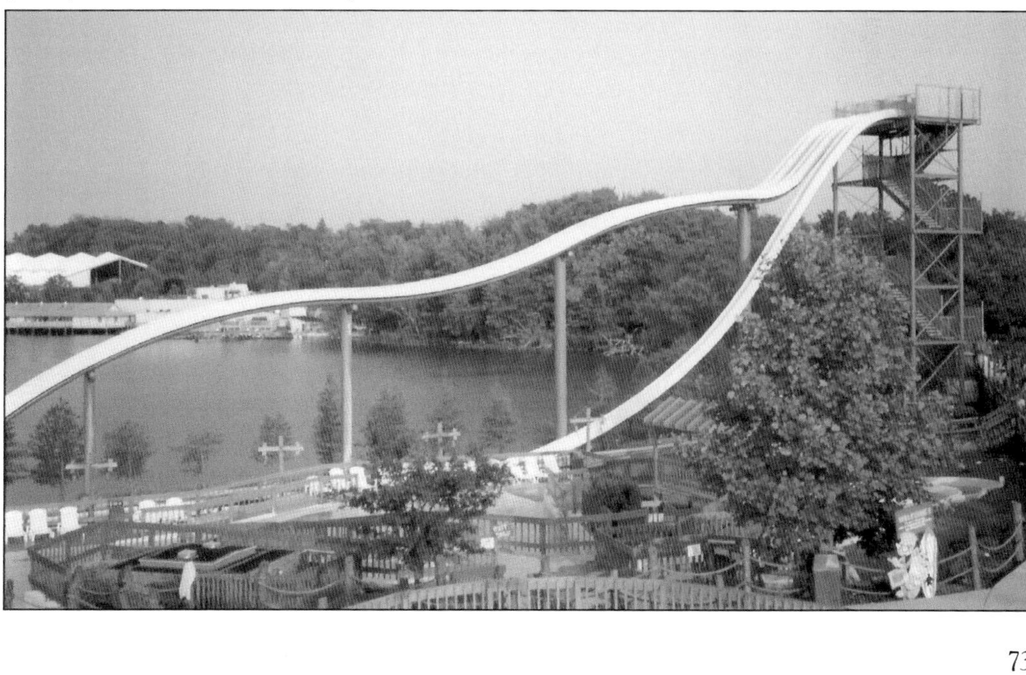

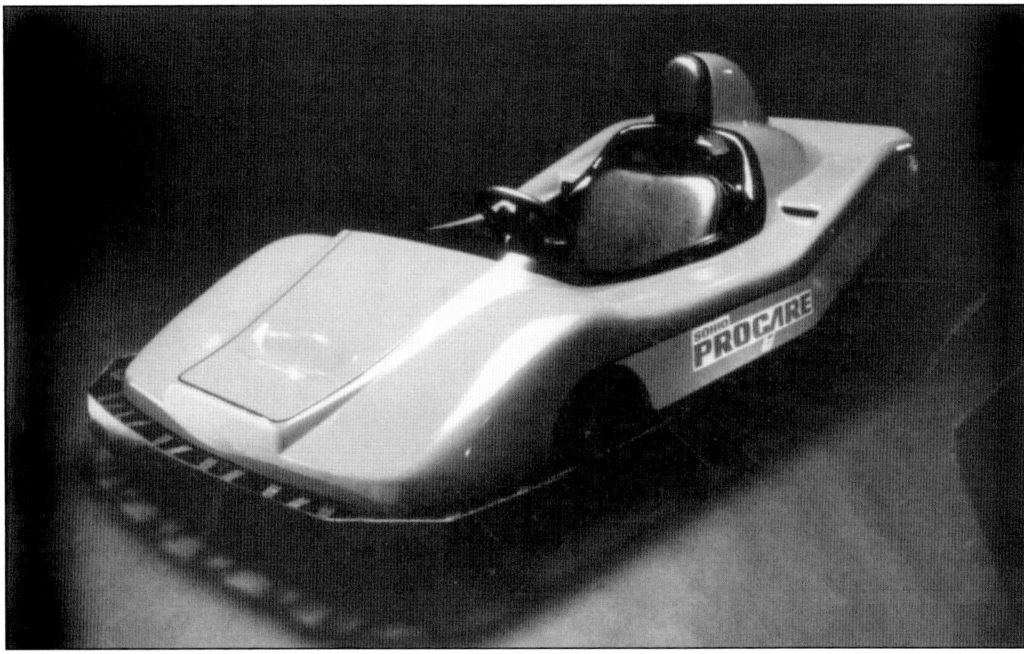

Also new for 1987 was the Euroracers Gran Prix racetrack. This 1,500-foot-long go-cart track featured cars that were patterned after sleek European-styled Formula 1 race cars. In an age when pay-one-price admission at amusement parks had largely replaced the old pay-as-you-ride ticket systems, Geauga Lake took the chance that guests would still pay for an "upcharge" attraction, even after paying admission to enter the park. And the gamble paid off, as the attraction proved to be quite popular—so much so that other parks took notice and began to offer similar attractions. (Above, Jim Futrell collection; below, Dave Hahner collection.)

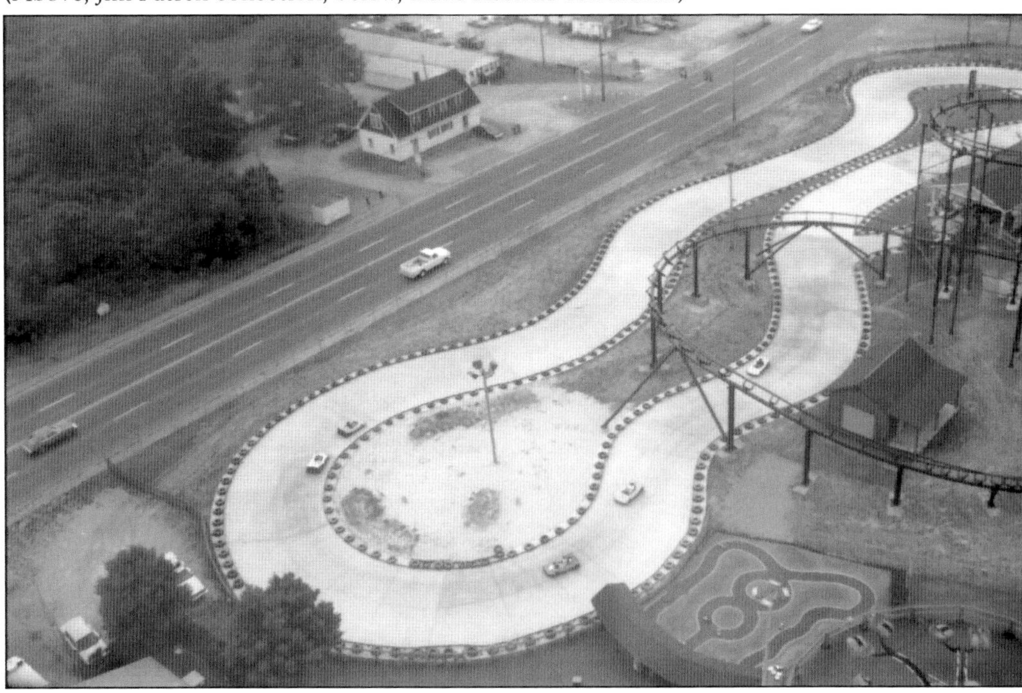

Five

Raging into Its Second Century 1988–1995

With the enormous popularity of the waterslides of Boardwalk Shores and the Wave, Funtime could have easily chosen to continue building upon the water park. It had become the trendsetter in the industry by being the first park to successfully merge water park and amusement park together as one. But at the end of the 1987 season, Funtime management decided to take the company private in a $63-million leveraged buyout. This would be the first time since 1968 that Geauga Lake would be owned by a single private entity, opening up possibilities for future expansion.

The first new investment after the buyout would be a huge one, with the addition of a brand-new wooden roller coaster to help commemorate what the park decided would be its centennial season, in 1988. A decade had passed since the park last installed a new roller coaster, and management decided the best strategy would be to re-create a lost classic. Based upon a legendary wooden coaster called the Bobs that once operated at Chicago's famous Riverview Park, the new ride would be built in a mostly undeveloped, marshy portion of the property. The new coaster would be a major coup for Funtime, as it finally would pass the one million annual visitors mark for the first time.

The following two seasons, park management focused back on the water park additions by adding Turtle Beach, a child-sized water park for the younger crowd. The addition of Turtle Beach would be a huge success, keeping the park's attendance over 1.1 million visitors.

The early 1990s were a bit more challenging, as recession hit the area in 1992. Creative promotions were attempted by the park to keep guests returning, including free bungee jumping for a brief period. As the economy improved in 1993, Funtime would add another innovative new ride to its lineup with Texas Twister, the first ride of its kind in the United States. But this would be its last major addition, as the entire Funtime chain would be sold during the 1995 season as the industry started to consolidate.

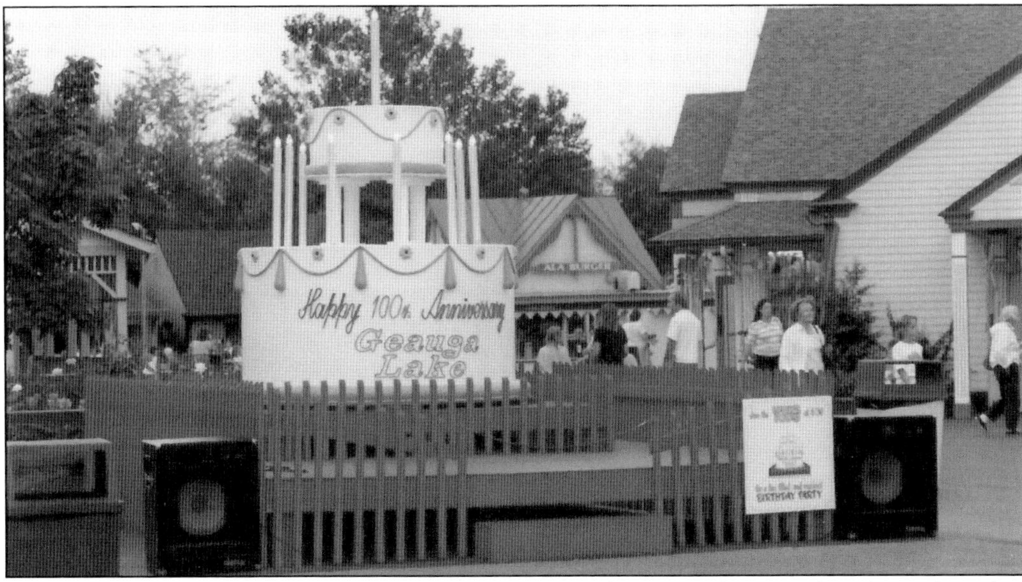

Geauga Lake never really had a true opening date, as evidenced in chapter 1, but the park evolved significantly since the 1870s. By 1988, Funtime thought that a centennial observation was in order and launched a huge, season-long centennial celebration, including special live entertainment, fireworks, and other activities throughout the season. At the park's entrance, a large, festive birthday cake welcomed guests to Geauga Lake's 100th anniversary. (Joel Styer collection.)

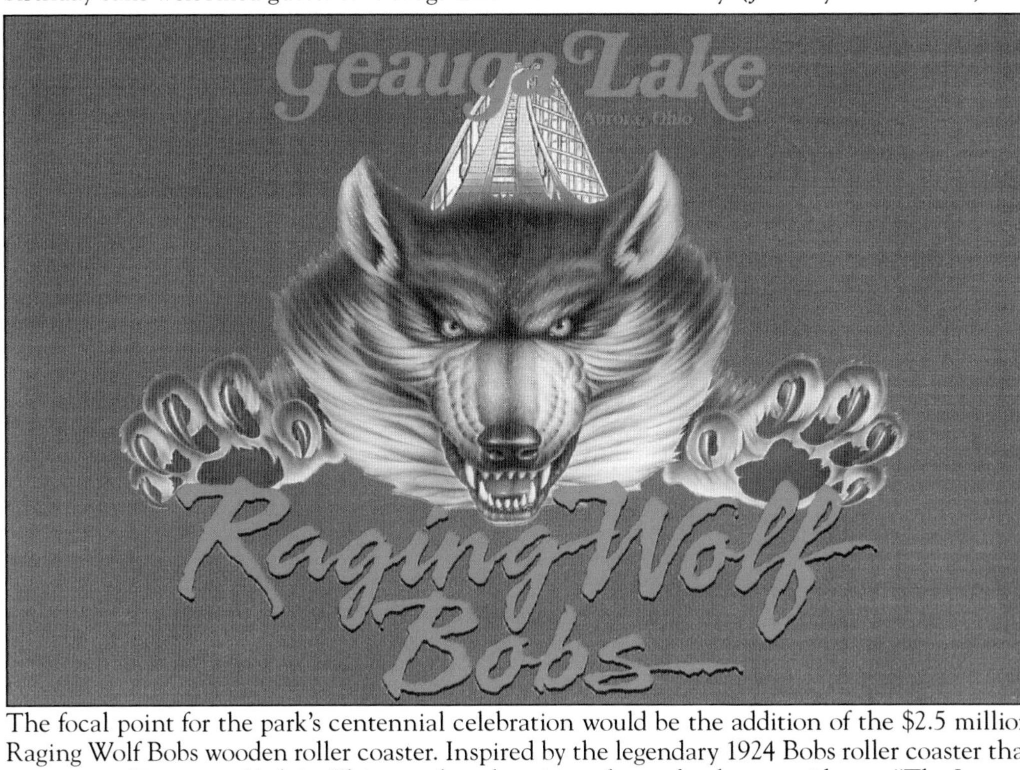

The focal point for the park's centennial celebration would be the addition of the $2.5 million Raging Wolf Bobs wooden roller coaster. Inspired by the legendary 1924 Bobs roller coaster that once ran at Riverview Park in Chicago, the advertising slogan for the new ride was "The Legend of Terror Returns." (Sam Shurgott collection.)

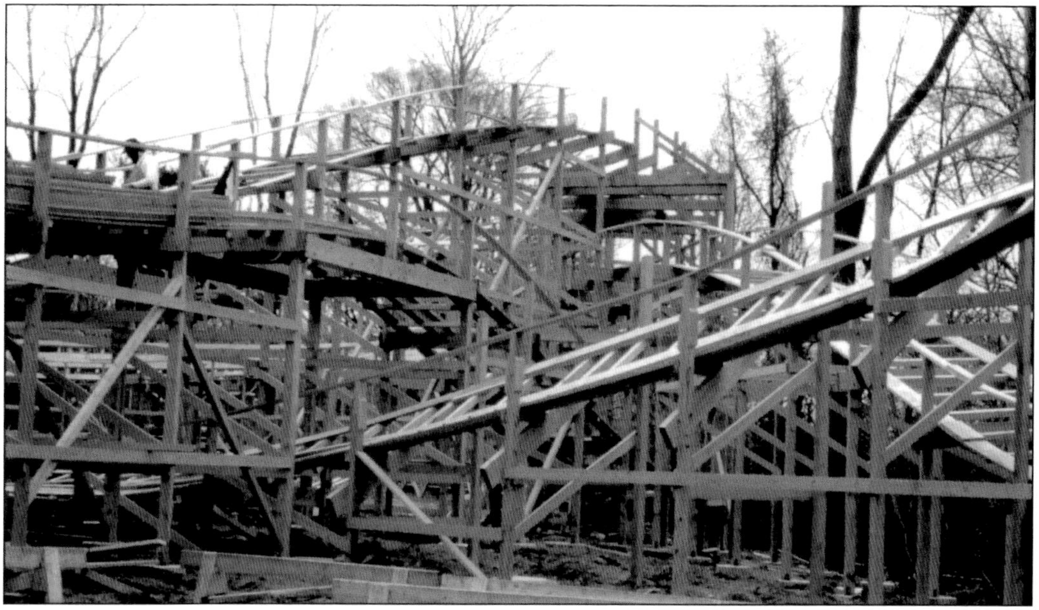

Construction of the new roller coaster began just after the end of the 1987 season. Designed by Curtis D. Summers and built by the Dinn Corporation, Raging Wolf Bobs was somewhat based on the layout of the original Bobs, which was designed by Frederick Church in 1924 for Riverview Park in Chicago. Ralph Lopez, founder of the National Amusement Park Historical Association (NAPHA), offered the Bobs' blueprints for use by Summers for the development of the ride. Charles Dinn supervised construction of the coaster during the 1987–1988 off-season. However, the ride layout would be radically modified by Summers when compared to Church's original 1924 design, mainly due to modern design methods and engineering standards. (Both, Jim Futrell collection.)

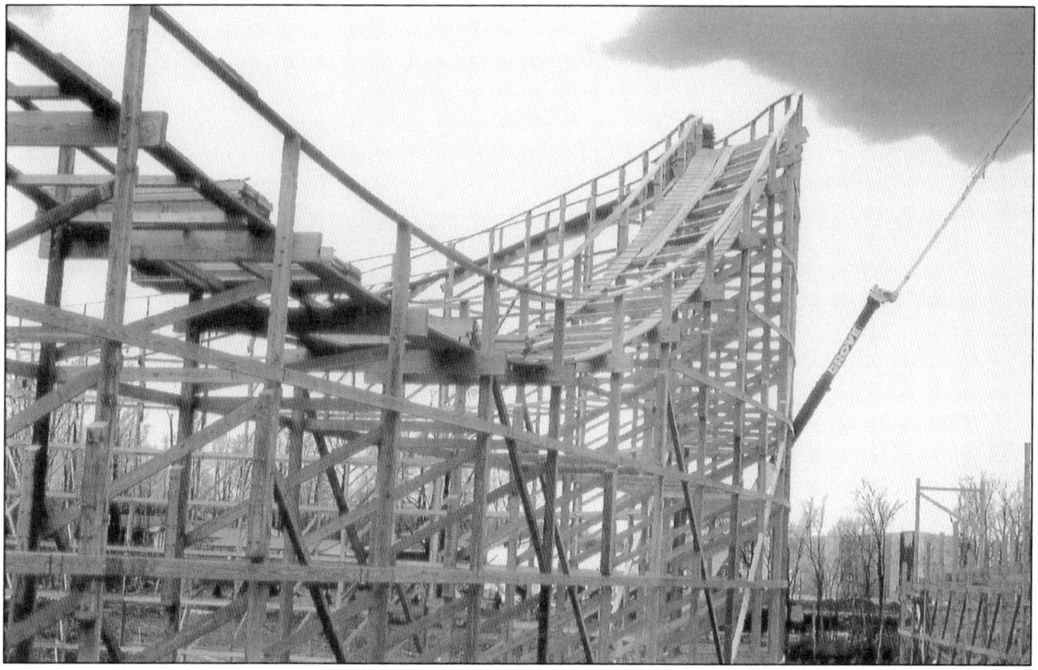

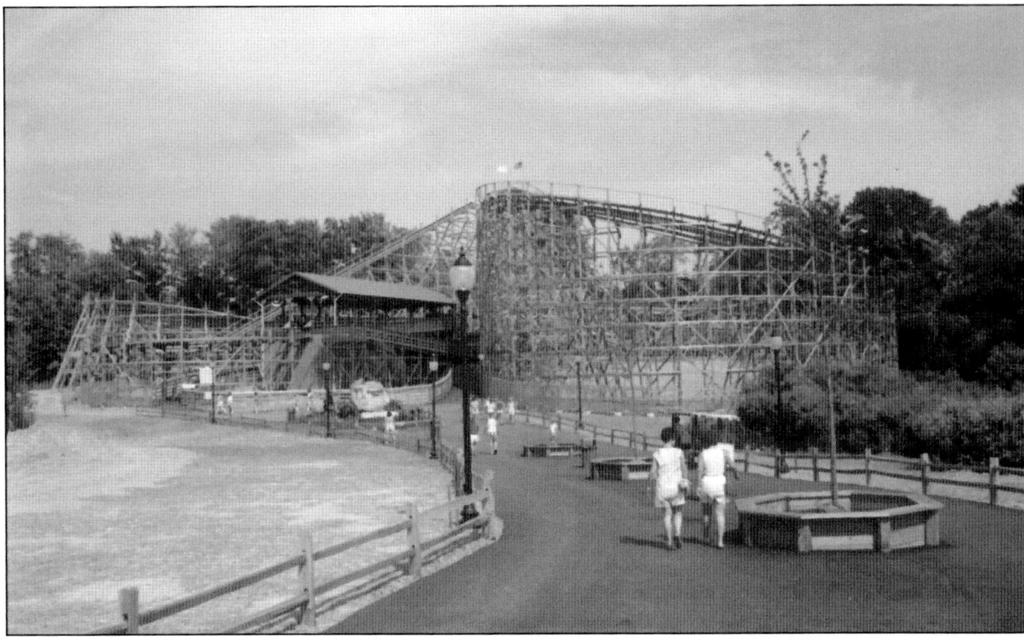

Raging Wolf Bobs would be located on formerly marshy area that was once home to a portion of the Big Ditch boat ride and would anchor a new expansion area beyond the Western Village. It would be located at the end of a long, sloping walkway, seemingly isolated from the rest of the park when it first opened. (Dave Hahner collection.)

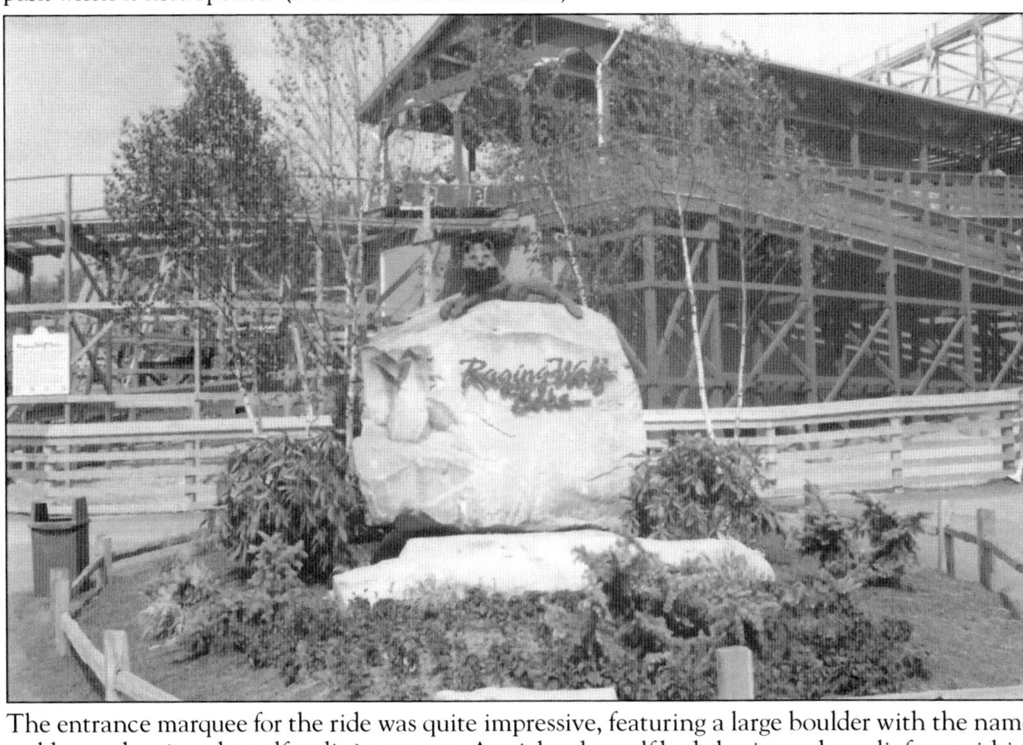

The entrance marquee for the ride was quite impressive, featuring a large boulder with the name emblazoned on it and a wolf reclining on top. At night, the wolf had glowing red eyes lit from within, giving the creature—as well as the ride—a more sinister look. (Dave Hahner collection.)

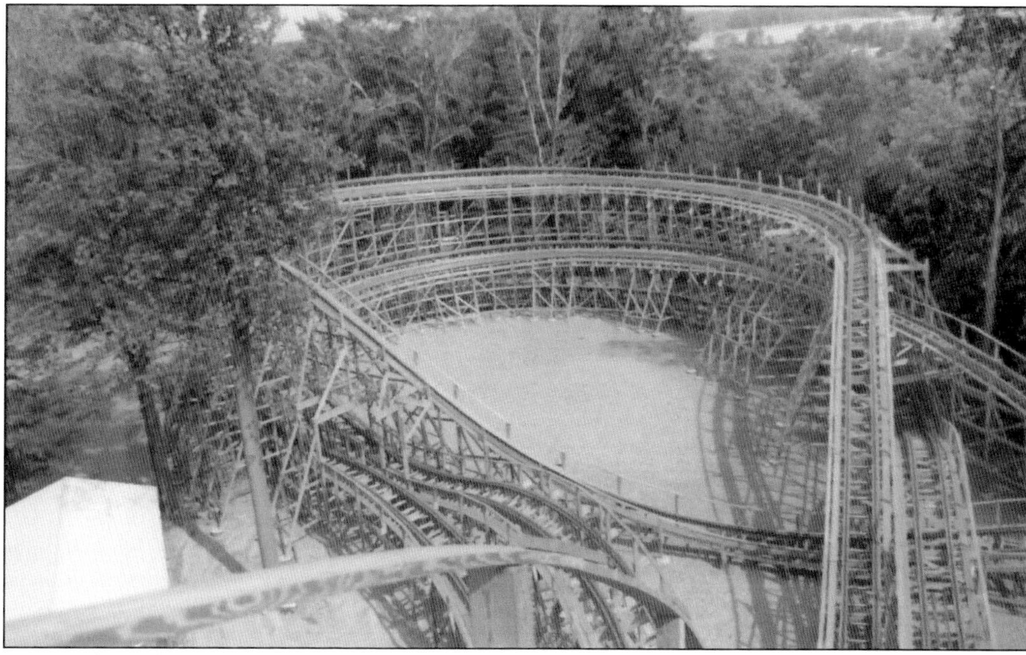

A view from the top of Raging Wolf Bobs' 80-foot-high lift hill, which was slightly higher than the original Bobs', shows the twisted track and triple-level curve structure found along the ride's 3,506-foot-long layout. At $2.5 million, it was the most expensive ride built by Funtime, Inc. at Geauga Lake. (Dave Hahner collection.)

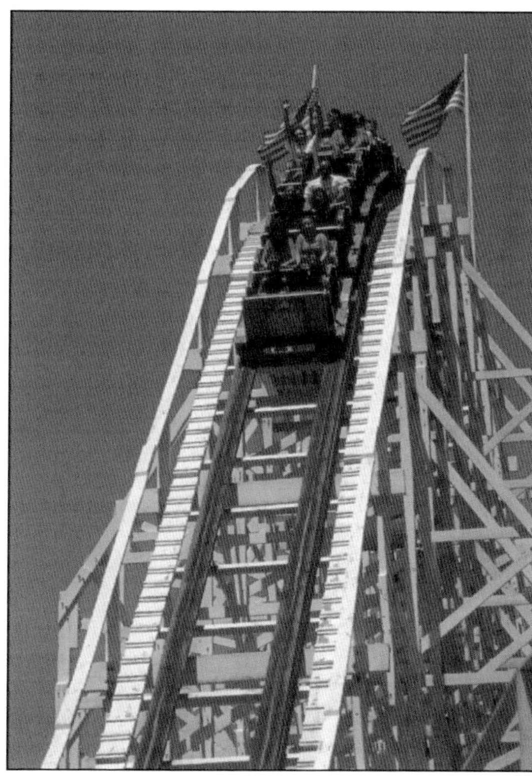

Riders are plunging down the 80-foot-high first drop of Raging Wolf Bobs, reaching a top speed of 50 miles per hour. Although never a true reproduction of the original Bobs due to all of the modern engineering modifications, it still proved to be quite successful for Geauga Lake. Its addition helped to push the park's annual attendance to more than one million guests. (Jim Futrell collection.)

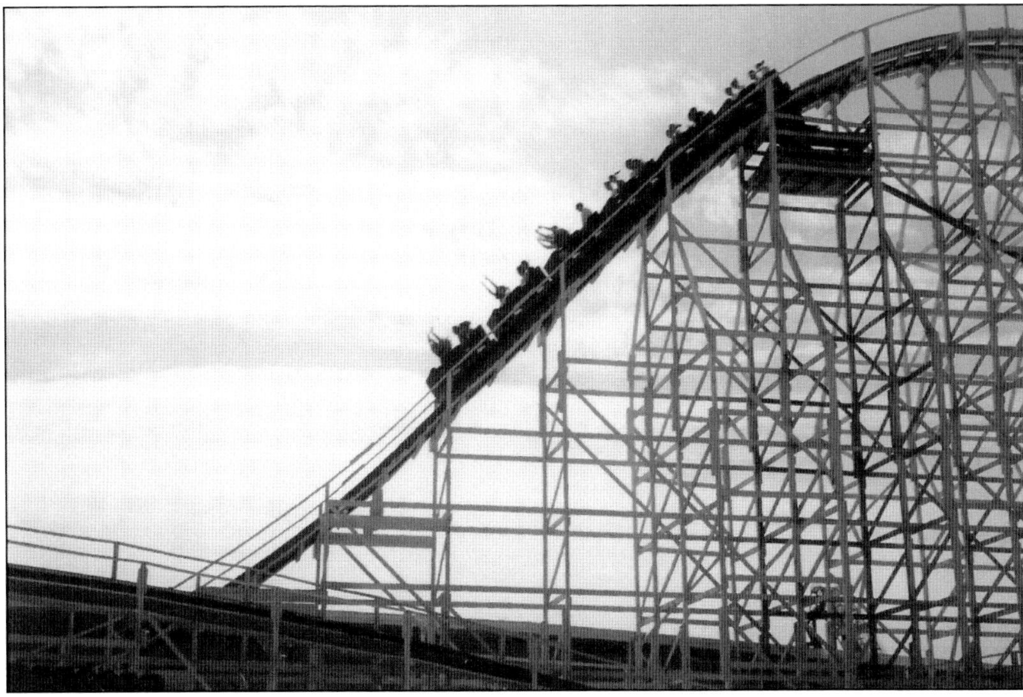

In the early 1990s, Raging Wolf Bobs would be painted white for greater visibility from neighboring SeaWorld. Sadly, the coaster stopped operation in June 2007 due to a mechanical issue and would never operate again. It was eventually torn down after Geauga Lake closed in 2007. Wood from the ride was purchased by Conneaut Lake Park in Pennsylvania to help maintain its historic Blue Streak coaster. (Dave Hahner collection.)

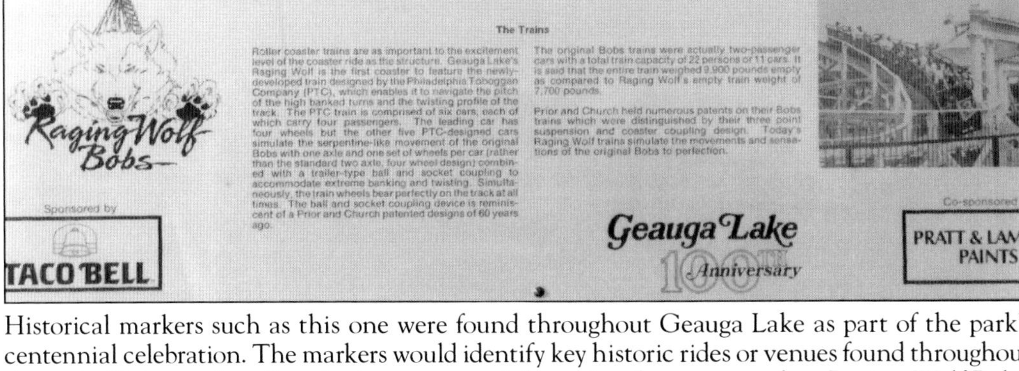

Historical markers such as this one were found throughout Geauga Lake as part of the park's centennial celebration. The markers would identify key historic rides or venues found throughout the park. This one describes the importance of the trains that were used on Raging Wolf Bobs, which were supplied by the Philadelphia Toboggan Company. (Joel Styer collection.)

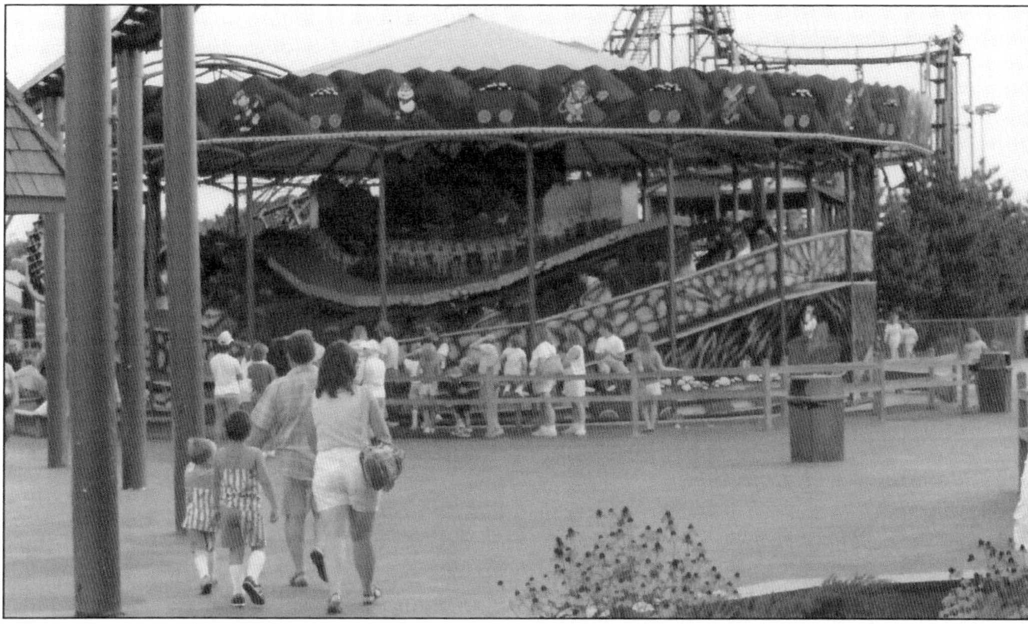

The park's Matterhorn ride was totally refurbished for the 1988 season and renamed Yukon Yahoo. Instead of an Alpine theme, the new paint scheme gave it a mining treatment, and the ride was placed near the Corkscrew roller coaster. In 2000, it would be moved and re-themed yet again as Haybaler, and it would be placed within a large barn-shaped building in the Western Village. (Joel Styer collection.)

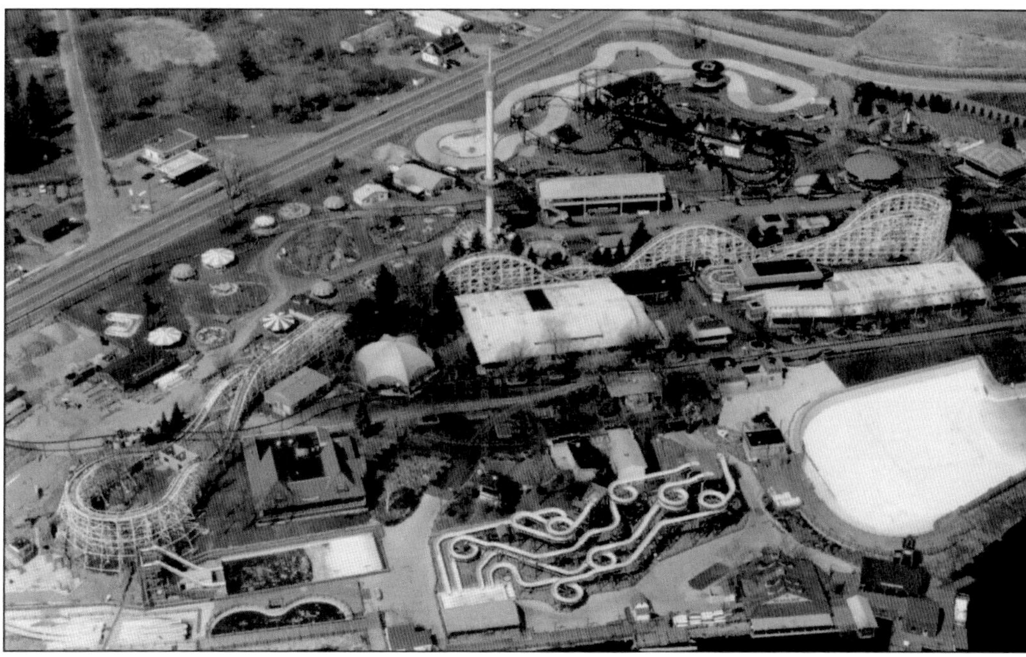

This 1989 off-season aerial view shows the Big Dipper area of the park just before the installation of the next major investment, Turtle Beach. Much of the cleared land on the left would be transformed into a children's water area. Turtle Beach would be a two-year reinvestment to the water park area of the park. (Jim Futrell collection.)

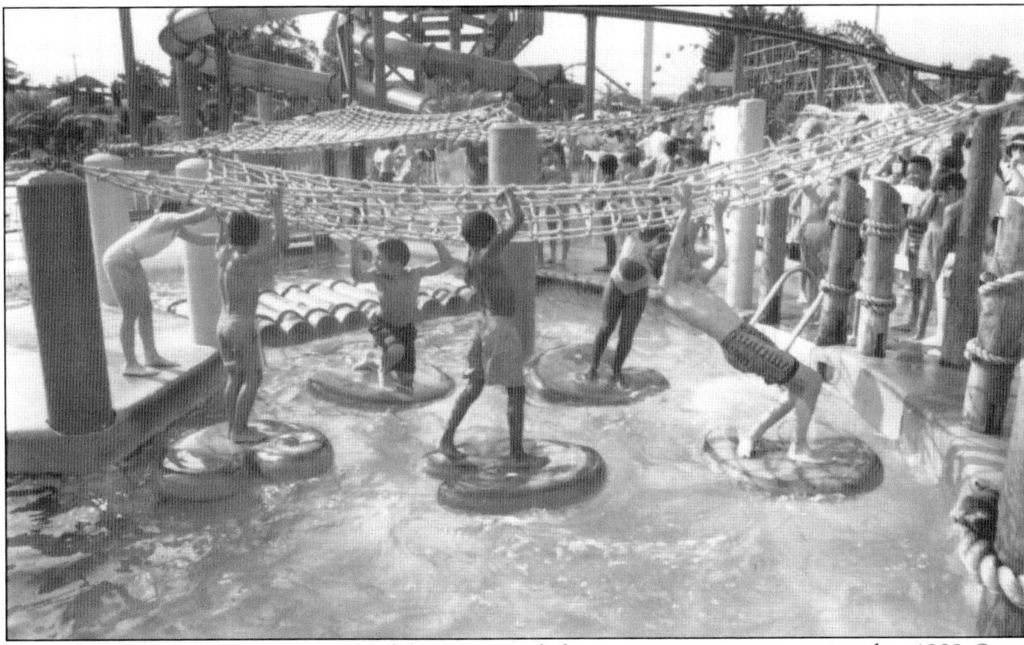

Turtle Beach, a 1.4-acre expansion of the water park for younger visitors, premiered in 1989. Since much of the existing water park was geared toward older children and adults, it was decided that a new area dedicated to younger children was much needed. It would be situated just beyond Rainbow Island, ideal for families to move from one children's area to the other. Costing more than $1.1 million, it would feature two different sections, one for preschool-aged children and the other for those of grade-school age. The new area would consist of four waterslides, a lazy river, and an interactive area within a shallow pool featuring lots of water jets that children could control. (Both, Jim Futrell collection.)

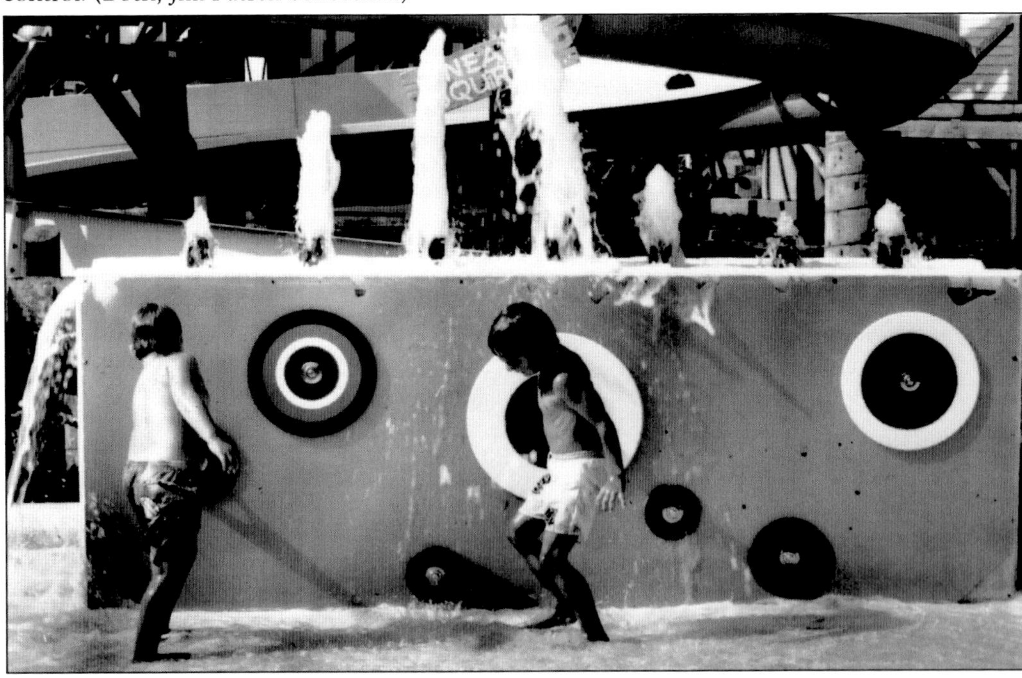

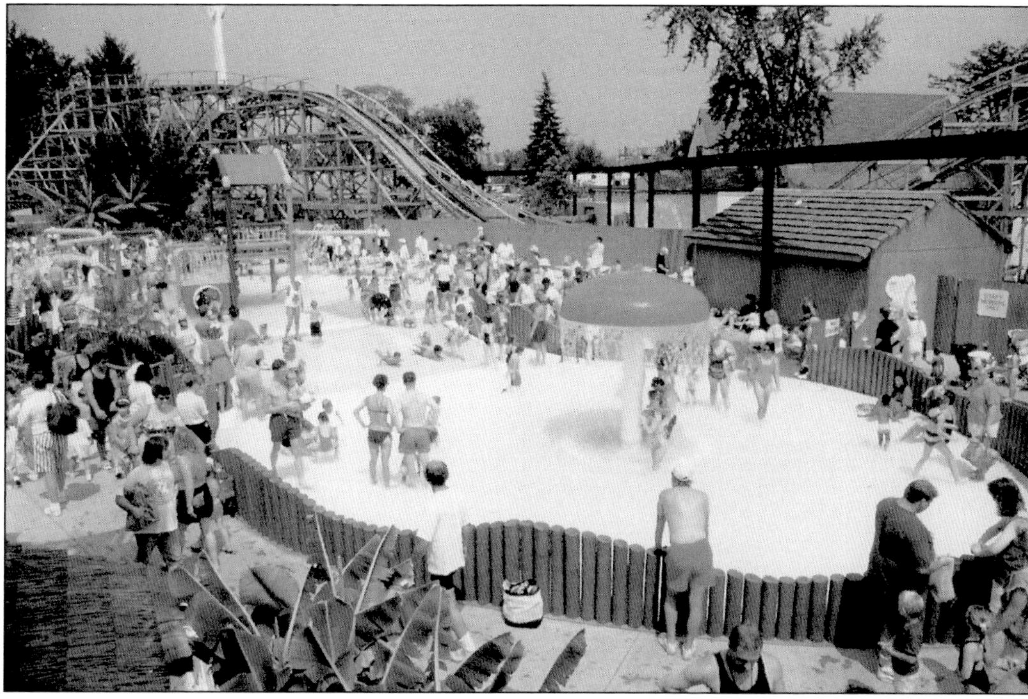

Turtle Beach was an instant success, with record-breaking attendance for the park, topping 1.15 million guests for the first time. Another $1.1 million would be invested by expanding Turtle Beach another 1.4 acres in 1990 to help accommodate the growing crowds. The new area featured additional water elements and an expanded interactive play area featuring various types of water jets and spray cannons, many of which could be operated by children. Other additions included a new sand volleyball court and 26 artificial palm trees to add to the theme. (Both, Sam Shurgott collection.)

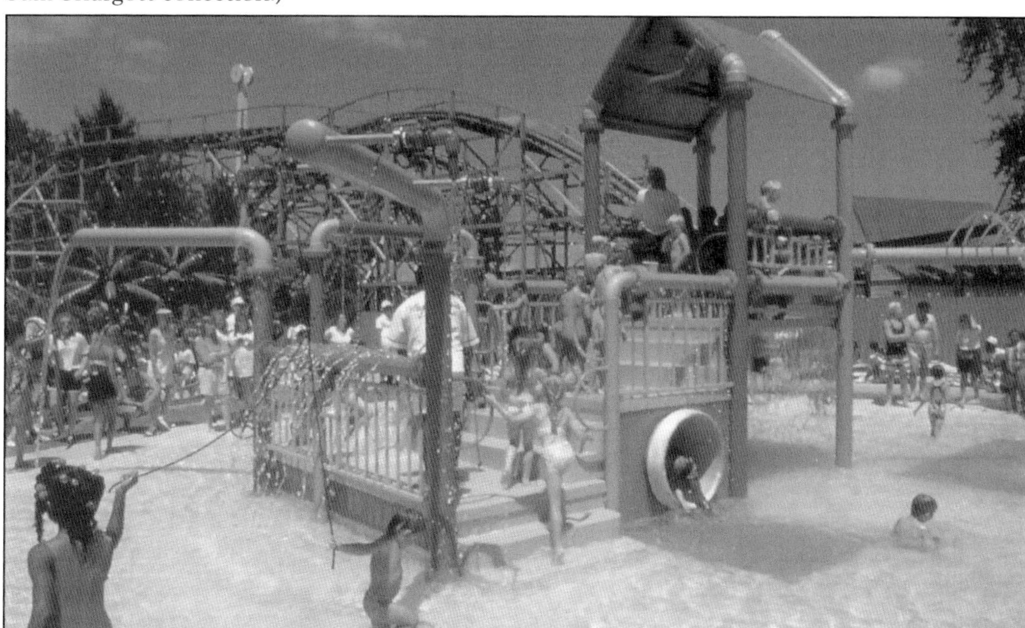

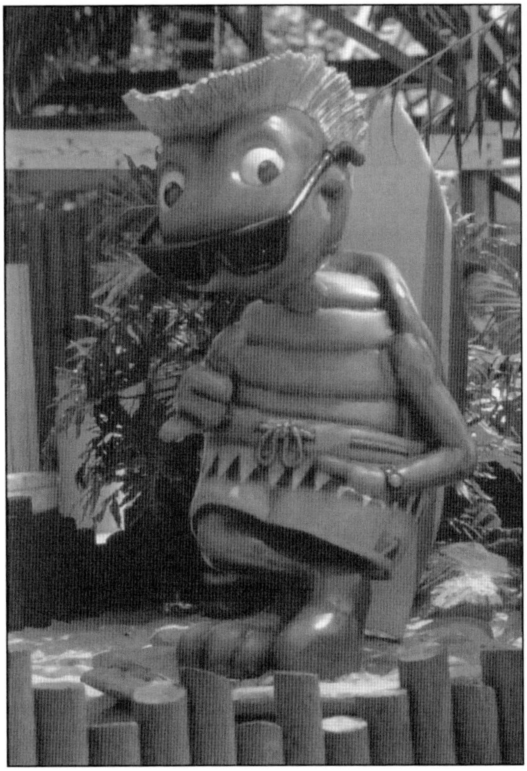

Turtle Beach's new mascot would be Butch Hightide, a surfer dude who happened to be one radical turtle. Butch's image would be featured throughout the new area, including a fiberglass figure near the far end of Big Dipper for photo opportunities. Souvenirs with Butch's image were a popular item at the park. (Sam Shurgott collection.)

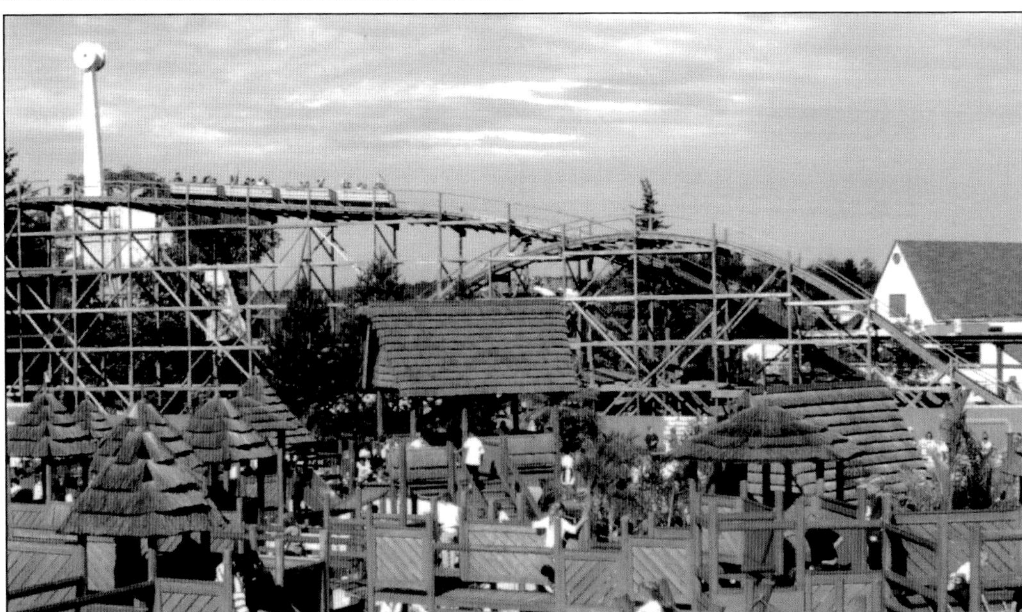

For those children who did not want to get wet, the 1990 Turtle Beach expansion also included an interactive children's dry-play area, Butch Hightide's Play Park. The tropical-themed play structure featured cargo nets, crawl tubes, elevated huts, small slides, and other playground equipment, which would be located along the fence near Highway 43. HAGS, a playground developer from Denmark, built the attraction. (Jim Futrell collection.)

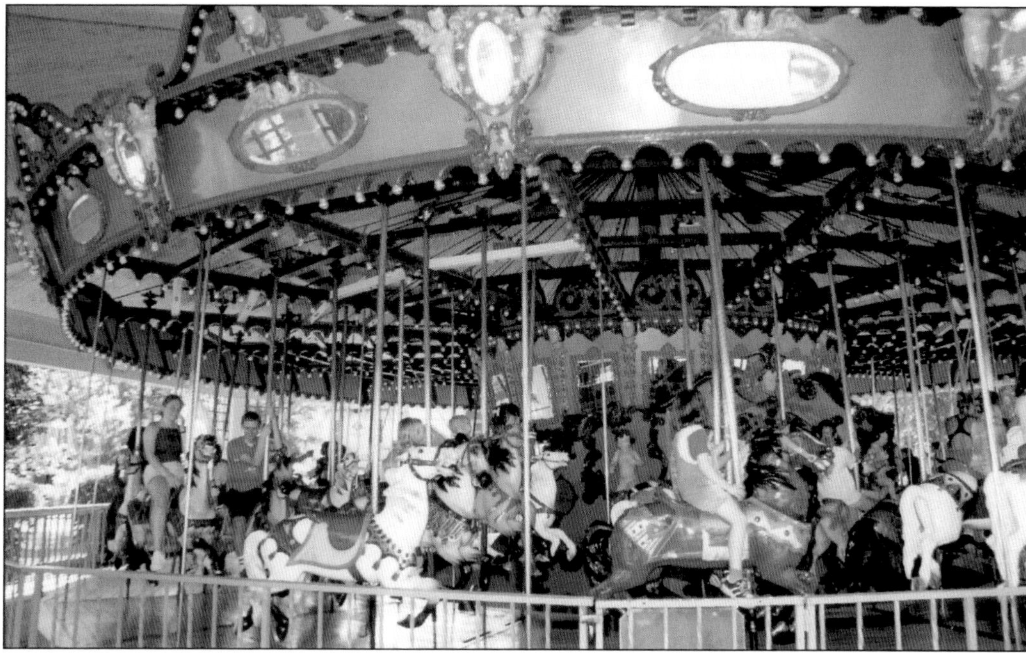

During the late 1980s, antique carousel horses were in high demand by collectors. Individual horses could sell for thousands of dollars, with entire antique machines selling for well over $1 million. Many parks had already sold their carousels to make a quick profit, and Geauga Lake considered selling its antique 1926 M.C. Illions carousel in 1989. (Joel Styer collection.)

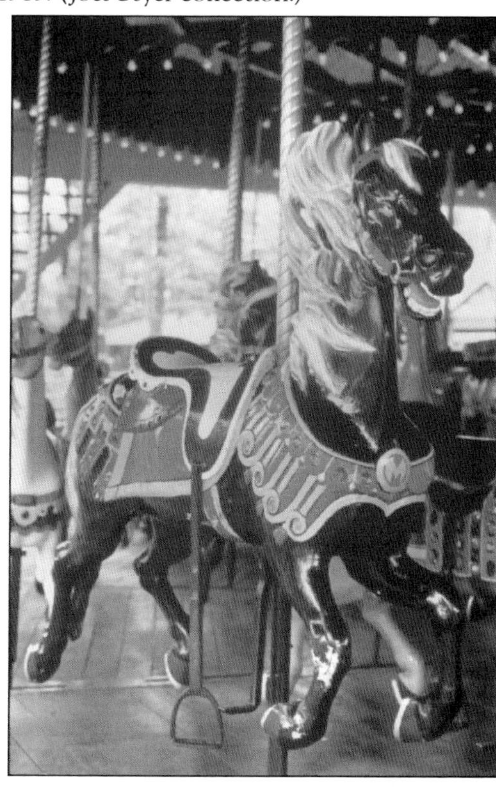

When the news of possibly selling the carousel got out, there was public outcry from both carousel enthusiasts and local residents against the sale. Geauga Lake management not only reconsidered the possible sale, but in 1990, purchased a new band organ for $38,000 from the Stinson Pipe Organ Company to once again serenade riders for the first time since 1951. (Jim Futrell collection.)

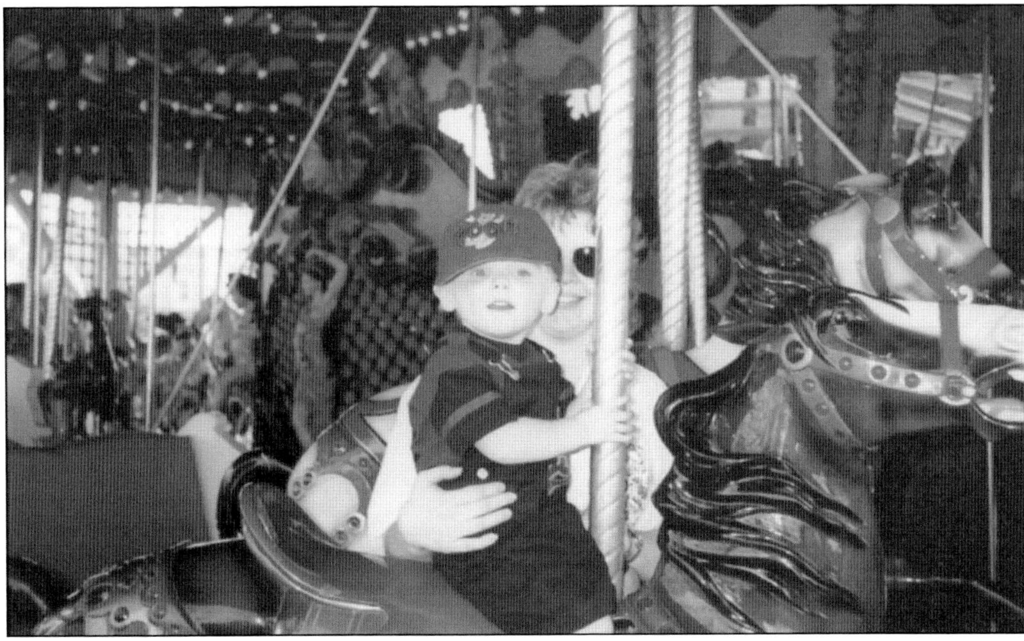

In 1994, the entire M.C. Illions carousel would be completely restored and repainted, and it remained a favorite until the park closed for good in 2007. The carousel sat in storage for several years, and in 2010 it was eventually moved by CedarFair to Worlds of Fun in Kansas City, Missouri, where it was completely restored again before its installation. (Dave Hahner collection.)

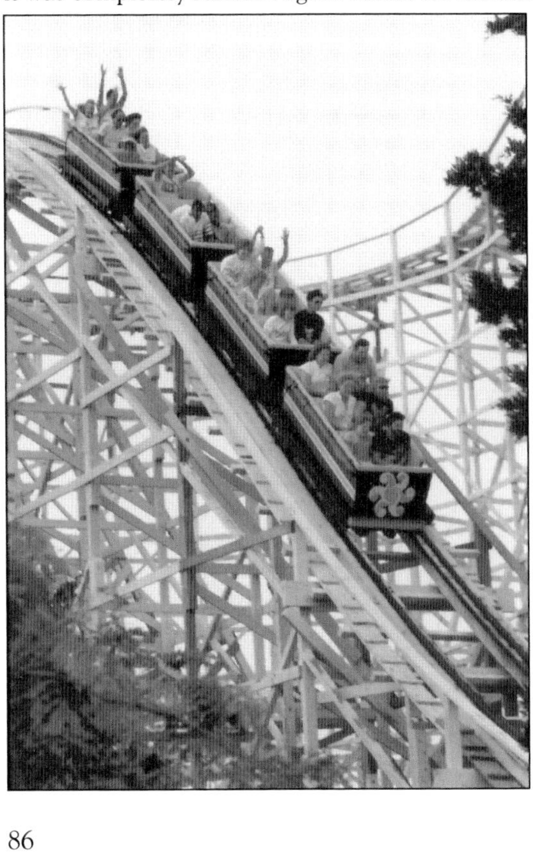

The carousel was not the only antique ride being restored during the early 1990s; the park's signature ride since 1925, Big Dipper, would undergo a five-year-long restoration. Each off-season, beginning in 1990, major sections of the ride would be torn down and rebuilt. This photograph captures how the ride appeared in 1988 just before restoration. (Joel Styer collection.)

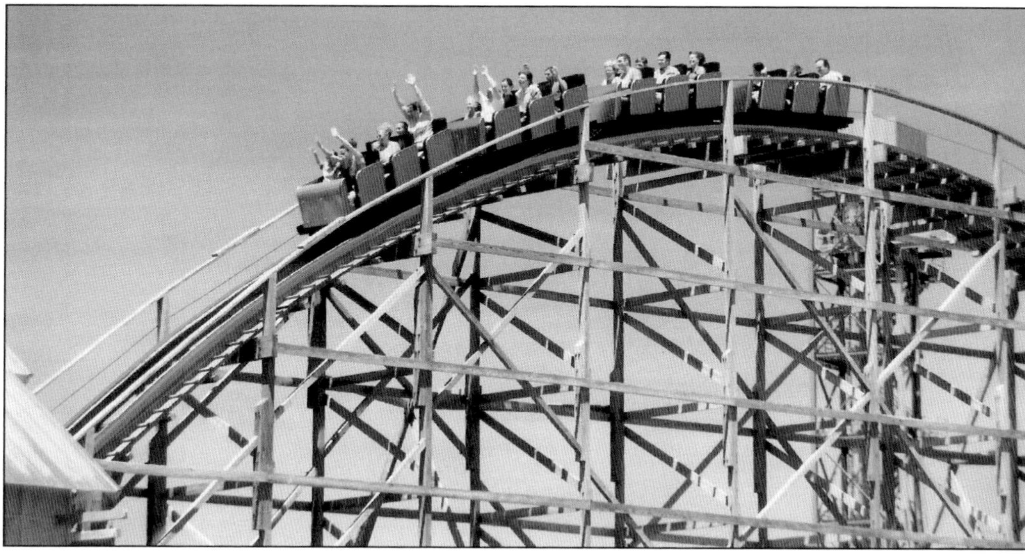

After five long years, the Big Dipper restoration would be complete in 1994. It was no longer painted white and featured the natural wood of the new, treated lumber used to rebuild it. The only parts of the structure that would be painted would be the twin beds of track that the trains ran upon. (Joel Styer collection.)

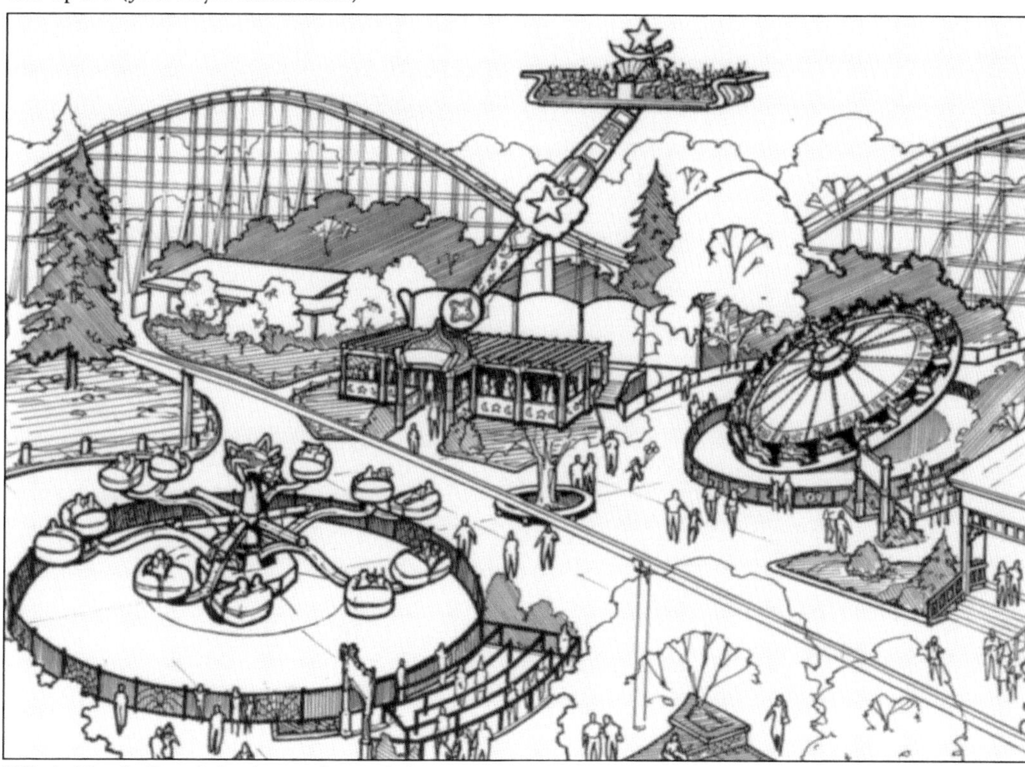

While Turtle Beach had transformed the property on the far end of Big Dipper near Highway 43, it was now turn for the lakeside midway near Big Dipper between the water park and coaster to get a makeover for 1991. Cinema 180 would be removed, while two new rides, Mirage (flying carpet) and Casino (Trabant), would be added and the park's Spider ride relocated. (Jim Futrell collection.)

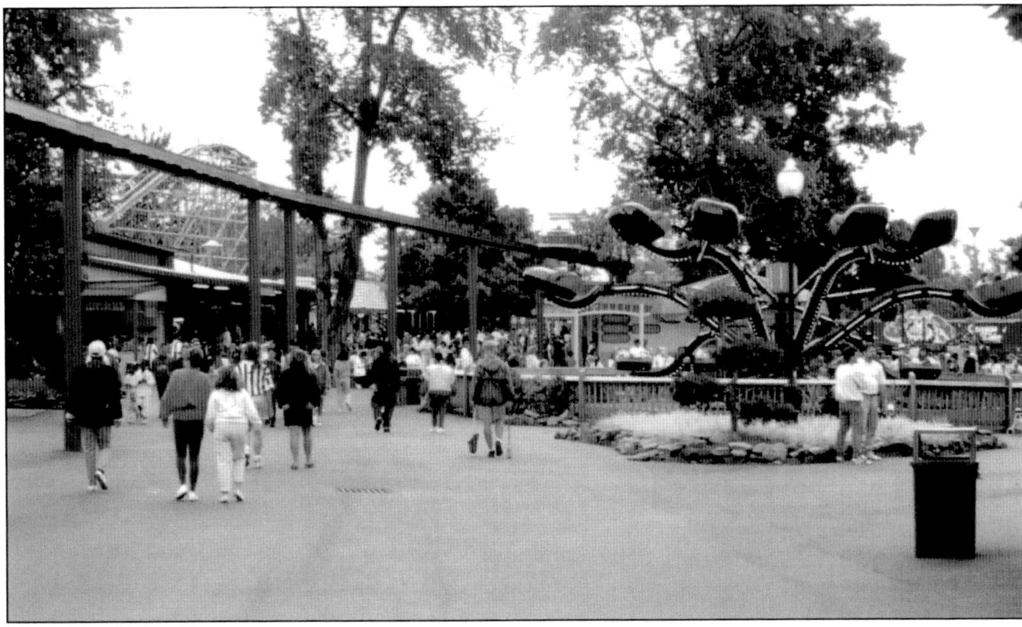

This image shows the relocated Spider ride in the newly laid-out lakeside midway for 1991. The entire new midway redevelopment cost over $1.65 million. Unfortunately, the economy started to slide down, and Geauga Lake had to redevelop its marketing strategy for 1992. Various promotions, such as carload specials, dive-in movies at the Wave, free children's admission, and buy-one-get-one promotions were common to bolster attendance. (Jim Futrell collection.)

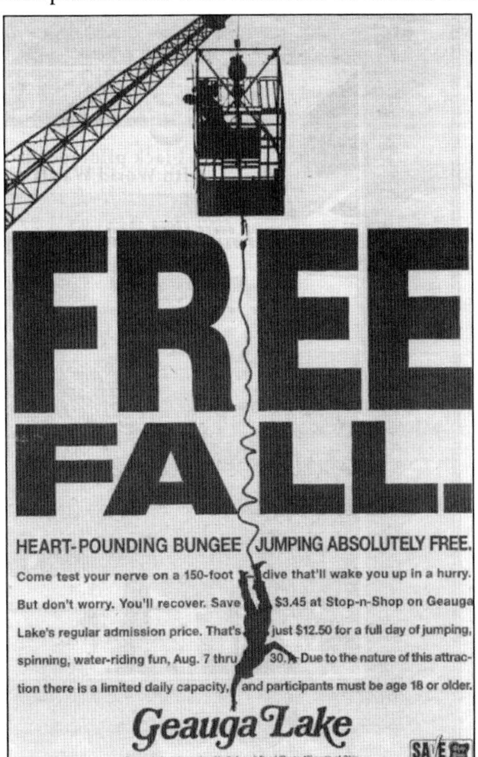

One of the more unusual promotions that Geauga Lake attempted during 1992 was free bungee jumping with park admission. Daring visitors would be hoisted 150 feet in the air on a platform by crane. Once there, they would literally jump off the platform with a bungee cord attached to their legs. The promotion only lasted a very short time, but it was extremely popular during its run. (Jim Futrell collection.)

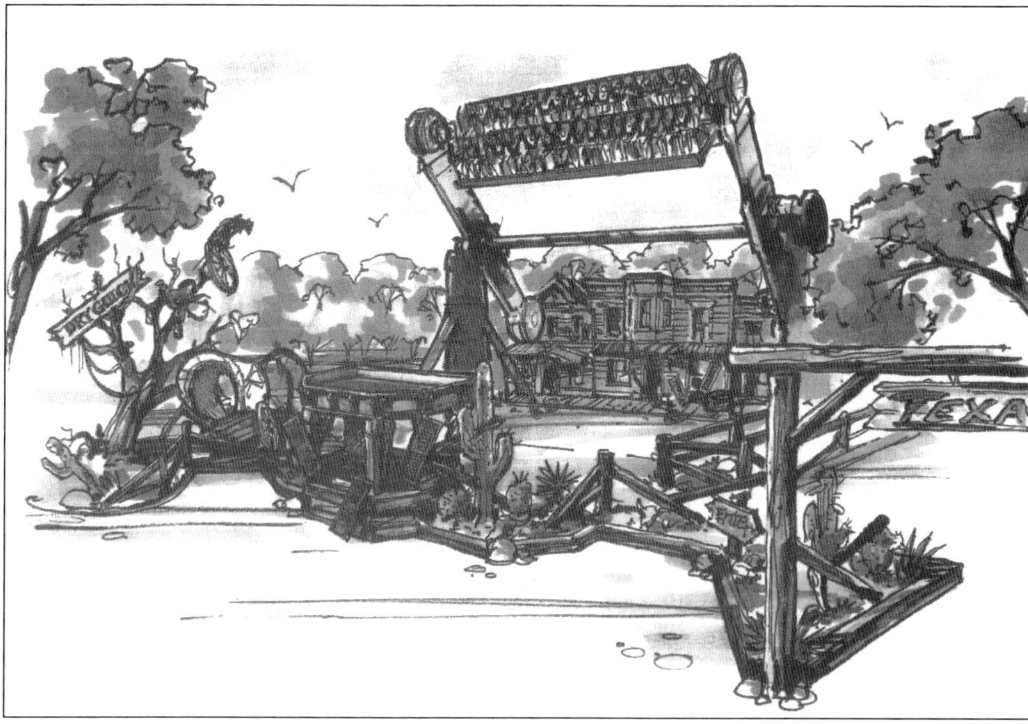

The final new ride to be added to Geauga Lake by Funtime before the park was sold was the Texas Twister, a Huss top-spin ride, for the 1993 season. To compete with other area theme parks, it was decided to give Texas Twister a full theme and story line rather than to just add only the ride. (Jim Futrell collection.)

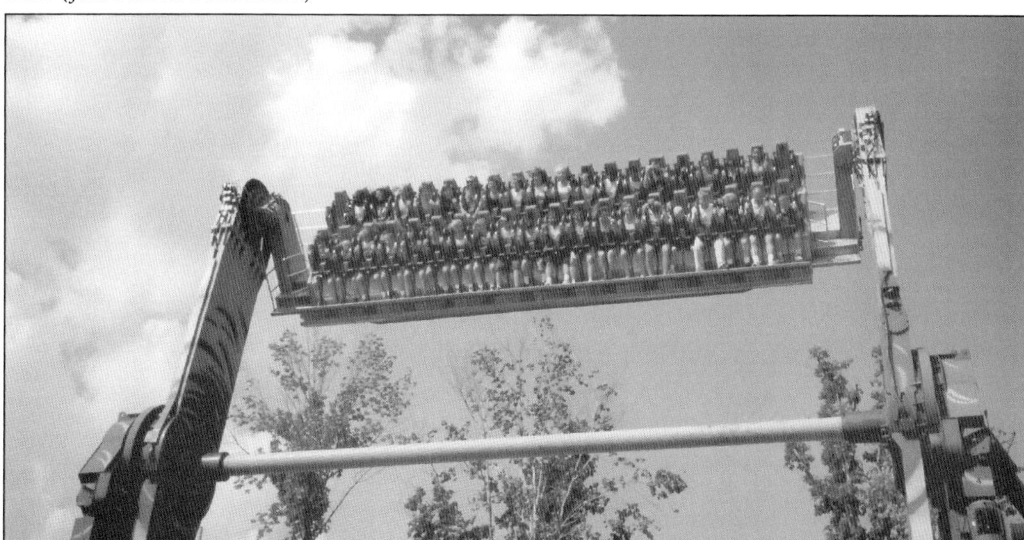

The new $2.1-million ride, complete with theme, would be the very first ride of its kind in the country. The ride would literally flip riders head-over-heel over and over while the giant arms would spin the ride up and down. The ride was programmed with 10 different patterns of flipping, including sudden stops, hold patterns, and dangling riders upside down. (Dave Hahner collection.)

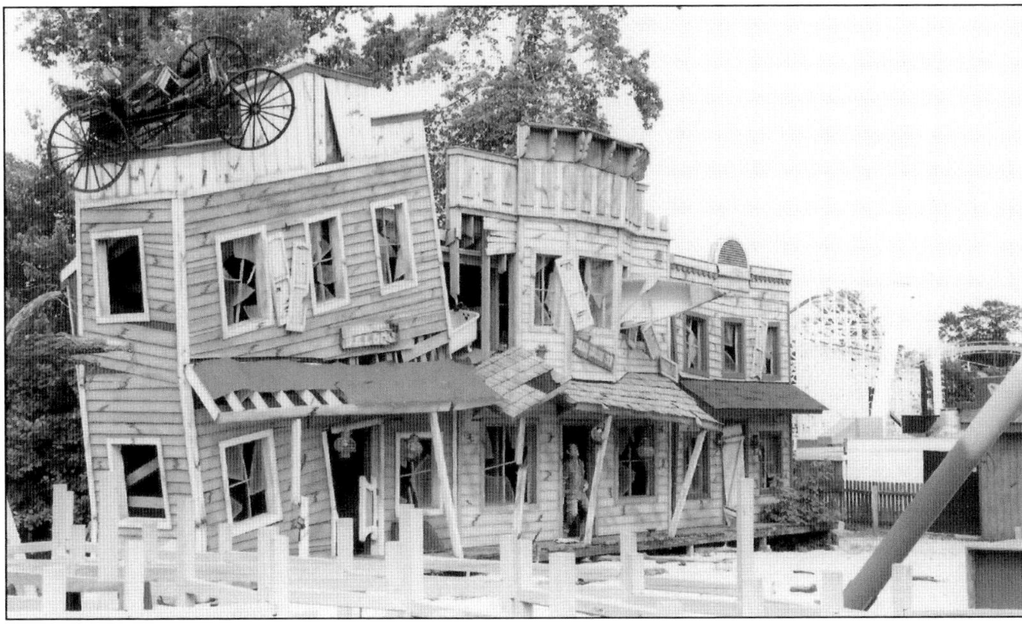

Although the attraction was thrilling for the rider, it was equally thrilling for those watching. The theme of the small Western town devastated by a tornado was quite convincing. The attention to detail was among the best that Funtime had ever added to a park. After the park's closure in 2007, the ride would be moved to California's Great America in Santa Clara, California. (Joel Styer collection.)

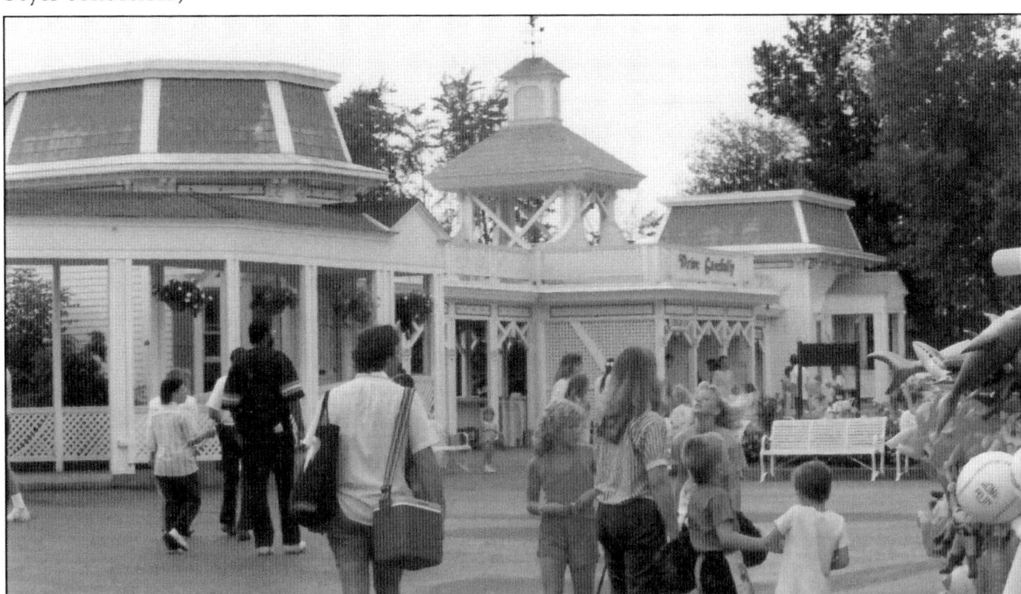

In August 1995, Funtime, Inc. would sell its chain of parks, including Geauga Lake, Darien Lake in Darien Center, New York, and Wyandot Lake in Columbus, Ohio, to Premier Parks of Oklahoma City, Oklahoma. Although the park would expand exponentially over the next few years, it would ultimately suffer from its rapid growth. The Funtime era had come to a close. (Joel Styer collection.)

Six

A Whale of a Neighbor
SeaWorld Ohio 1970–2000

In March 1964, SeaWorld, a state-of-the-art marine life park, opened its gates in San Diego, California, and a new type of theme park experience was created. Visitors flocked from across the country to visit the new creation, which housed all types of exotic sea animals, including performing dolphins and sea lions. In 1965, the introduction of the first captive killer whale to a marine park made SeaWorld an almost overnight sensation. The addition of the world-famous Shamu made SeaWorld one of the premier marine life parks in the world.

The success of SeaWorld prompted Earl Gascoigne, marketing director at Cedar Point, to ask SeaWorld executive George Millay to consider building a second park near Sandusky, Ohio. Uncomfortable with the location and sales agreement, Millay chose not to build there. Two years later, Gascoigne, who had become involved with Funtime, Inc., convinced Millay and his team to build the second SeaWorld across the lake from Geauga Lake in Aurora. After two years of planning and construction, SeaWorld Ohio opened during Memorial Day weekend in May 1970. It cost $5.5 million to build, but that first year, more than 1.1 million guests visited SeaWorld, more than doubling expectations for the new park.

For 30 years, SeaWorld entertained and educated guests from all over the region with its unique collection of marine life displays, killer whales, dolphins, sea lions, and its famous water-ski show. It shared a unique synergy with neighboring Geauga Lake during that time to help both parks succeed in a very competitive market, offering a unique two-park weekend getaway for visitors.

SeaWorld had several owners during its lifetime, including publishing company Harcourt Brace Jovanovich in 1976 and Anheuser-Busch in 1989. The park was sold in March 2001 to Six Flags Corporation, which merged both Geauga Lake and SeaWorld into one park called Six Flags Worlds of Adventure. When the struggling mega park was sold to CedarFair, LLP, in 2004, the marine life side of the park would close and be converted into a water park named Wildwater Kingdom in 2005, thus ending the 33-year history of a marine life park in northern Ohio.

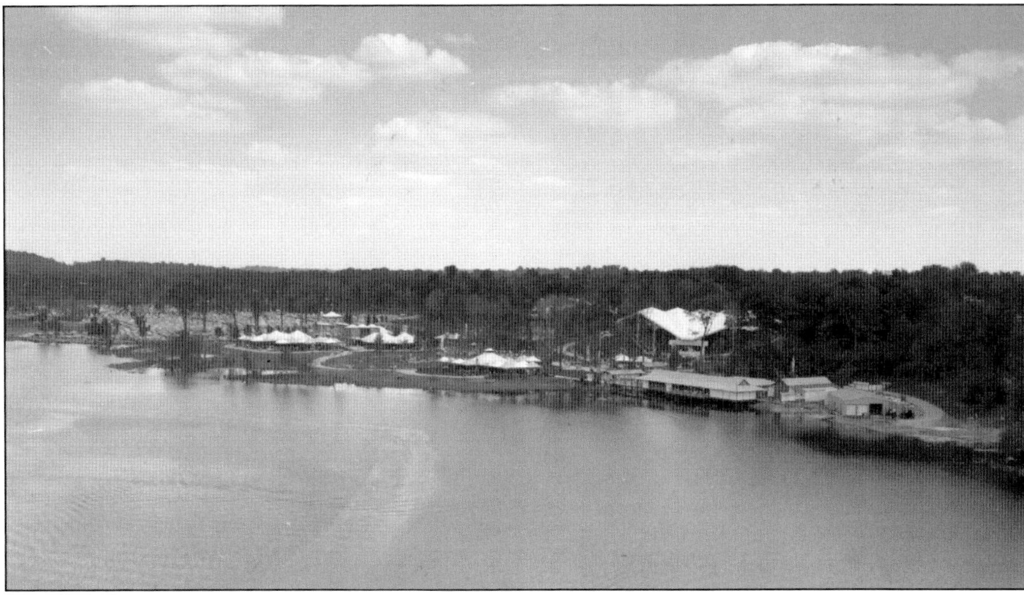

Pictured here is SeaWorld Ohio during its inaugural season in 1970. The park was built at a cost of over $5 million—more than twice the estimated cost when the project was publicly announced in November 1968. The new oceanarium featured a sea lion stadium, dolphin/killer whale stadium, and a Japanese-themed shopping village among its attractions. (Amusement Park Books Collection.)

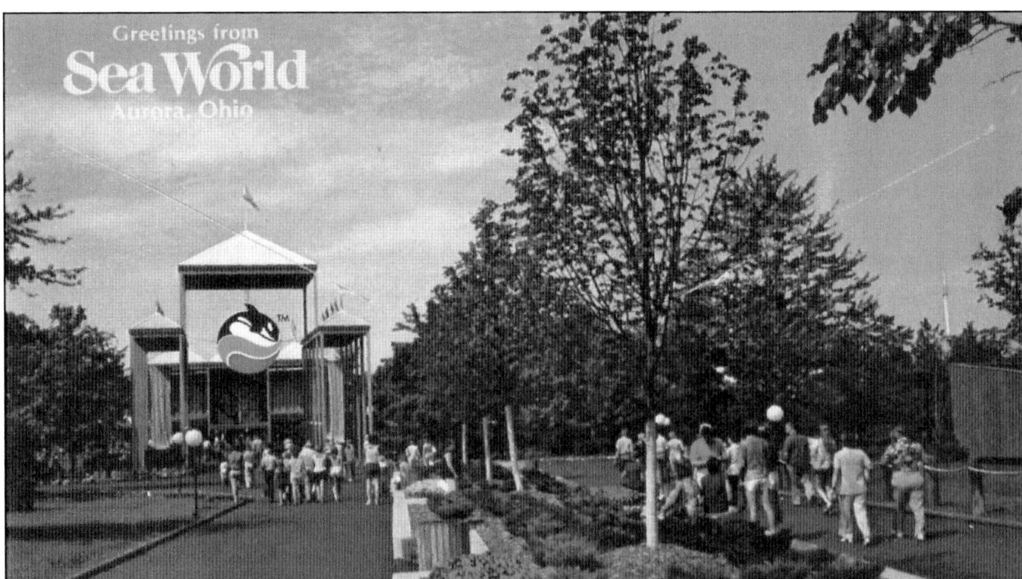

SeaWorld Ohio launched on May 29, 1970, with over 5,500 guests celebrating the grand opening of the new marine life park. This would be the second SeaWorld park built, after the original debuted in San Diego in 1964. This postcard gives a view of the main entrance promenade in the early 1970s. (Jim Futrell collection.)

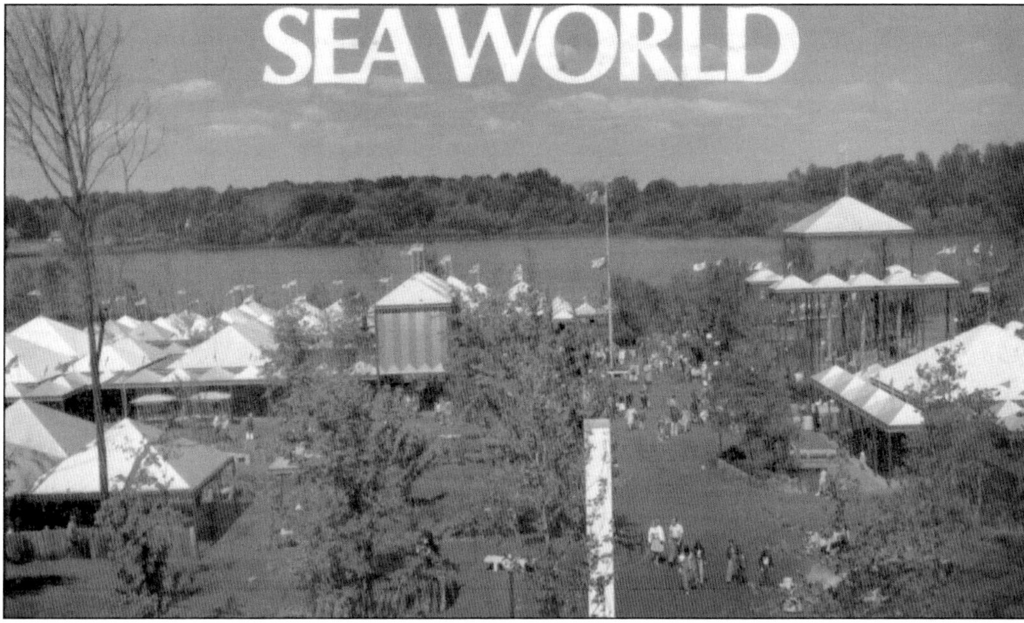

This overview shot of SeaWorld's entrance plaza captures its appearance in its early days. The plaza featured festive, brightly colored pyramid-topped structures throughout, giving SeaWorld a modern, world's fair look. The entrance plaza buildings housed various shops and eateries for the thousands of tourists that visited the park each day. The initial size of SeaWorld when it opened was just 25 acres. (Jim Futrell collection.)

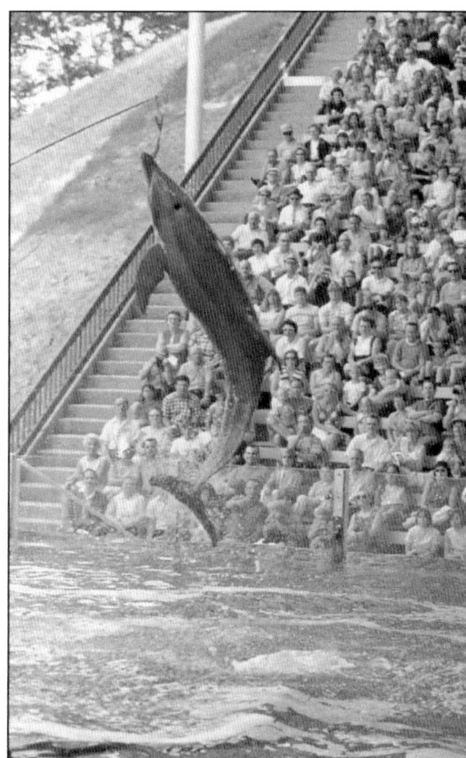

Atlantic bottlenose dolphins were some of the more popular species of marine mammals that performed at SeaWorld Ohio during the park's 30 years of operation. They exhibited many daring maneuvers during their shows, including high jumping, skilled synchronous acrobatic flips and jumps, and of course, jumping through hoops. (Dave Hahner collection.)

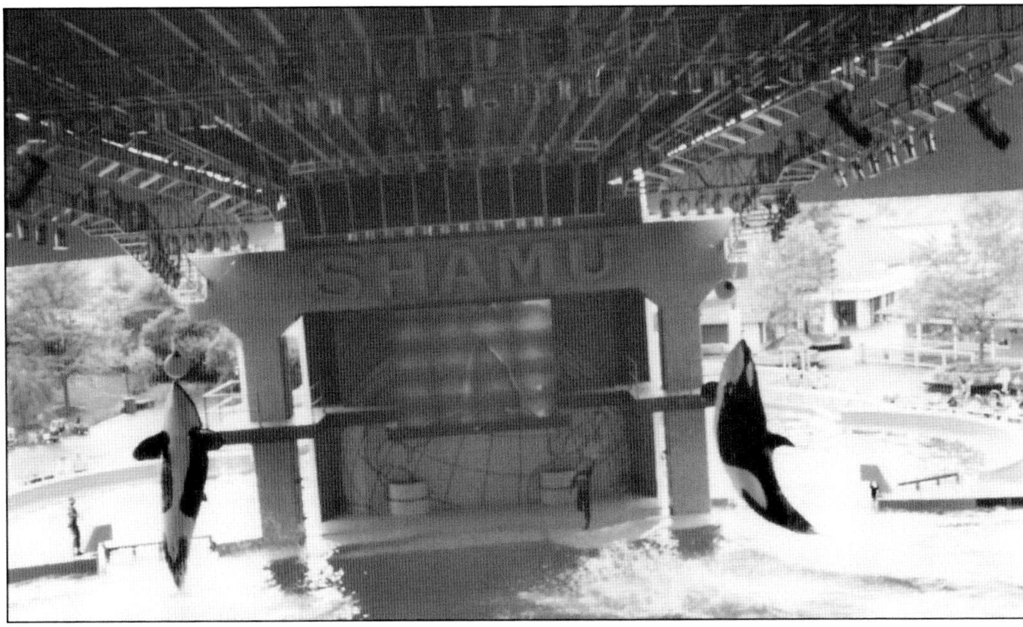

The large tank and stadium that the dolphins performed in was also home to the park's star attraction, Shamu, a 1.5-ton killer whale. Since killer whales are natural predators of other sea mammals, the orcas and the dolphins were held in separate holding tanks on either side of the main performance tank. Eventually, the tank was enlarged and, in 1982, converted to only house orcas. (Sarah Windisch collection.)

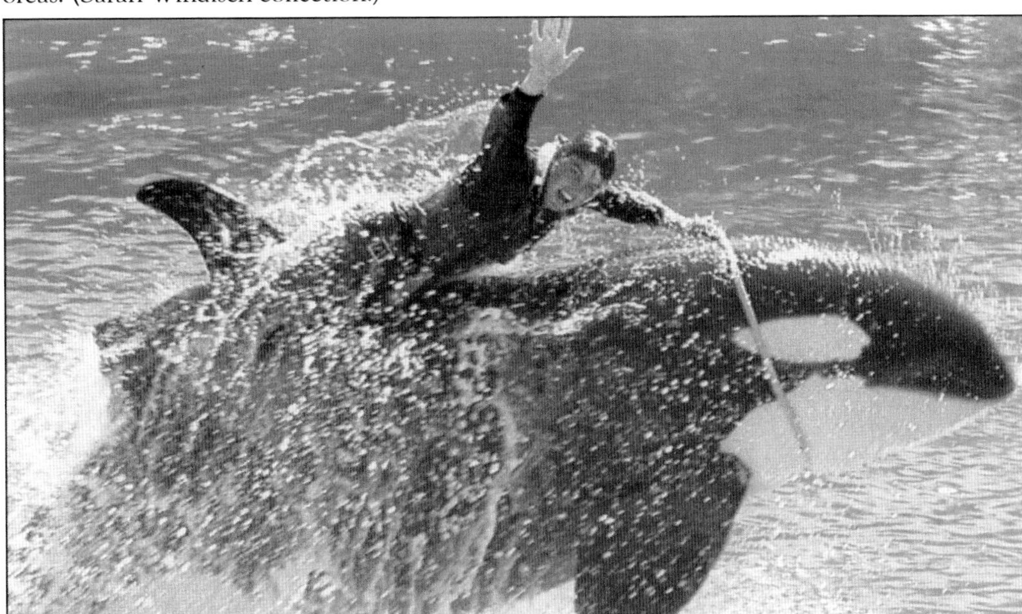

The sheer power of the two-ton orcas and their impressive agilities at swimming and jumping were the main appeal of the shows. Interactivity with the trainers in the tank also helped to add a level of excitement. The first few rows of spectator seats were known as the splash zone, often drenching viewers in those rows from the voracious splashing by the giant sea mammals. (Dave Hahner collection.)

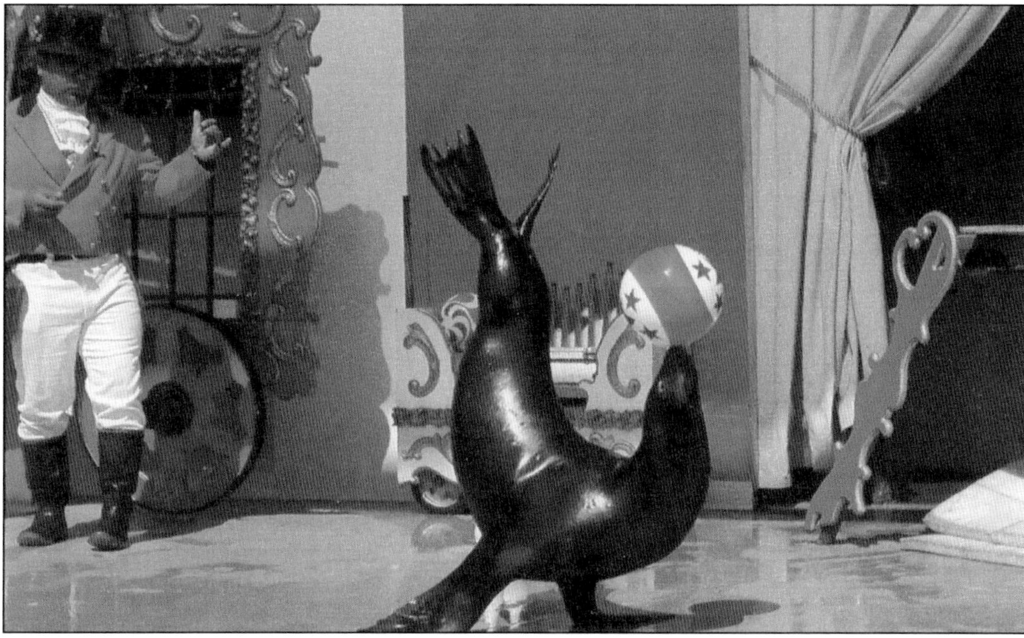

The other large stadium in the park to the left of Shamu Stadium housed the sea lion and otter show. Usually themed to a comedic story line, the shows featured a host of sea creatures such as penguins, otters, and walruses performing with sea lion hosts Clyde and Seamore. This particular show's theme was the Dingaling Bros. Circus during the early 1970s. (Dave Hahner collection.)

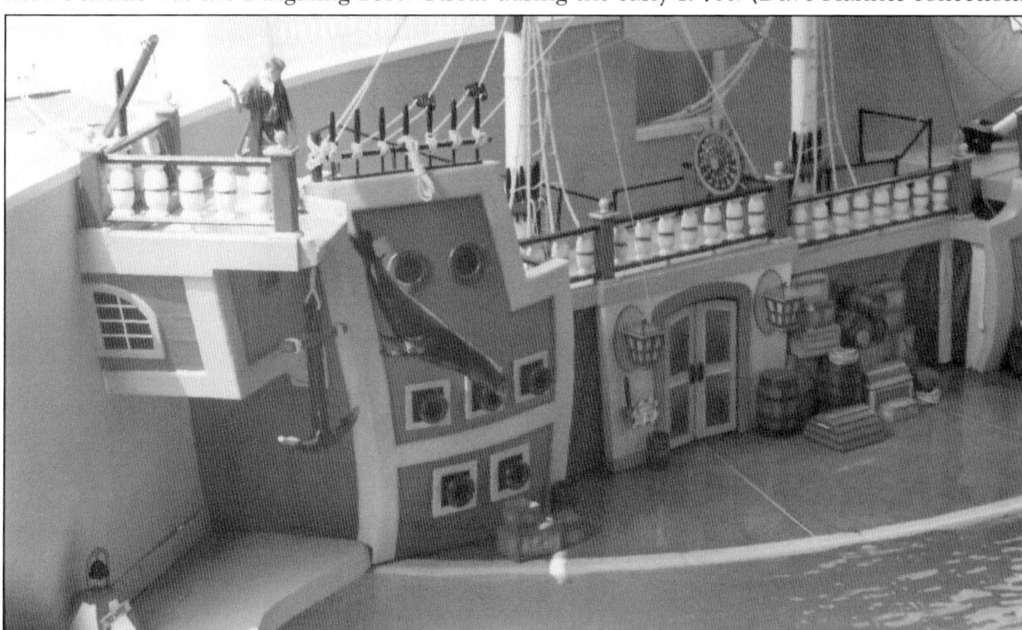

Although comic in nature, the show's story line would showcase some of the natural abilities of the marine performers. During the Pirates of Pinniped shows of the 1990s, one daring sea lion shows off his ability to high dive about 30 feet into the tank below. Educational descriptions of a performing animal would be provided by the trainer during the entertaining show. (Dave Hahner collection.)

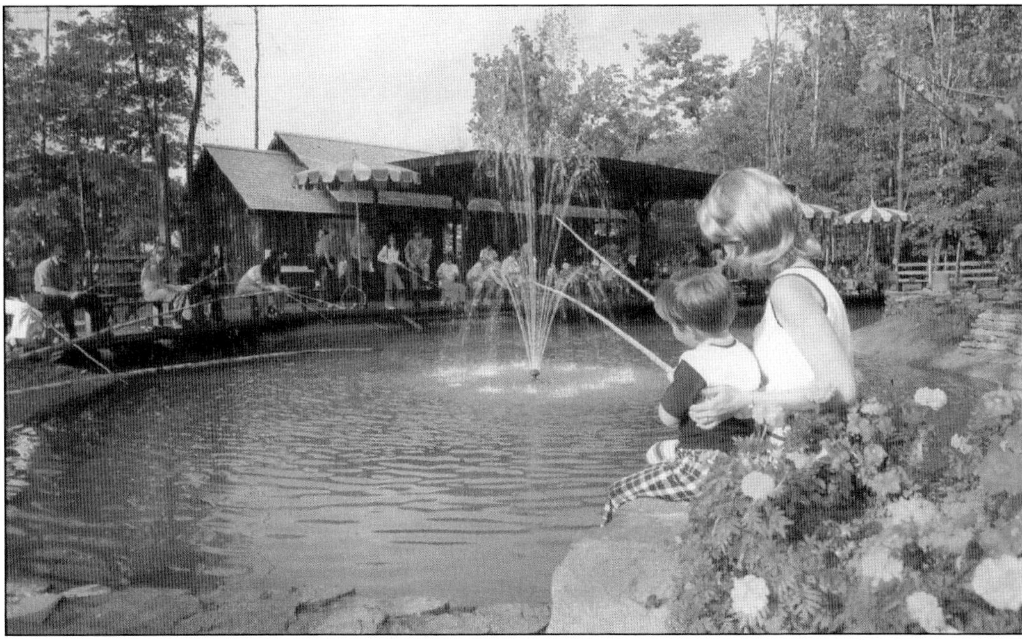

One of the more unusual attractions was that SeaWorld offered a fishing pond. The pond was stocked with live trout daily by SeaWorld's staff. For a small fee, guests had the opportunity to fish without the need of a fishing license. Guests were then allowed to take their catch home inside a provided bag of ice. (Dave Hahner collection.)

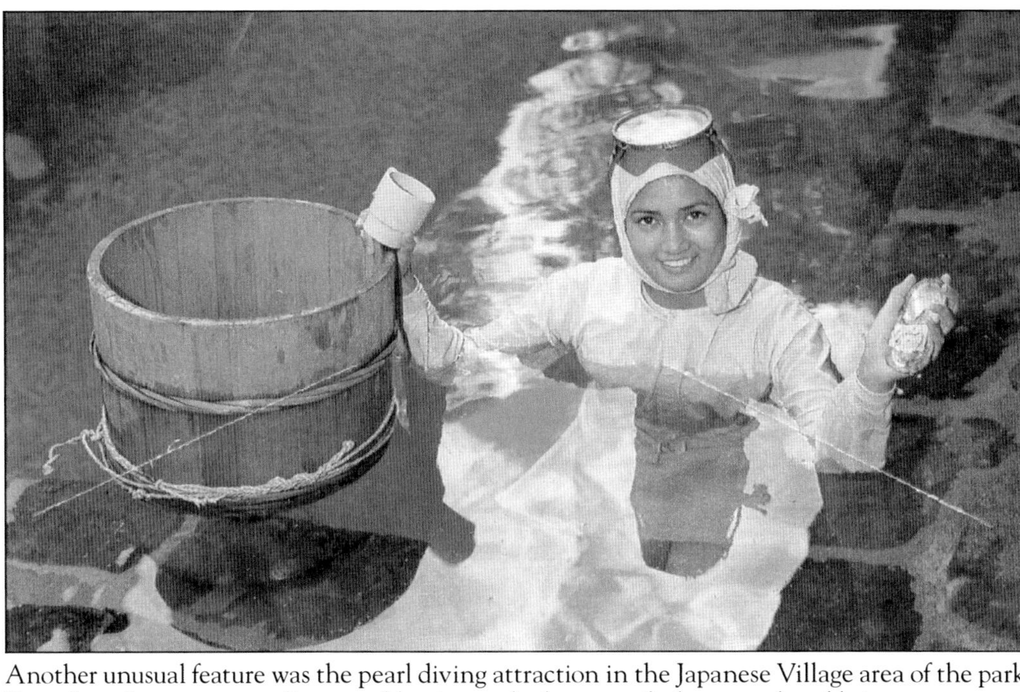

Another unusual feature was the pearl diving attraction in the Japanese Village area of the park. For a fee, a Japanese ama diver would swim to the bottom of a large pool and bring up an oyster for a guest. The oyster would then be opened at a counter and the natural pearl removed and mounted, offering a unique and decorative souvenir. (Dave Hahner collection.)

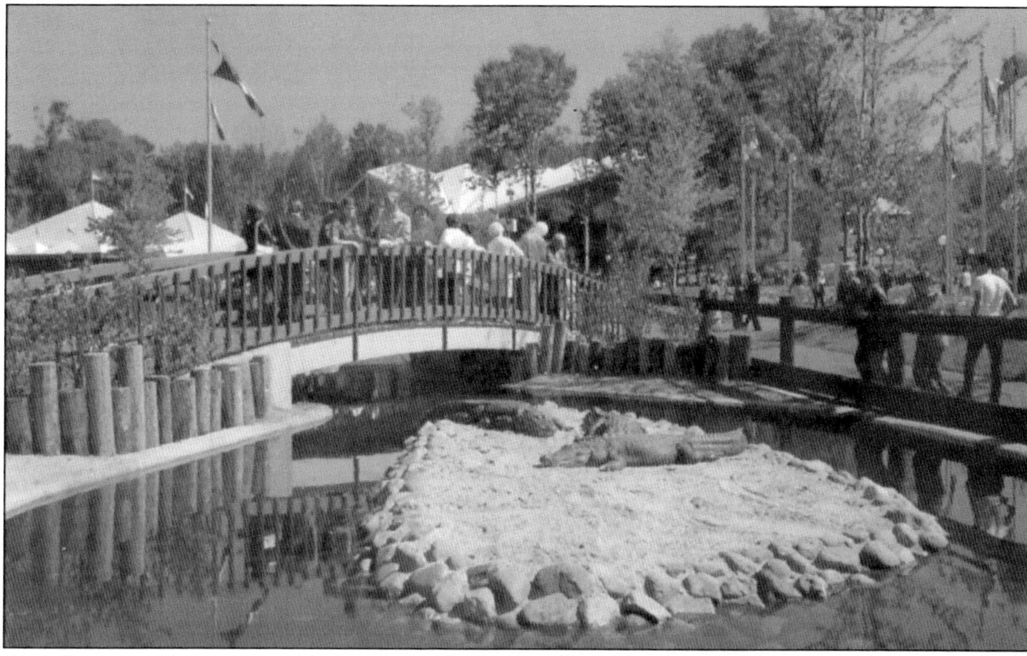

An alligator exhibit was added as part of a $1.5-million expansion in 1971, but it was removed by the 1980s. In the distance is the stadium that would eventually be renamed Shamu Stadium. The building to the left housed many concessions, including a gift shop and refreshments. Nearby, a Hawaiian village–themed eatery sponsored by Hawaiian Punch would open in 1972. (Dave Hahner collection.)

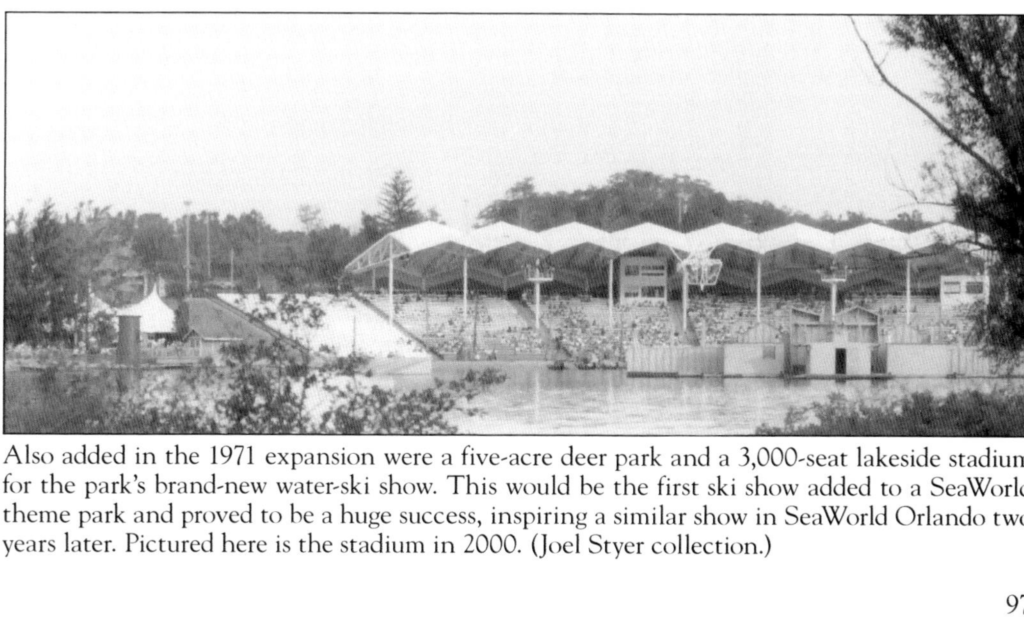

Also added in the 1971 expansion were a five-acre deer park and a 3,000-seat lakeside stadium for the park's brand-new water-ski show. This would be the first ski show added to a SeaWorld theme park and proved to be a huge success, inspiring a similar show in SeaWorld Orlando two years later. Pictured here is the stadium in 2000. (Joel Styer collection.)

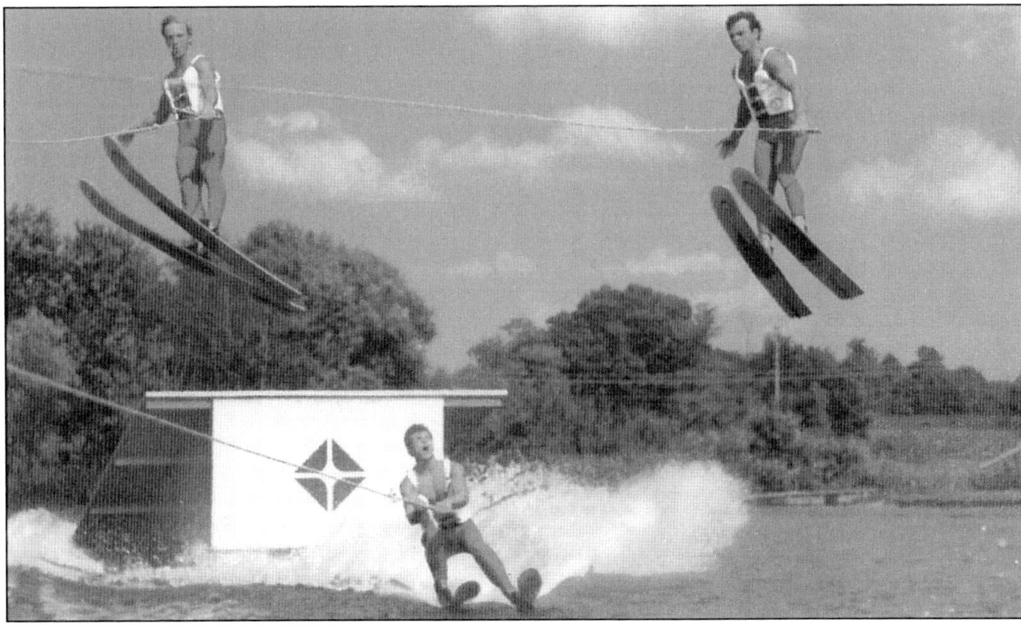

SeaWorld management hired legendary water-ski show producer Tommy Bartlett to create the new show for SeaWorld Ohio. Bartlett was famous for water-ski shows in the Wisconsin Dells and at Ontario Place in Toronto, Canada. His assistant, Dick Rowe, was given the assignment, and the show proved an instant hit among SeaWorld's guests. SeaWorld began producing the shows in-house in 1975. (Jim Futrell collection.)

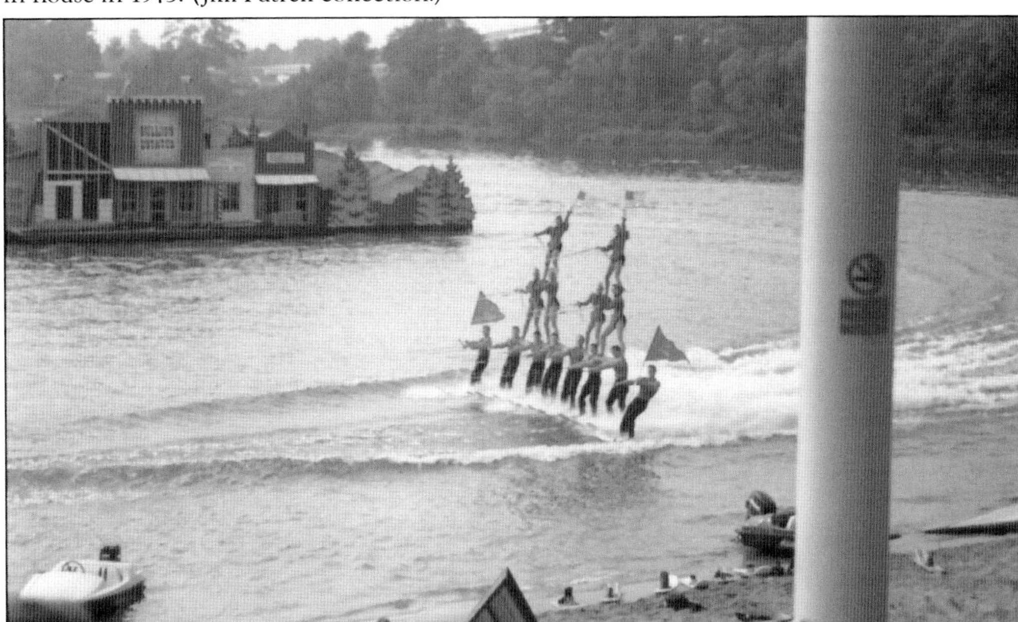

The water-ski stadium was expanded a few years later due to the enormous popularity of the show. In later years, the 3,500-seat stadium would be used for other entertainment in conjunction with the ski show, including live musical acts as well as a nighttime laser and firework show called "Mermaids, Myths, and Monsters" in the waters of Geauga Lake. (Dave Hahner collection.)

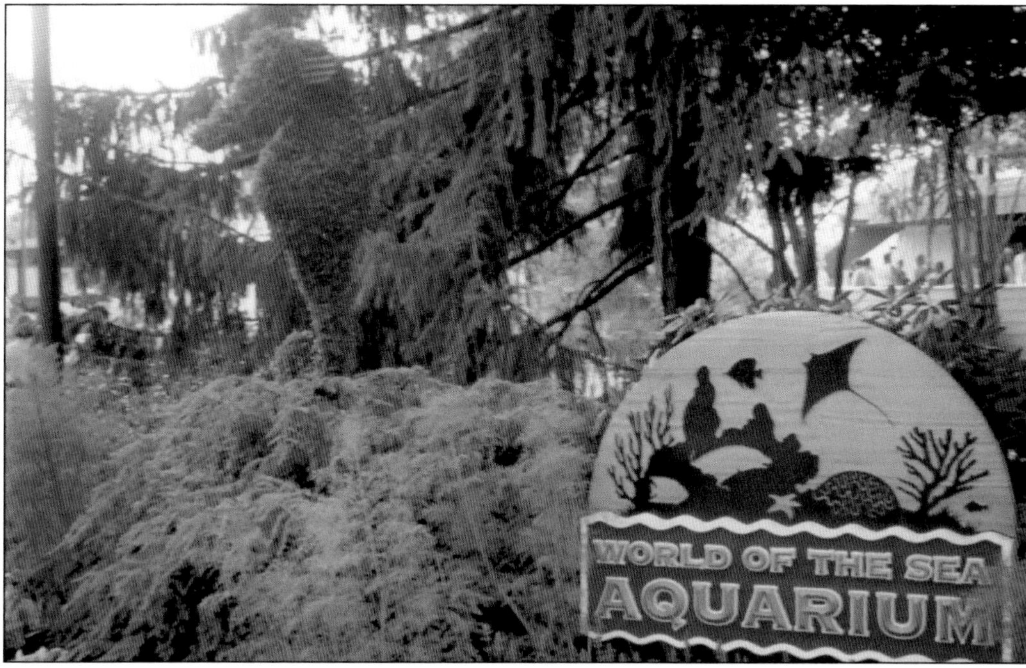

The World of the Sea Triquarium opened in 1973. The unique triple-pyramid structure featured many displays of marine life from all over the world. The facility cost over $1 million to construct and was built on a pier along the shoreline. The bright hues of blue painted on the structure were used to help advertise the new attraction to visitors at Geauga Lake across the way. (Dave Hahner collection.)

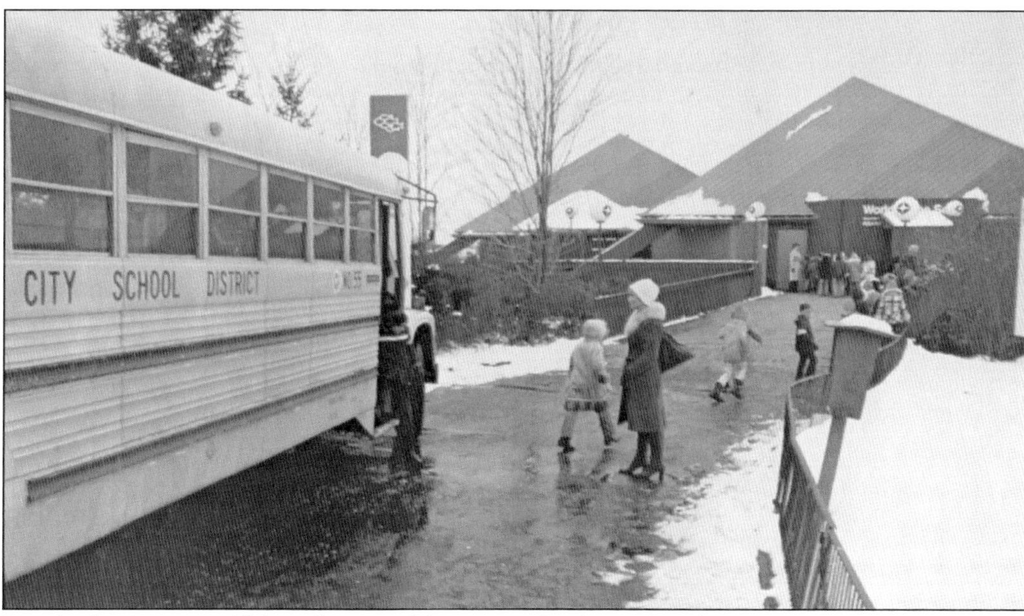

Hundreds of species of fish and marine life were on display within the World of the Sea Triquarium. The facility also featured a small, shallow pool where visitors could touch sea stars, rays, and other sea creatures just outside the building's entrance. In this photograph, a Cleveland-area school group takes a midwinter field trip to the Triquarium. (Sam Shurgott collection.)

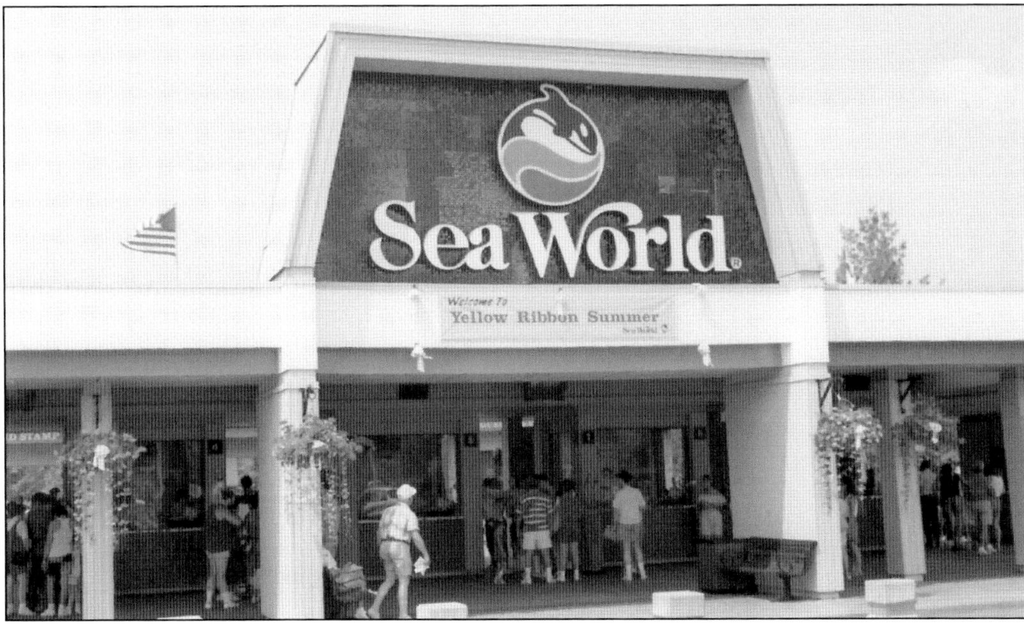

In 1976, the entire SeaWorld chain of parks, including the parks in Orlando and San Diego, were sold to publisher Harcourt Brace Jovanovich (HBJ). As part of the new owner's makeover of the newly acquired parks, SeaWorld Ohio would receive a brand-new expanded entrance gate in 1977 to help convey a grand sense of wonder and adventure of what lay beyond. (Dave Hahner collection.)

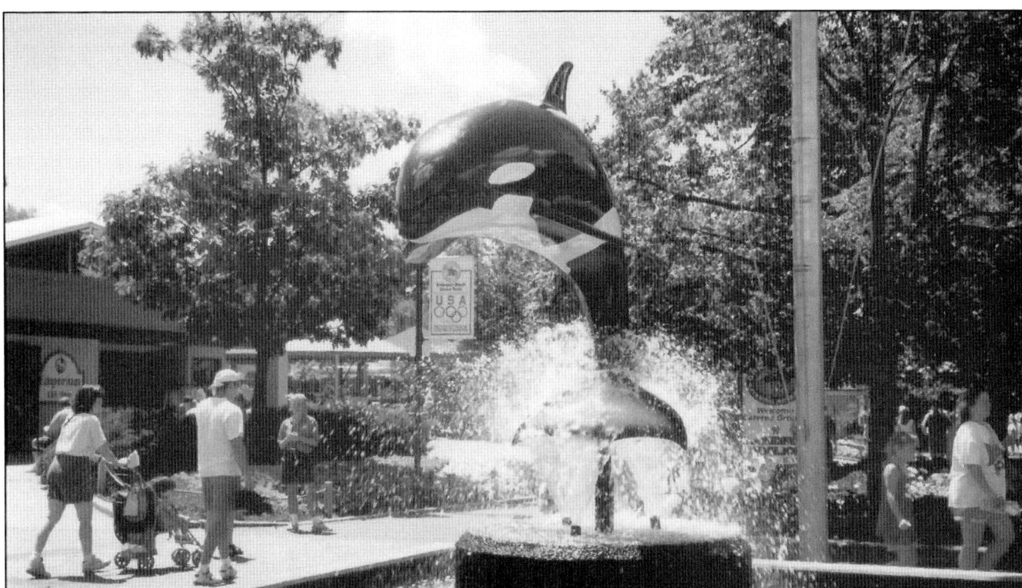

The first image that greeted guests when entering SeaWorld was this impressive statue of a killer whale leaping over a fountain. Many guests over the years used this popular fountain as a meeting point for their families. This photograph was taken in 1996, when SeaWorld and its parent company Anheuser-Busch were sponsors of the US Olympic team at the Summer Games in Atlanta, Georgia. (Dave Hahner collection.)

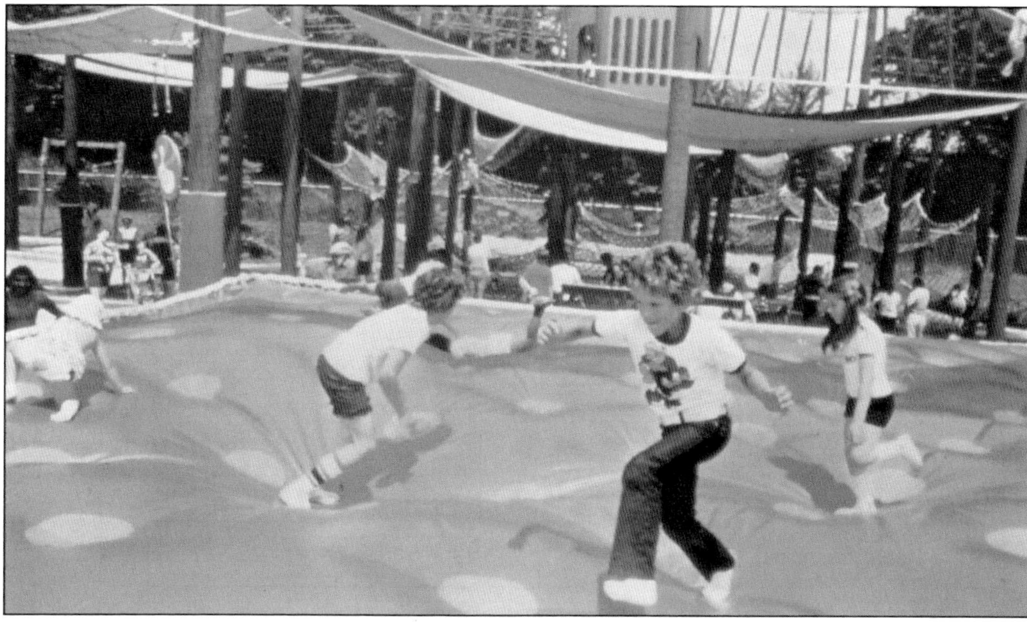

Since the park opened in 1970, small playgrounds were located within the picnic areas of the property. A larger play area with climbing nets and other play structures known as Cap'n Kids' World opened not far from the water-ski stadium in 1975. Because of a no-compete clause in the park's property lease agreement with neighboring Geauga Lake, no mechanical rides could be added to SeaWorld. (Sam Shurgott collection.)

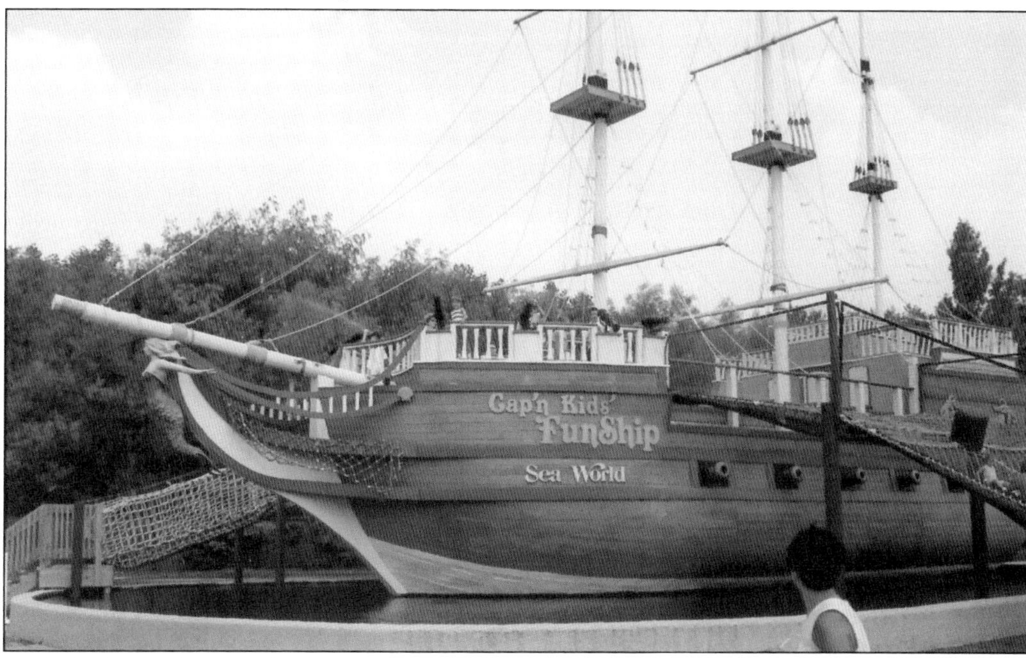

Cap'n Kids' World proved to be extremely popular among the children who visited SeaWorld over the years. In 1981, Cap'n Kids' Fun Ship was added to the area. The life-sized pirate ship featured cargo nets to climb and several places to explore while on board. The play structure became an iconic location for families to take photographs of young buccaneers. (Dave Hahner collection.)

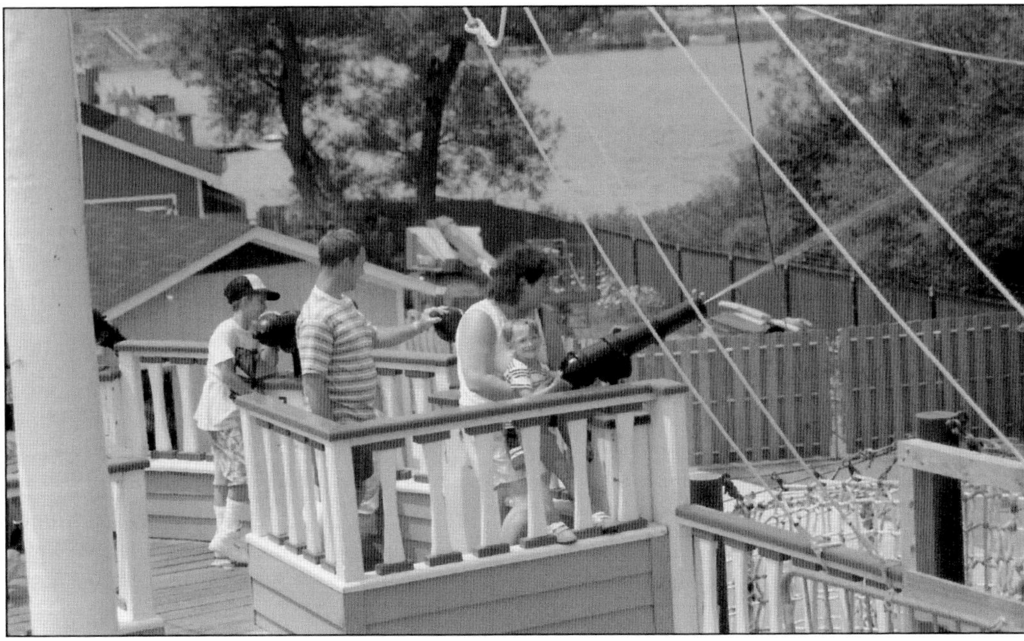

The Fun Ship also had cannons that squirted water, helping kids stay cool on those hot summer days. Unwary passersby often became unexpectedly wet from the new recruits of Cap'n Kids' crew. In 1992, the Fun Ship would become part of an even larger expanded children's play area known as Shamu's Happy Harbor, featuring a three-story-tall climbing structure. (Dave Hahner collection.)

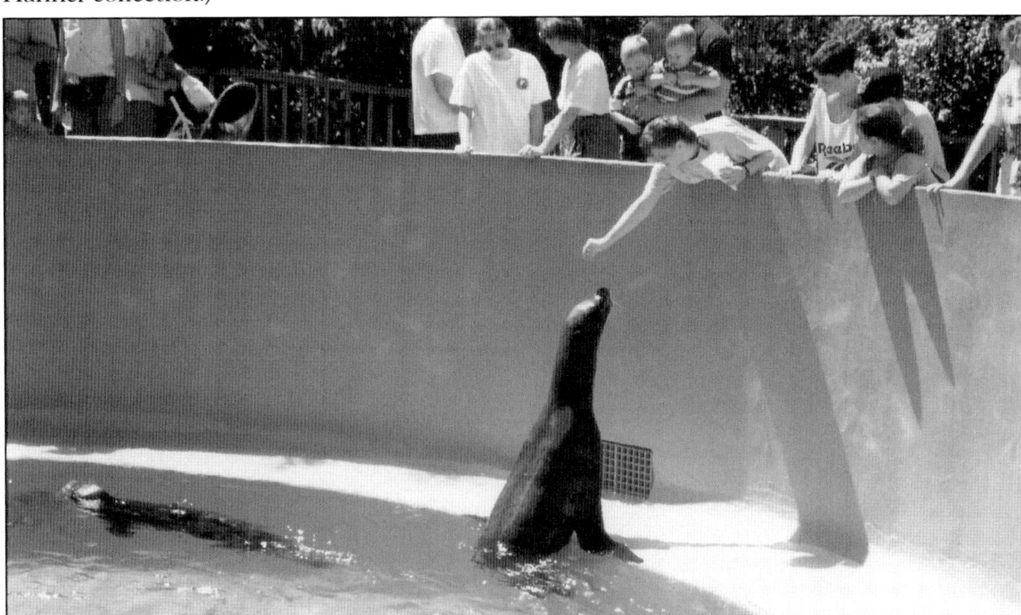

The sea lion pool was one of the longest-running exhibits at SeaWorld. The playful sea mammals could be fed by guests who were not too squeamish to handle the fishy morsels. A refrigerator magnet boasting "I Fed the Sea Lions at SeaWorld" would be included in the small fee to feed the hungry pinnipeds. (Dave Hahner collection.)

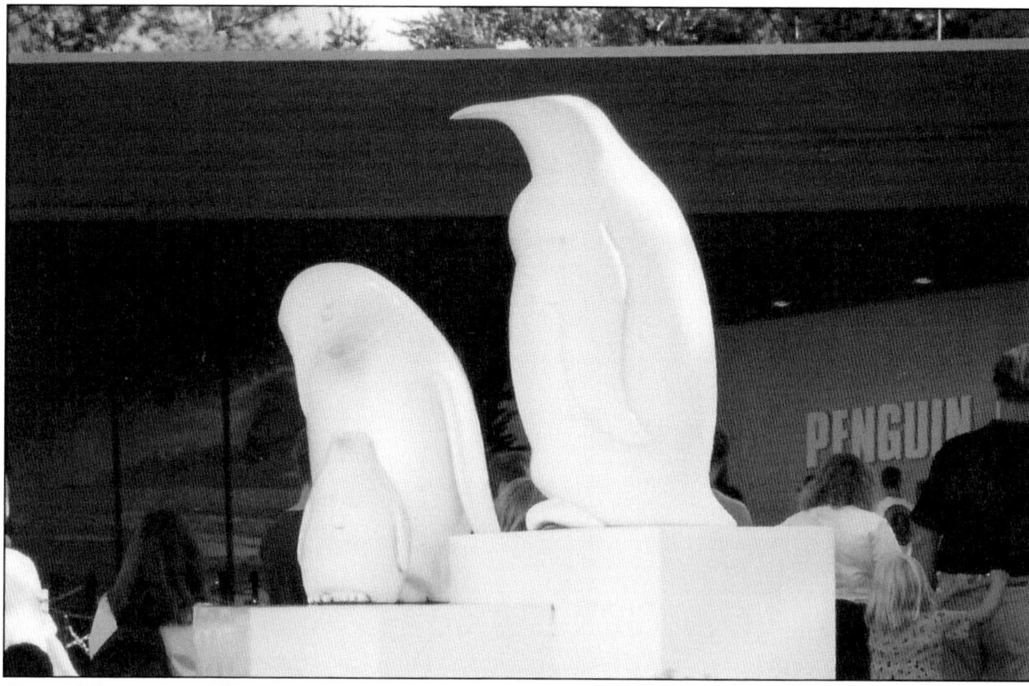

One of the most ambitious SeaWorld additions, Penguin Encounter, opened in 1985. At a cost of over $3.5 million, the state-of-the-art structure would house six species of Antarctic penguins, simulating their natural environment. Guests would view the penguins from a moving sidewalk, allowing up close encounters with the playful birds. (Dave Hahner collection.)

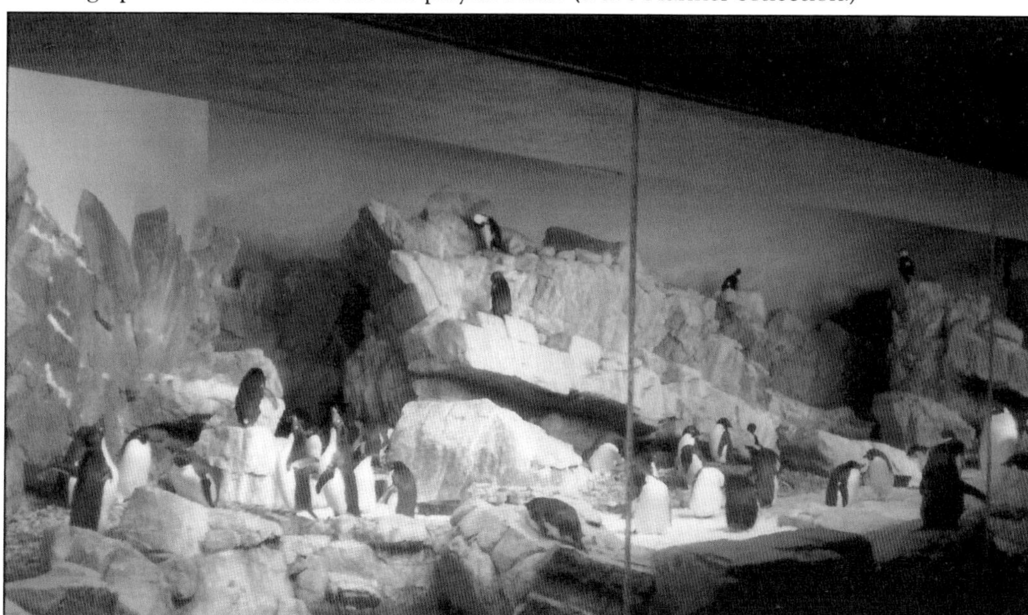

Penguin Encounter boasted over 100 penguins on display and simulated the harsh, eternal winter environment of Antarctica. The temperature remained a constant 26 degrees, featured 50,000 gallons of water, and produced 5,000 gallons of snow within the exhibit. The new attraction replaced the deer park near Shamu Stadium. (Sarah Windisch collection.)

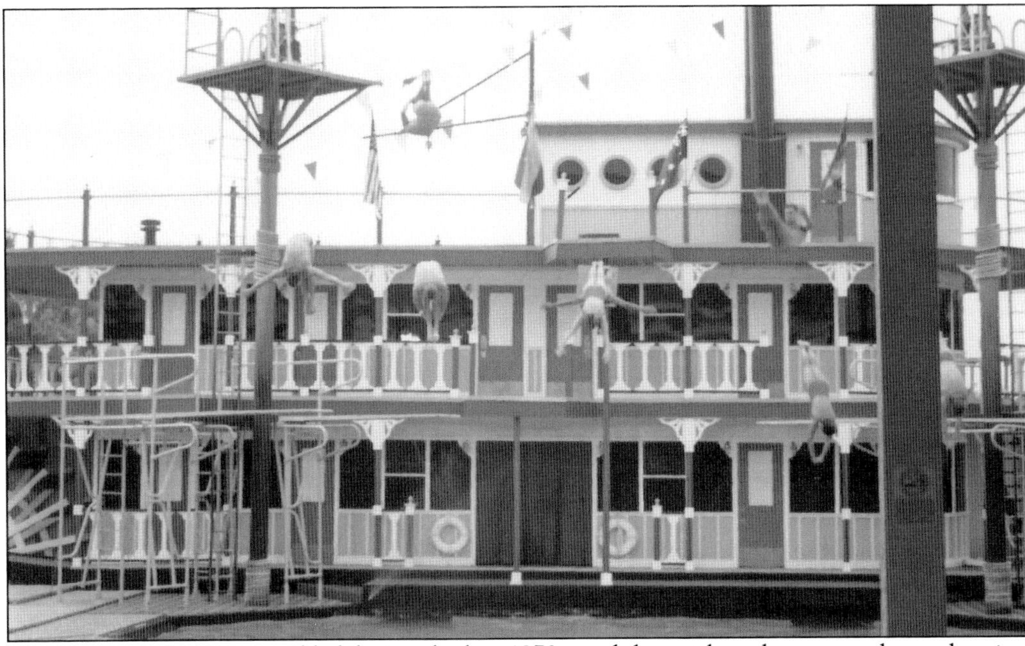

The Nautilus Theater was added during the late 1970s, and the outdoor show venue housed various acts over the years. Among these were lumberjack shows, stunt shows, bird shows, Chinese acrobats, pet shows, and even an appearance by the Sesame Street characters. This photograph captures a high-dive act featuring some of the nation's top divers in 1991. (Dave Hahner collection.)

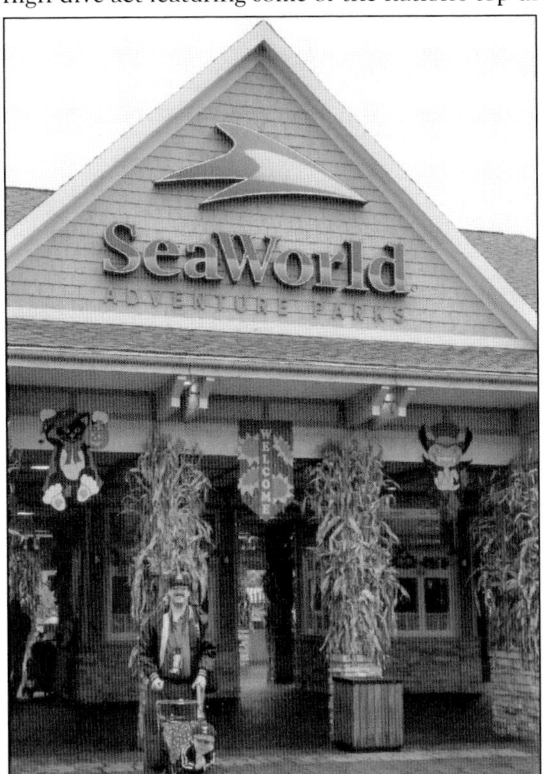

In 1989, publisher Harcourt Brace Jovanovich decided to exit the theme park business and sold the SeaWorld chain to Anheuser-Busch, which already owned and operated two successful Busch Gardens theme parks in Williamsburg, Virginia, and Tampa, Florida. Although this New England–style entrance gate would not be built until 1998, the park began to see many new additions under Anheuser-Busch ownership. (Theresa Hahner collection.)

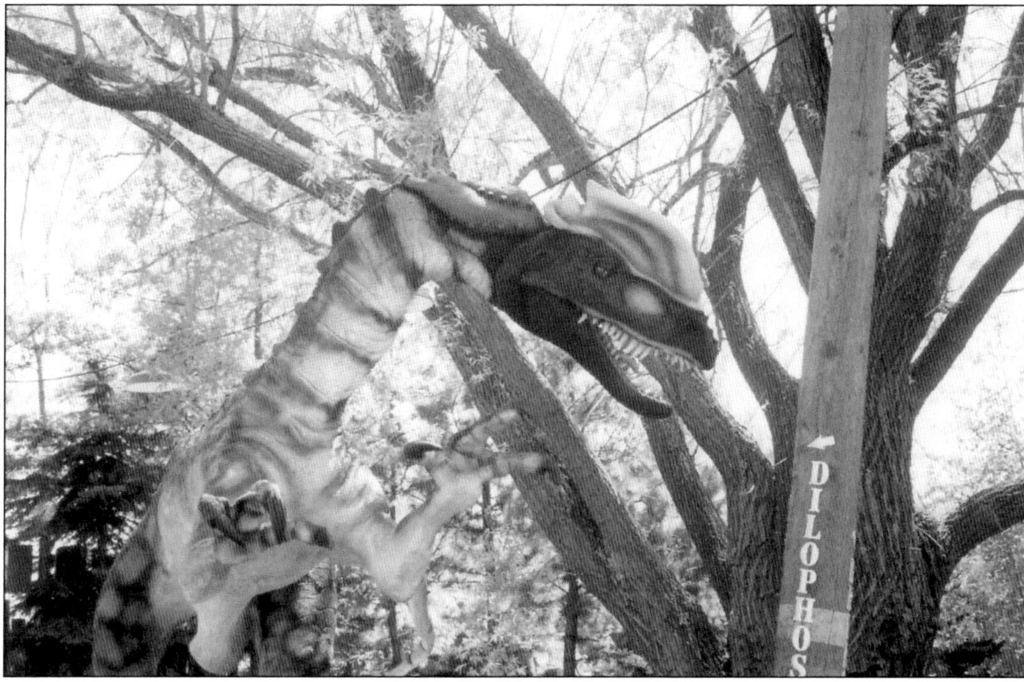

SeaWorld featured many temporary exhibits over the years within the park. In 1992, SeaWorld added Monster Marsh, a five-acre animatronic dinosaur exhibit through a primeval landscape. The attraction only lasted two seasons, but it returned for another two seasons as Carnivore Park in 1998, loosely inspired by the 1993 hit movie *Jurassic Park*. (Dave Hahner collection.)

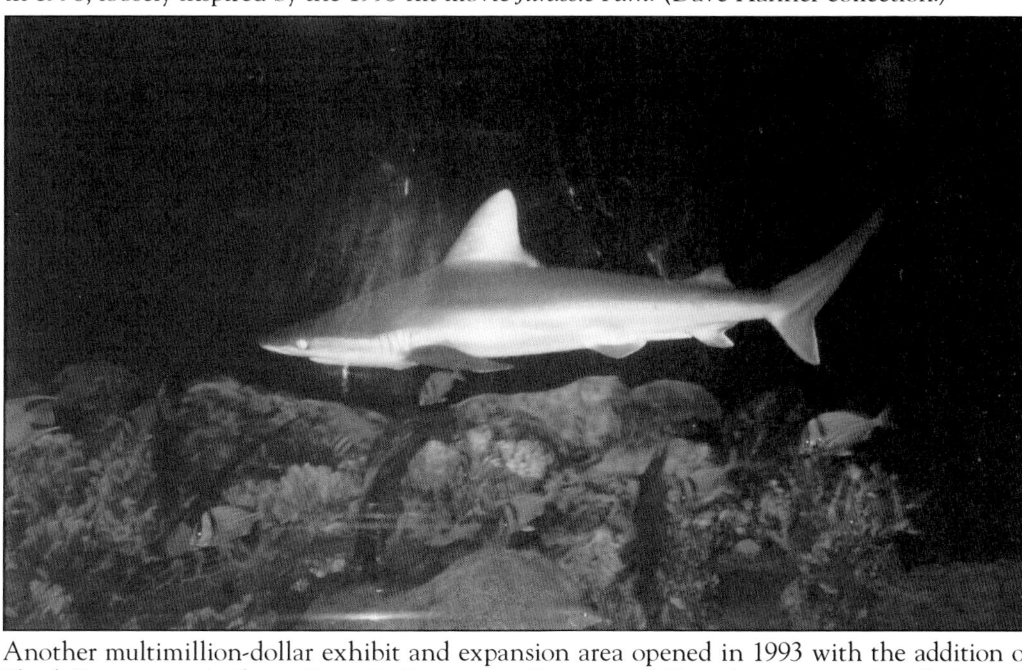

Another multimillion-dollar exhibit and expansion area opened in 1993 with the addition of Shark Encounter, similar to Penguin Encounter. Guests would board a moving sidewalk through a partially surrounding acrylic tube to view four species of sharks and other sea life up close and personal within a 340,000-gallon tank. (Dave Hahner collection.)

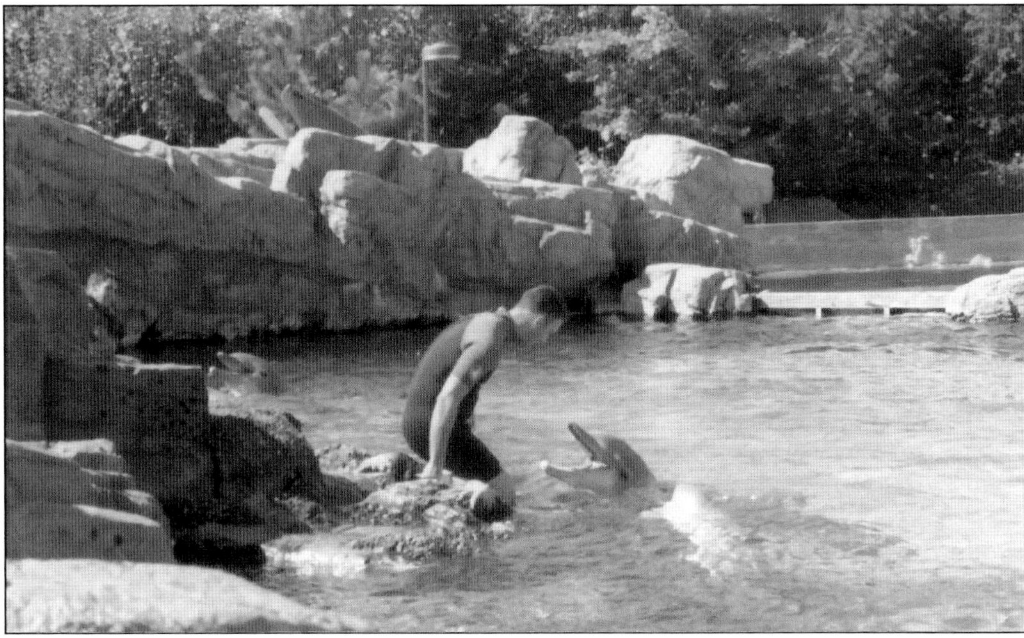

Although dolphins had been a major draw to SeaWorld since the park had opened in 1970, they had always had to share a venue with the killer whales. In 1995, a new 375,000-gallon habitat known as Dolphin Cove, featuring a realistic rocky shoreline, gave the park's 12 bottlenose dolphins a new home. (Sarah Windisch collection.)

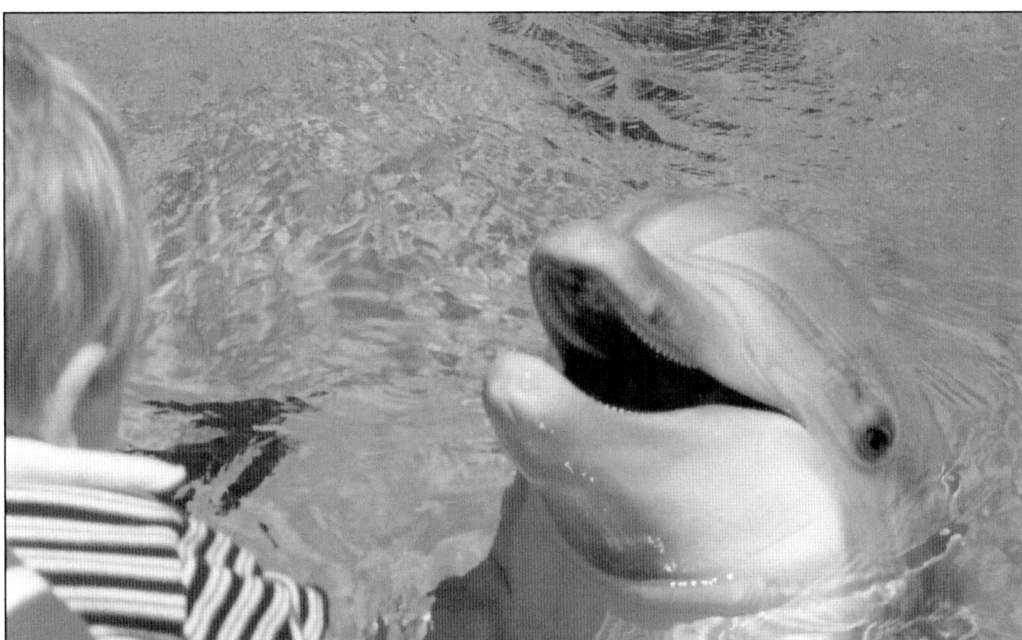

Dolphin Cove not only gave the dolphins a much larger, friendlier habitat to live in, but it also gave guests a better opportunity to interact with the friendly sea mammals. Visitors could literally reach in and touch the dolphins as well as feed them. Dolphin Cove quickly became one of the park's most popular attractions. (Dave Hahner collection.)

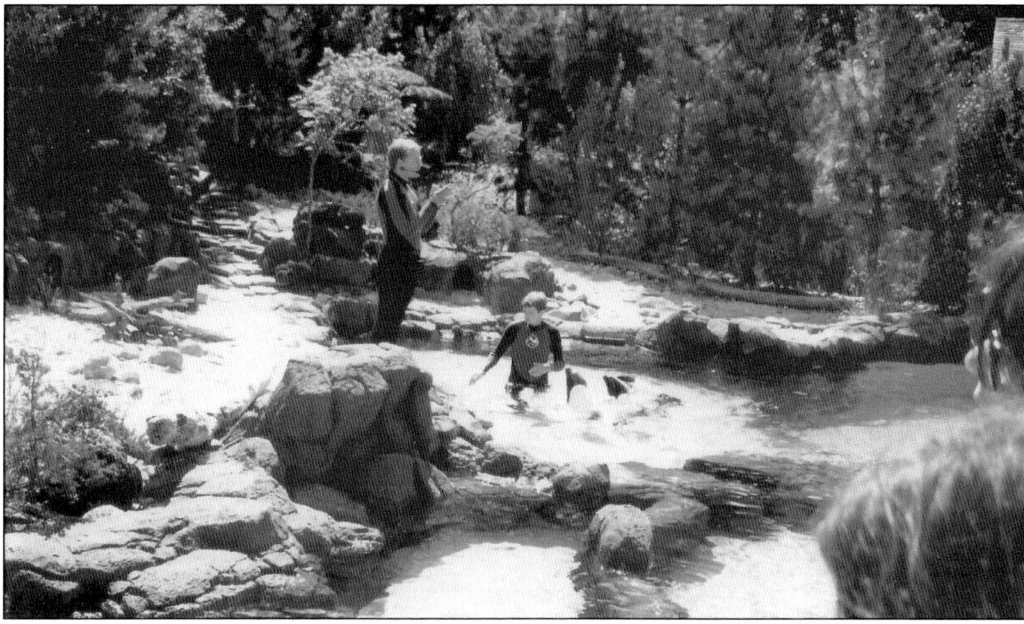

Another new outdoor exhibit area known as Patagonia Passage opened in 1996. Replicating the rocky coastal waters off the southern tip of South America, the new exhibit featured Commerson's dolphins, a smaller black-and-white-skinned species of dolphin found mainly in that part of the world. In this photograph, trainers are demonstrating some of the sea mammal's abilities within the rocky exhibit. (Dave Hahner collection.)

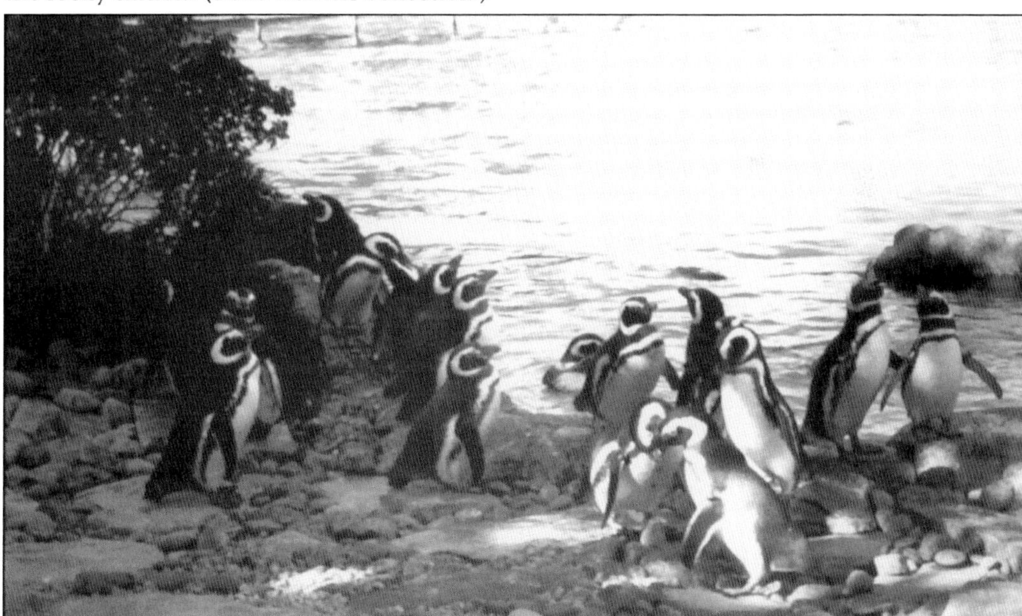

Also found within the Patagonia Passage exhibit were Magellanic penguins. This warm-weather species of penguin is found in the southern waters off the coast of South America. Dozens of the unique waterfowl could be observed swimming and walking within the rocky environments of the exhibit. (Jim Futrell collection.)

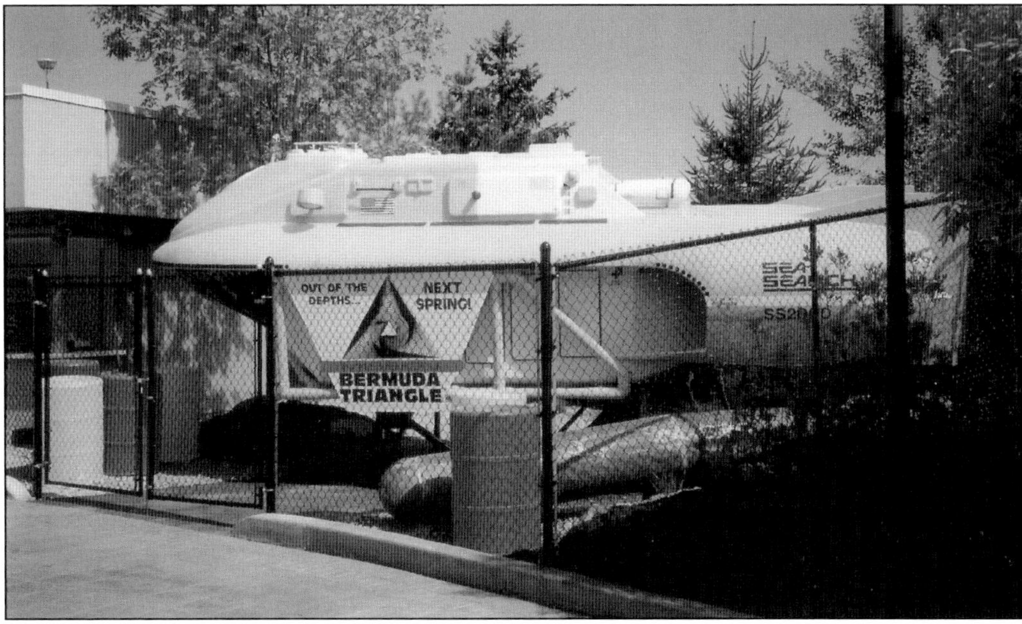

In 1997, a hilarious new *Pirates* 4-D movie starring Leslie Nielsen and Eric Idle was added in the just-built Harbor Theater. In 1999, SeaWorld had a small yellow exploration submarine on display near the Shark Encounter gift shop. This was a teaser for what would essentially be SeaWorld's only ride ever installed, Mission: Bermuda Triangle, which opened in May 2000. (Dave Hahner collection.)

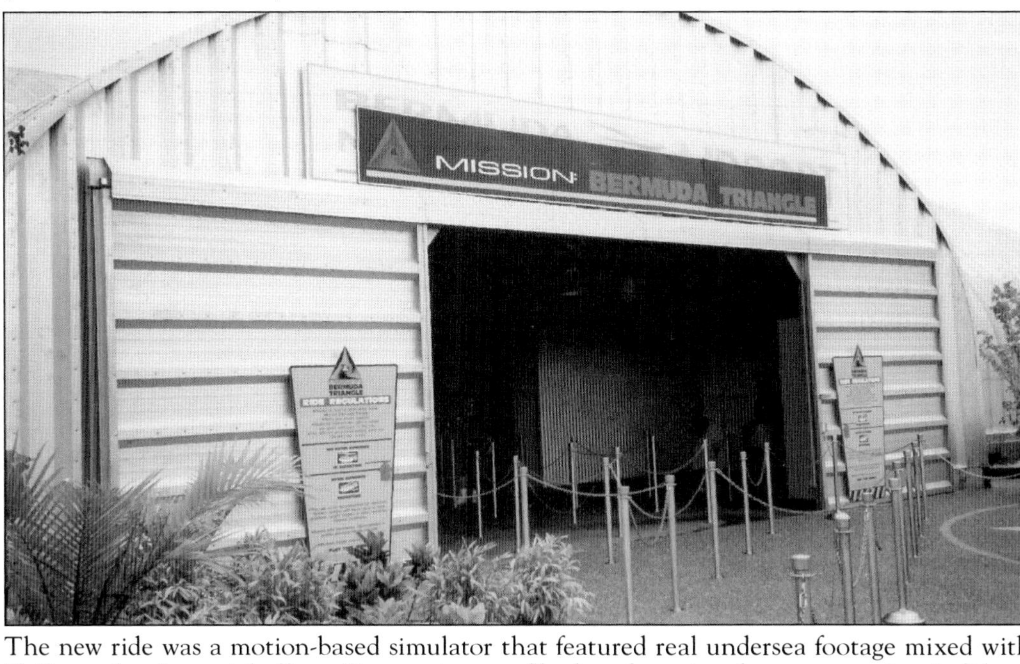

The new ride was a motion-based simulator that featured real undersea footage mixed with Hollywood-style special effects. Because it was a film-based moving theater attraction, it did not violate the non-compete clause that SeaWorld had with Geauga Lake. Ironically, this would be the final season for SeaWorld Ohio, as the property would be sold to the Six Flags Corporation in March 2001. (Dave Hahner collection.)

Seven

Epilogue 1996–2007

Most amusement parks when they near the end of their existence usually slowly fade away. But this would not be the path that eventually ended Geauga Lake and neighboring SeaWorld. Rapid expansion would be both parks' undoing. Like a supernova, the fate of Geauga Lake and SeaWorld would explode them both into one massive mega park and suddenly shrink in size until only a water park remained.

The final decade for Geauga Lake looked promising. Funtime, Inc. would sell its properties to Premier Parks, a theme park operator from Oklahoma City, Oklahoma, in August 1995. Premier Parks began to invest in the park almost immediately after the park closed for the 1995 season, with the addition of a roller coaster and white-water raft ride in 1996. More additions in subsequent years continued, including another new coaster in 1998. That same year, Premier Parks purchased the Six Flags chain of theme parks and became the Six Flags Corporation.

In 1999, several properties, including former sister Funtime park Darien Lake in New York, would be re-branded as Six Flags parks. Geauga Lake would follow suit in 2000 with a $40 million makeover to become Six Flags Ohio that would include several new rides, including four roller coasters. Another new coaster would be added in 2001, but the biggest addition was not a new ride, but the purchase of neighboring SeaWorld for $110 million. The newly combined mega park would be re-branded into Six Flags Worlds of Adventure. But the rapid expansion proved to be the park's undoing. Massive debt and lower than expected attendance proved to be too much for the struggling park.

By 2004, the debt load was too much, and competing CedarFair, LLP, offered to purchase the property for $145 million. The former SeaWorld side would close permanently and become a water park in 2005. The Geauga Lake name would return, but attendance remained low. CedarFair, LLP, began to remove rides, downsizing the park into a family amusement park. Eventually, the decision was made in 2007 to close the ride side of the park, with only Wildwater Kingdom remaining.

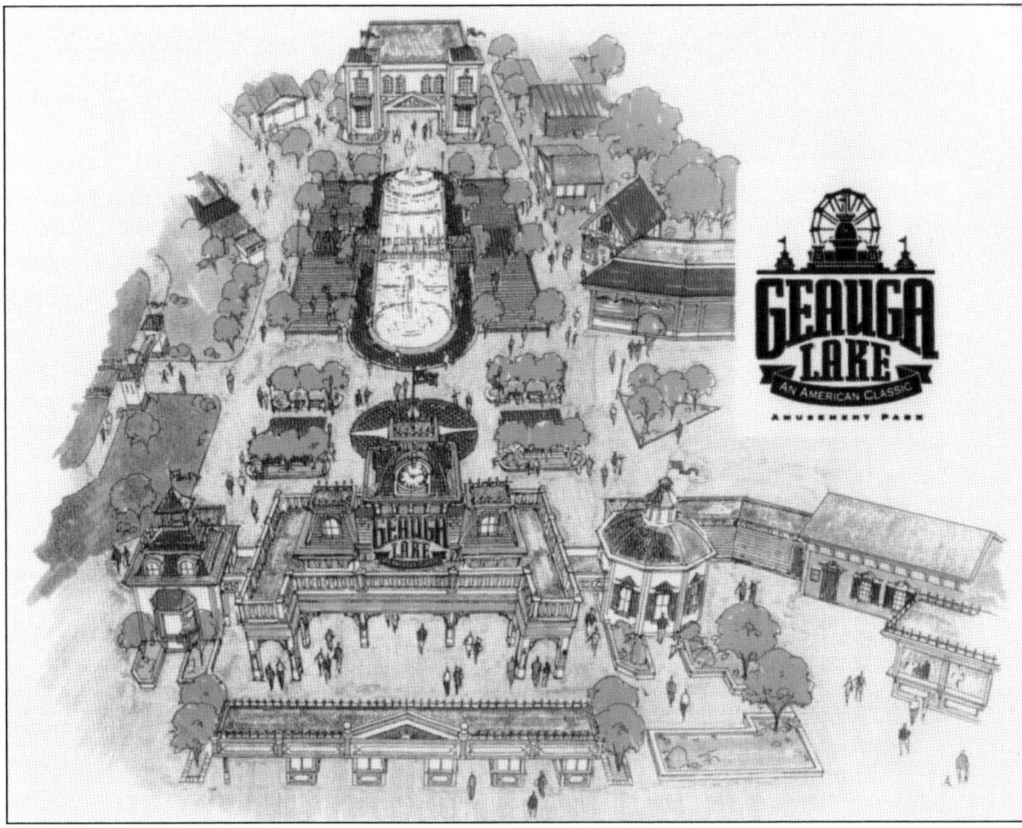

Once the sale of Geauga Lake to Premier Parks was complete, a new master plan was drafted for the redevelopment of the park. This image shows the reimagined front gate and entry plaza, which would resemble a Victorian-era town square. A new logo featuring the newly designed front gate and a Ferris wheel behind it would show the changes that were coming to the park. (Jim Futrell collection.)

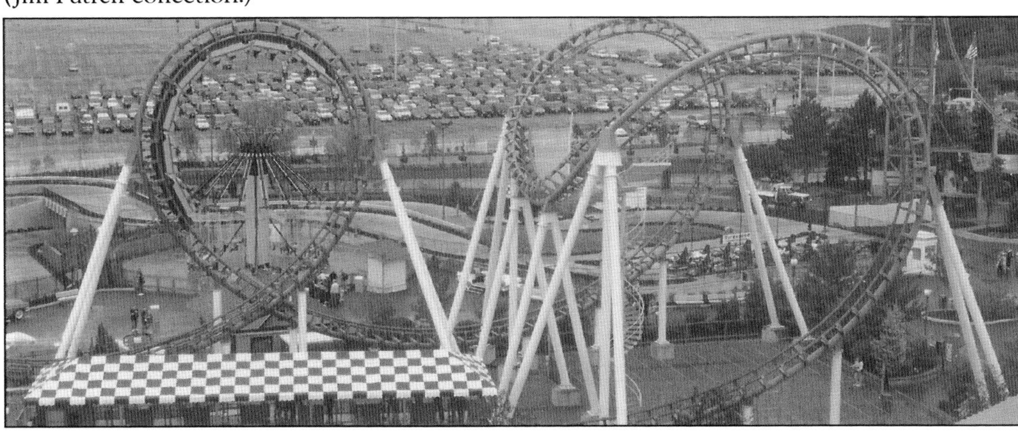

With new ownership at the helm, change would be inevitable. Two beloved attractions were removed during that first year, including the Arrow-designed Corkscrew looping coaster and the classic Harry Traver Rocket Ships from the 1920s. Replacing Corkscrew would be a new Vekoma boomerang shuttle coaster called Mind Eraser. Corkscrew was sold to MGM Dizzee World in Muttukadu, India, where it still operates today. (Jim Futrell collection.)

Mind Eraser riders were lifted backwards up a 116-foot lift hill, then released, traveling up to 45 miles per hour through three inversions (a double-looping cobra roll and a vertical loop). The train would then be pulled up another lift hill and traverse the same three inversions backwards. The ride was renamed Head Spin in 2004, and it eventually moved to Carowinds, near Charlotte, North Carolina, in 2009. (Joel Styer collection.)

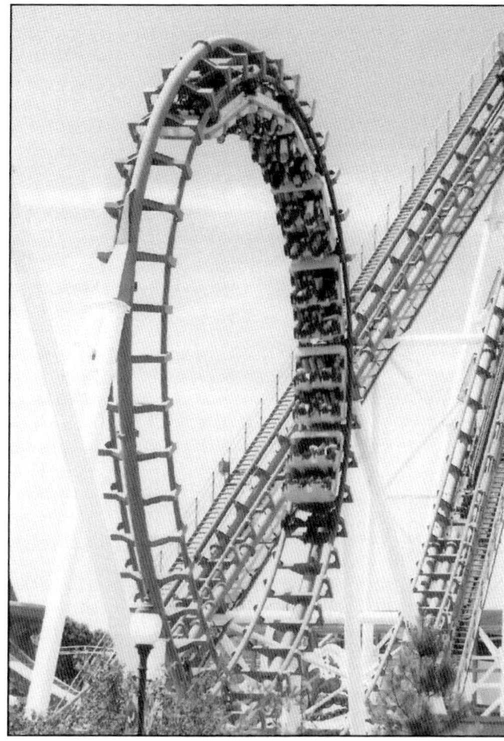

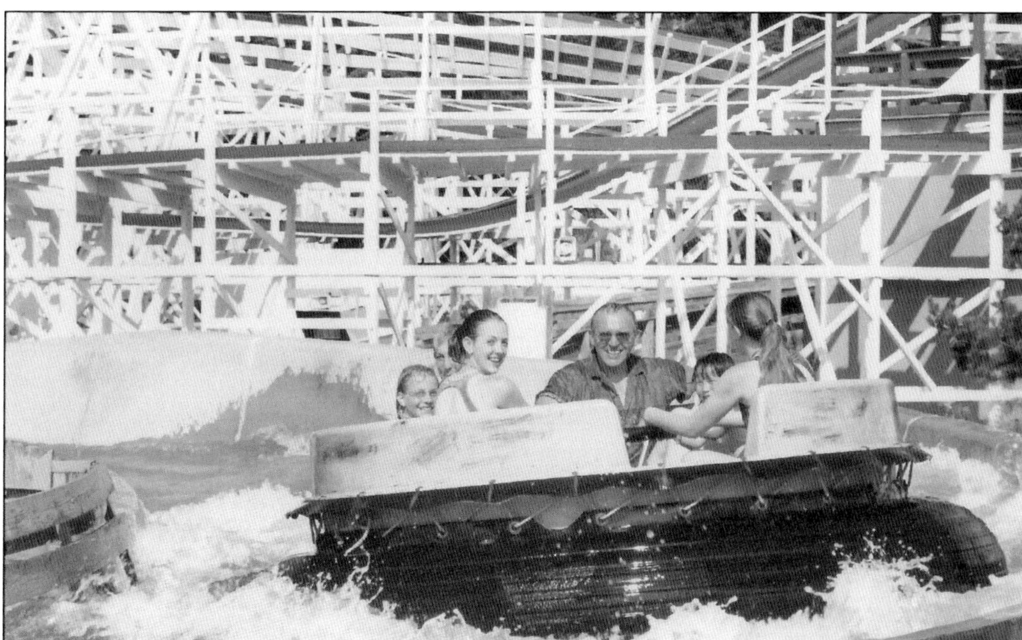

Also opening in 1996 was Grizzly Run, a river rapids ride from Intamin AG of Switzerland. Simulating a trip aboard a white-water raft, this extremely wet water ride offered passengers the perfect option for cooling down on those hot summer days in northeastern Ohio. The addition of Mind Eraser and Grizzly Run, along with other improvements, cost over $9 million. (Joel Styer collection.)

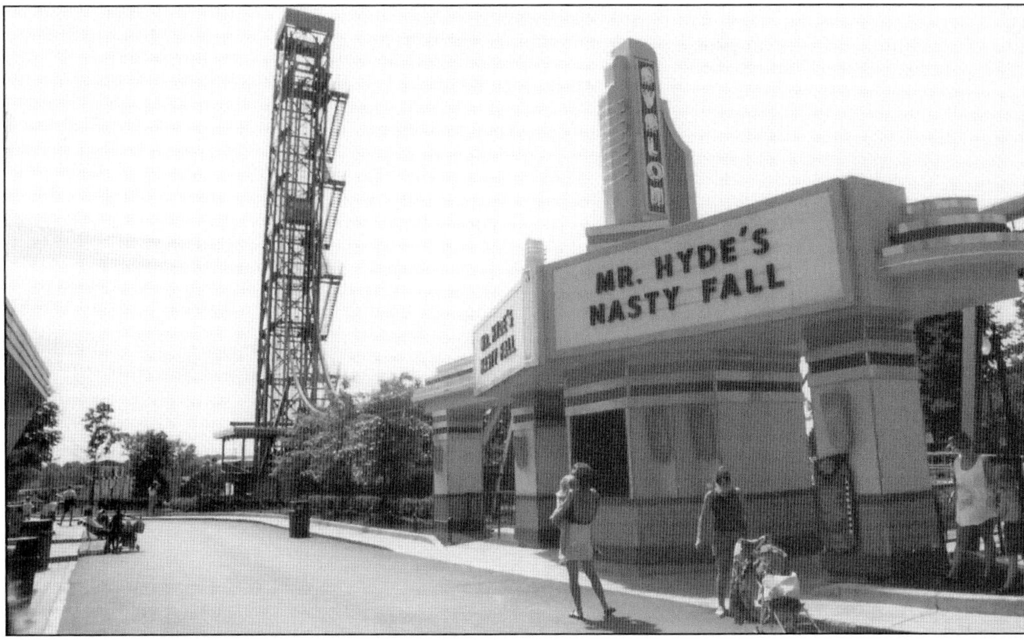

In 1997, Mr. Hyde's Nasty Fall, a 13-story free fall tower ride from Intamin AG, was added to the Geauga Lake skyline. This ride had originally operated at Six Flags Great America in Gurnee, Illinois, and was then sold to Rocky Point Amusement Park in Warwick, Rhode Island. Premier Parks acquired the ride in 1996 after the closure of Rocky Point. It was scrapped after the 2005 season. (Joel Styer collection.)

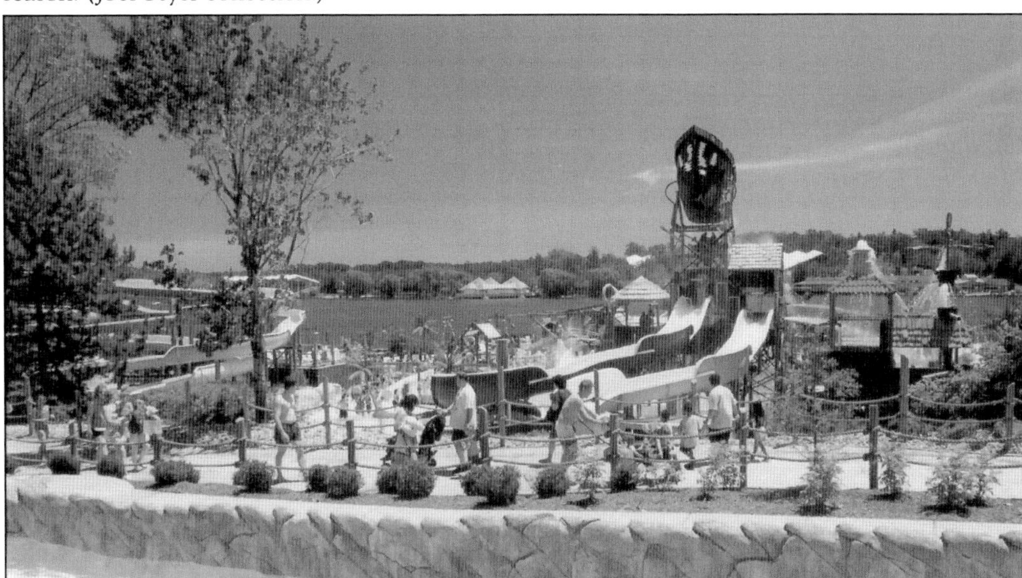

Also added for the 1997 season was a new interactive five-story-tall water park play structure called Hook's Lagoon. Featuring a 1,000-gallon tipping bucket shaped like a ship's bow, plus several small body slides and other water spray features, this would be the first phase of a multimillion-dollar rejuvenation to the existing Boardwalk Shores and Turtle Beach water park sections of the park. (Joel Styer collection.)

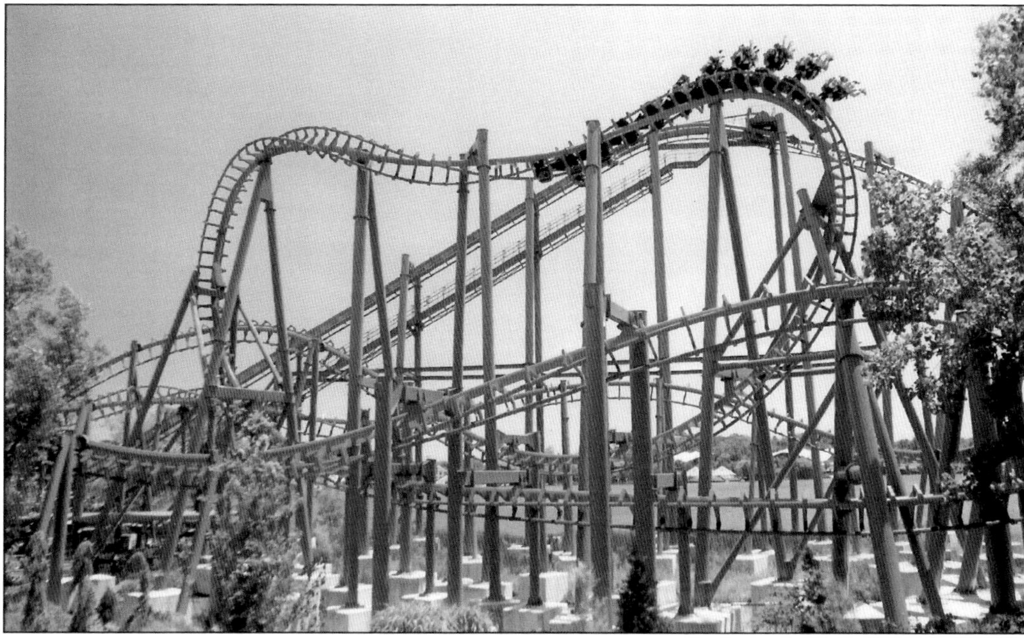

The waterfront area of the park beyond the Wave would drastically change in 1998 with the addition of Serial Thriller. This large, suspended looping roller coaster from Dutch ride manufacturer Vekoma featured 2,260 feet of twisting track with five upside-down inversions. The addition of such a large ride along the park's waterfront was a deliberate attempt to entice visitors from neighboring SeaWorld to Geauga Lake. (Joel Styer collection.)

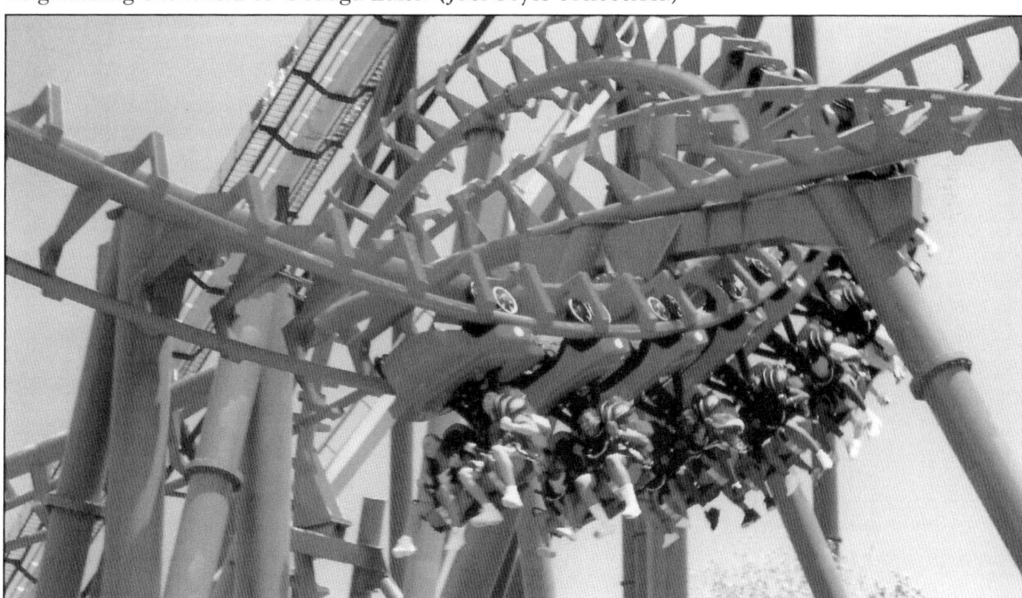

Unlike traditional roller coasters, Serial Thriller's trains traveled underneath the ride's track while maneuvering through its various twists, drops, and inversions. Traveling at speeds reaching 50 miles per hour, the 109-foot-tall ride proved to be a popular addition during its inaugural season. The ride was renamed Thunderhawk after the CedarFair purchase of the park and moved to Michigan's Adventure in Muskegon, Michigan, in 2008. (Joel Styer collection.)

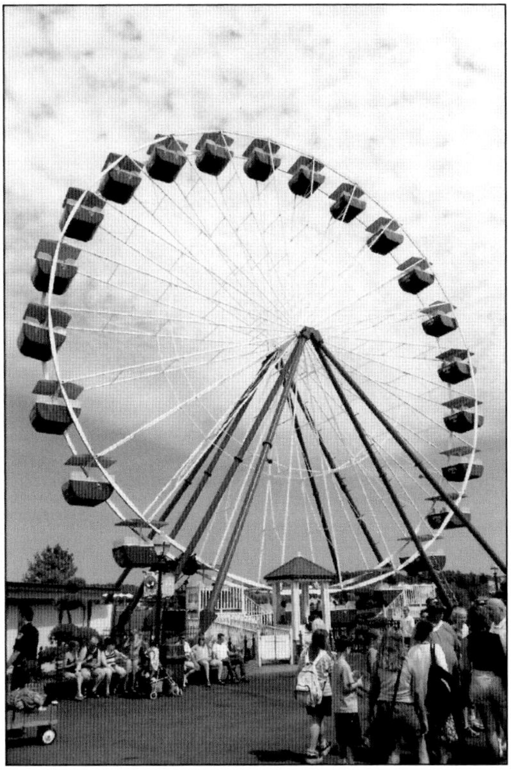

Americana, a 120-foot-tall giant Ferris wheel, was purchased from defunct Old Indiana Fun Park in Thornton, Indiana, in 1997. It was refurbished and added to Geauga Lake's ride lineup in 1999 and placed in line with the park's main entrance, which ironically matched the park's logo. It would be moved to Kings Dominion in Doswell, Virginia, in 2009. (Joel Styer collection.)

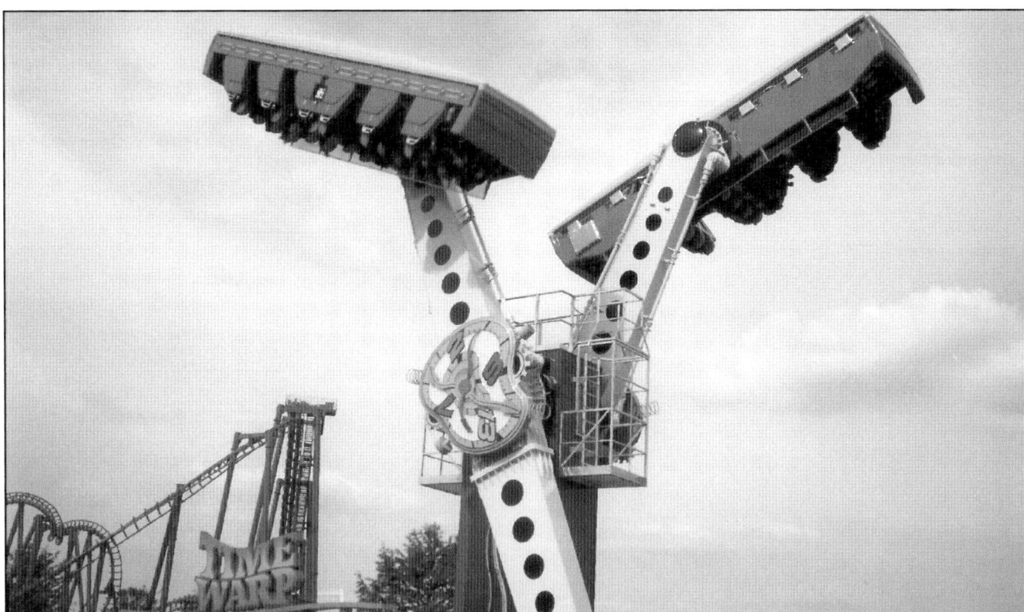

Also added for 1999 was an inverter ride from Chance Rides of Wichita, Kansas. Called Time Warp, this wickedly demented ride turned its riders upside-down at speeds reaching 35 miles per hour. The cars would stop at the apex in the upside-down position midway through the ride's cycle, then reverse direction. Loose items and change fell from riders' pockets on almost every ride. (Dave Hahner collection.)

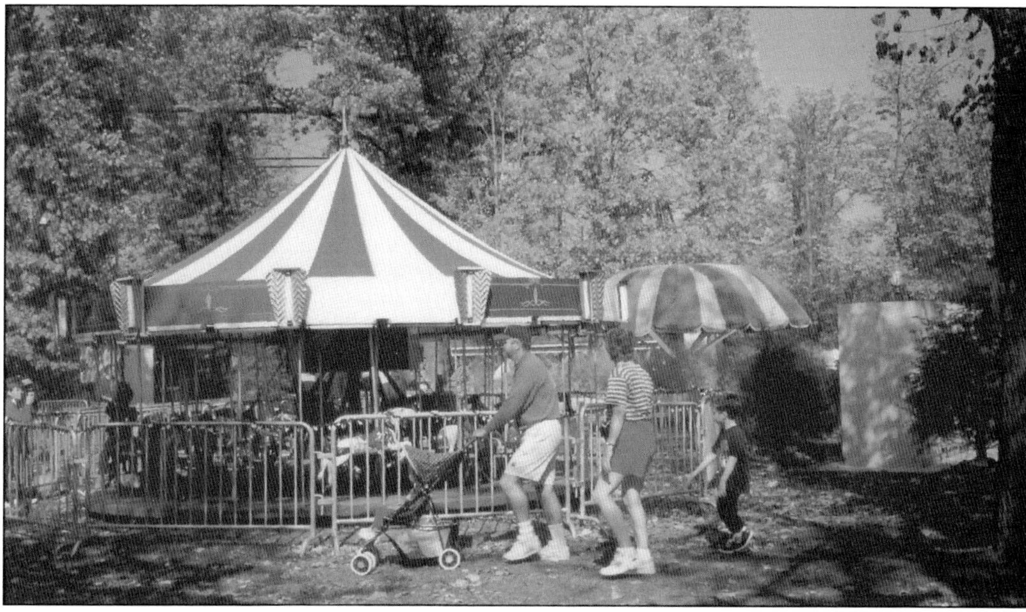

At the end of the 20th century, Geauga Lake would begin to undergo a massive transformation. Quietly, at the end of the 1999 season, many of the kiddie rides from Rainbow Island were temporarily transplanted to the parklike area near the main gate that once housed a miniature golf course. It was apparent that something major was happening within the park for the 2000 season. (Dave Hahner collection.)

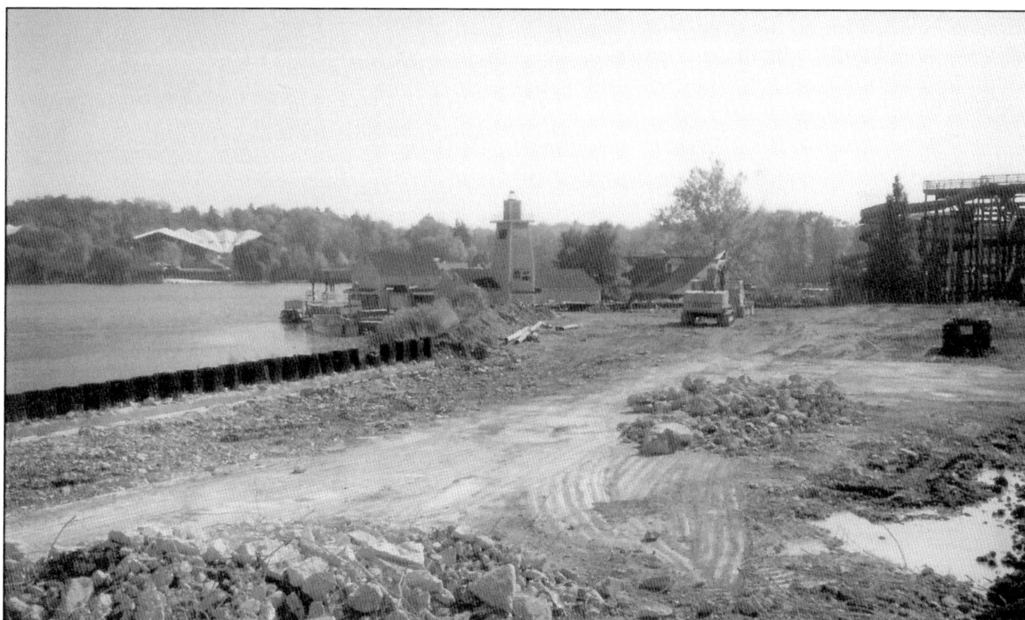

With the acquisition of Six Flags, Premier Parks, whose corporate name had also been changed to the better-known brand, had started transforming several of the facilities acquired in the 1990s to Six Flags–branded attractions. Geauga Lake's turn at the transformation would happen at the dawn of the new millennium. The Wave, once one of the nation's largest wave pools, would be no more. (Dave Hahner collection.)

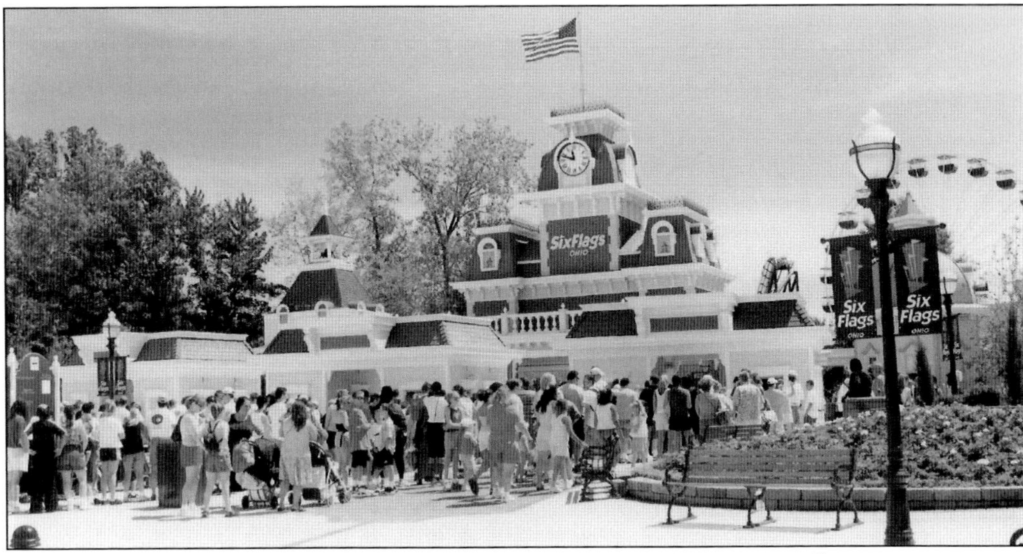

In May 2000, the park would have a new name and a new identity, as well as new attractions costing $40 million. Geauga Lake would now only be used in reference to the large body of water separating SeaWorld Ohio from the region's newest theme park, Six Flags Ohio. Crowds would flock to the new park for the 2000 season, resulting in record attendance. (Joel Styer collection.)

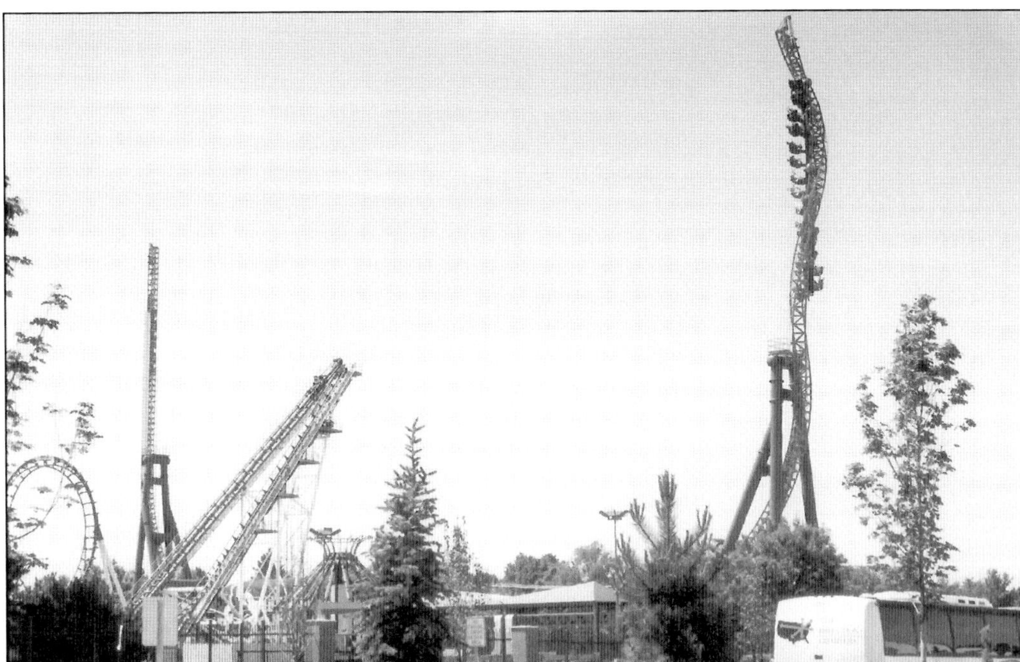

Four new roller coasters were added, including Superman: Ultimate Flight. This first-of-its-kind magnetic-launched coaster by Intamin featured a suspended train that would launch from zero to 70 miles per hour in just three seconds. It had a vertical twisting spiral on one end, with holding brakes on the other to add an extra thrill. It was renamed Steel Venom in 2004 and eventually moved to Dorney Park in Allentown, Pennsylvania, in 2008. (Joel Styer collection.)

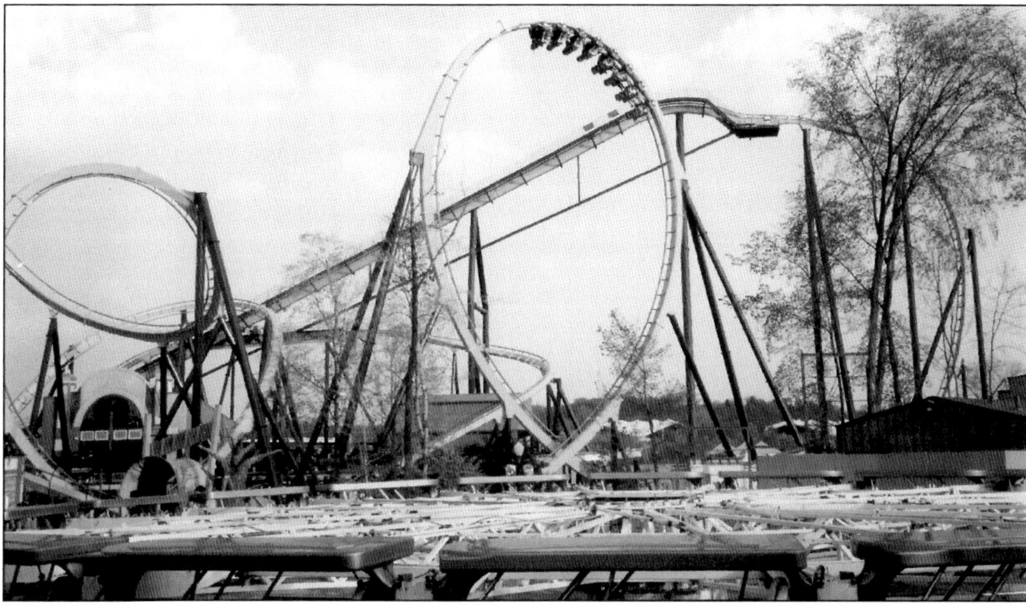

Among the largest investments during Six Flags Ohio's inaugural season was the addition of Batman Knight Flight. This massive, 147-foot-high steel roller coaster from Swiss coaster designers Bolliger & Mabillard featured floorless trains, speeds reaching 65 miles per hour through five hair-raising inversions, including what was then the world's tallest loop at 135 feet. Like Serial Thriller before it, Batman Knight Flight would be built along the lake's edge, essentially becoming a massive beacon to entice guests at neighboring SeaWorld to visit the new and improved theme park on the other side of the lake. After CedarFair purchased the property in 2004, the ride would be renamed Dominator, and it eventually moved to Kings Dominion in Doswell, Virginia, in 2008. (Above, Dave Hahner collection; right, Joel Styer collection.)

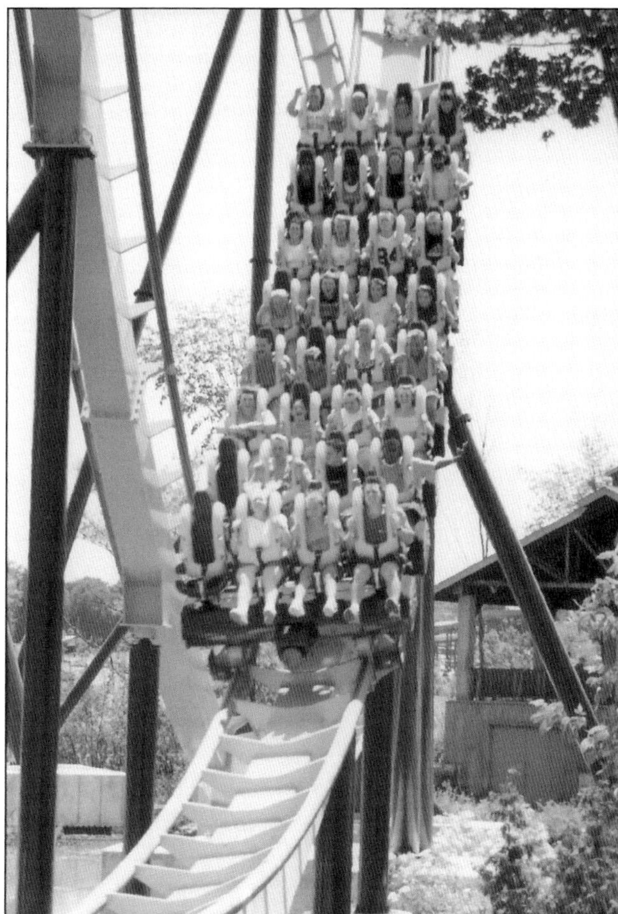

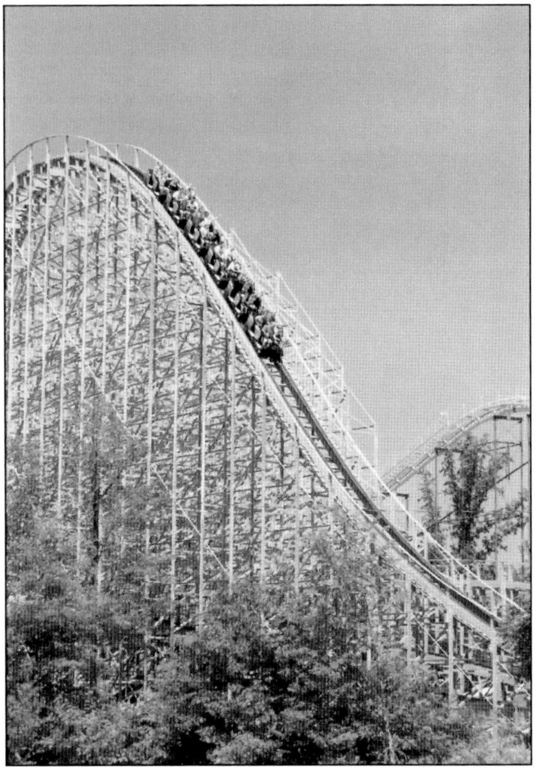

The third of four new coasters added in 2000 was the Villain, a large, 108-foot-tall, 3,980-foot-long wooden roller coaster built on a steel structure. Designed by Custom Coasters International, Inc., the Villain lived up to its moniker as a wild, intense traditional-style roller coaster. Sadly, the colossal ride would be sold for scrap metal along with the Double Loop coaster at a June 2008 auction. (Joel Styer collection.)

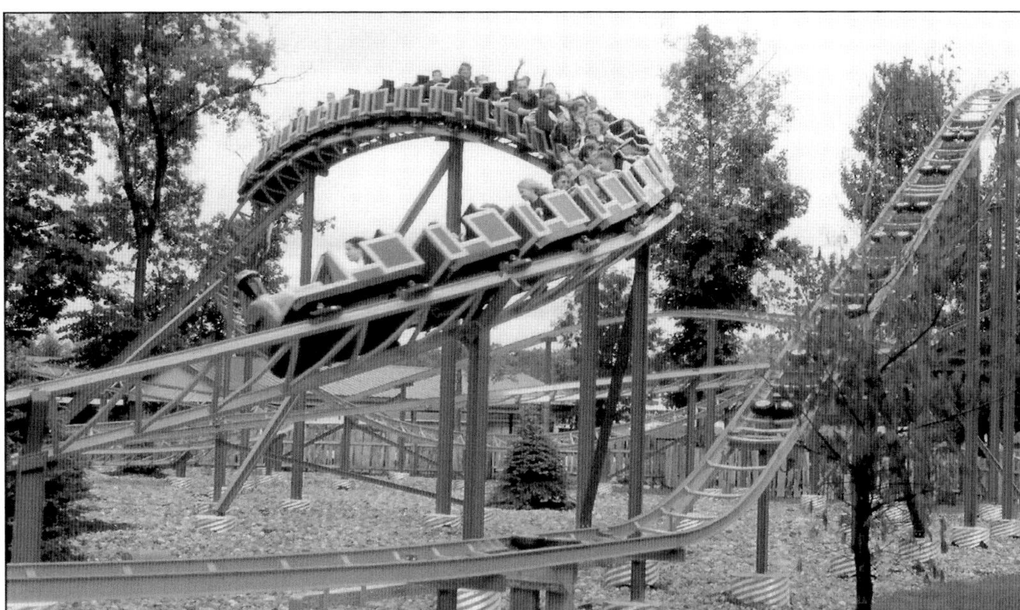

The final new coaster was a family ride from Zierer Rides of Germany called Road Runner Express, after the famous Looney Tunes character. The 25-foot-high coaster featured a long, 20-car train that traversed mildly swooping turns and drops along a 1,181-foot-long course. It would be renamed Beaver Land Mine Ride in 2004, then move to Papéa Park in France in 2009. (Jim Futrell collection.)

Another new ride for 2000 was Shipwreck Falls, a 50-foot-tall shoot-the-chute ride from O.D. Hopkins Company. It would serve as the gateway to a brand-new water park, Hurricane Harbor, which featured a new wave pool built on the location of the former Rainbow Island children's area. The ride would be sold to Celebration City in Branson, Missouri. (Joel Styer collection.)

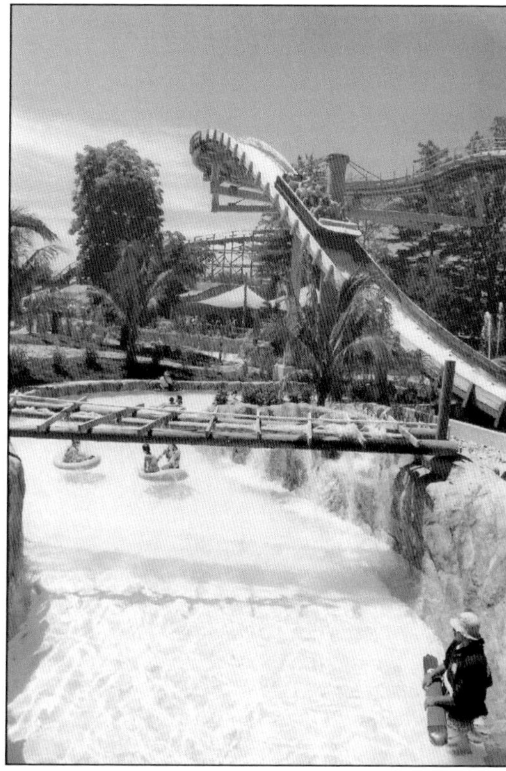

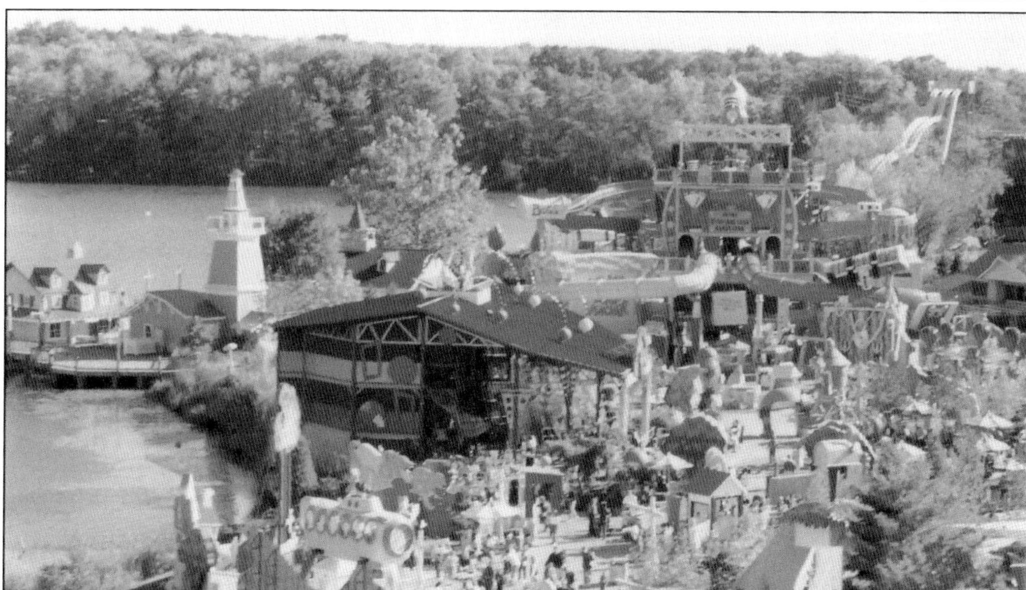

Where the Wave once stood, a new Bugs Bunny–themed children's area called Looney Tunes Boomtown would emerge. It would feature seven children's rides from Italian manufacturer Zamperla, a re-creation of Bugs Bunny's house where children could meet the "wascally wabbit," and the Foam Factory play fortress, complete with foam-ball-shooting cannons. The seven children's rides would move to Cedar Point after Geauga Lake's closure. (Dave Hahner collection.)

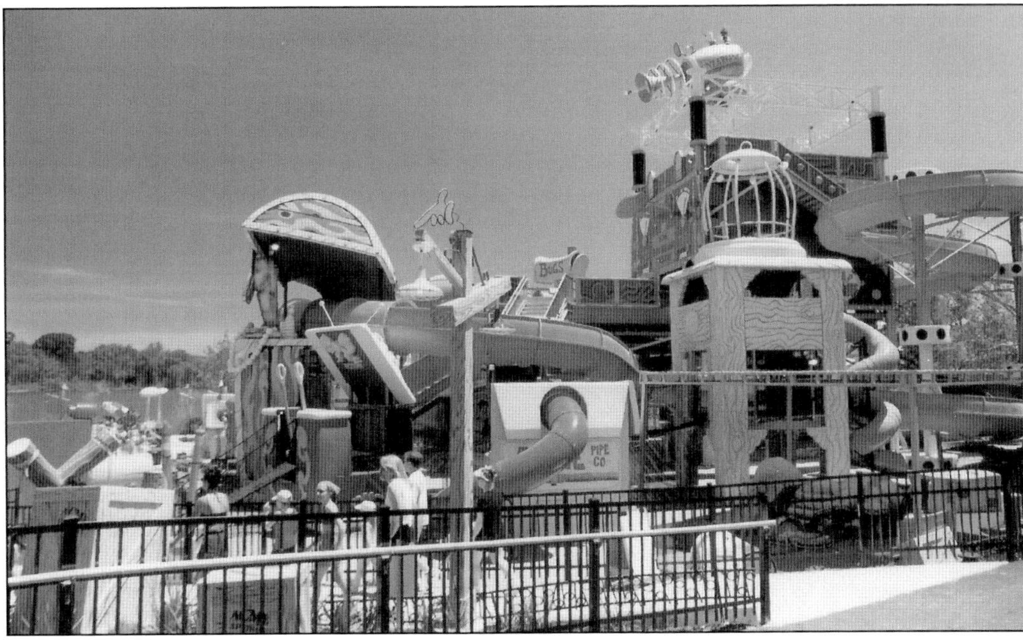

Looney Tunes Boomtown also featured the Larger Than Life Nets children's climbing structure. Themed to giant-sized cartoon-like objects stacked upon one another, it also featured the Great Acme Raft Race. The twin twisting dry waterslides featured two-passenger rubber rafts that raced down through the giant play area. (Joel Styer collection.)

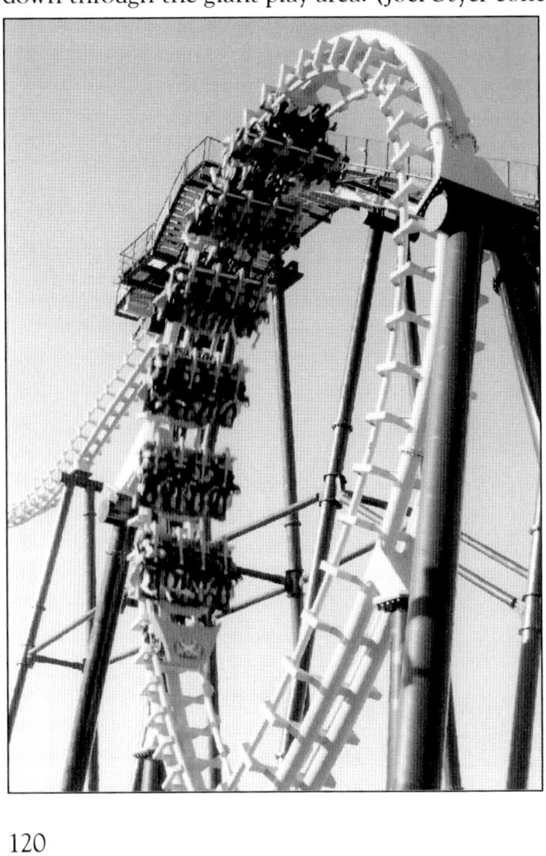

Six Flags Ohio's first season was a successful one, with 1.7 million guests visiting, a 14 percent increase. In January 2001, the park announced X-Flight, a 115-foot-high flying coaster from Vekoma in which riders would lie down as if flying. It would feature five looping inversions along its 3,340-foot track. After the sale to CedarFair, the ride would be moved to Kings Island near Cincinnati in 2007. (Dave Hahner collection.)

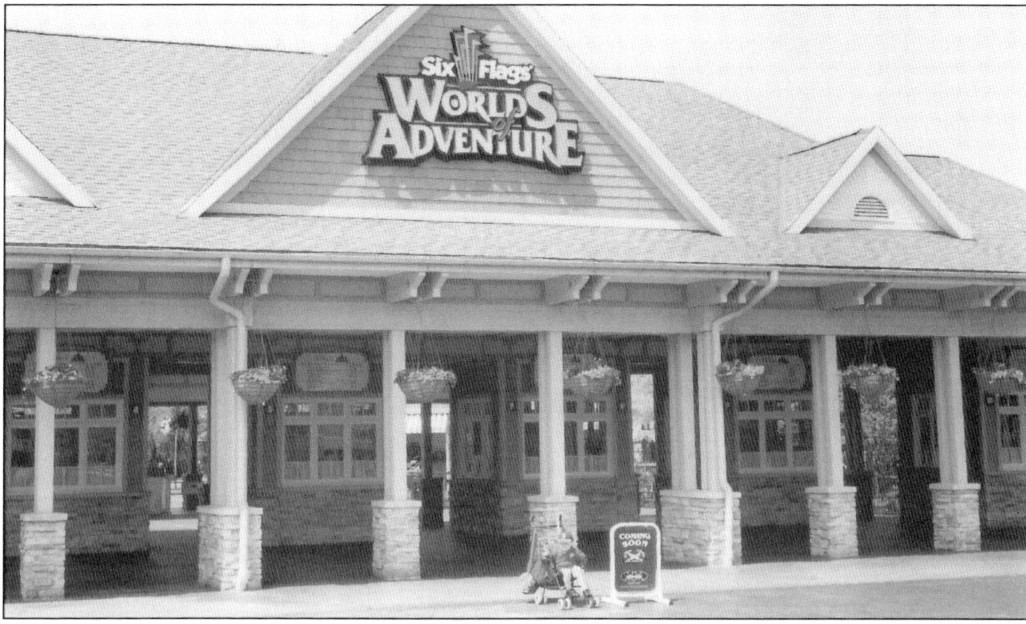

The biggest surprise came in February 2001 as neighboring SeaWorld was purchased by Six Flags for $110 million. Instead of keeping it as a separately gated facility, it was decided to merge the two parks into one, a move that may have eventually sealed the fate of the new mega park. The new complex would be renamed Six Flags Worlds of Adventure, featuring "Wild Life & Wild Rides." (Dave Hahner collection.)

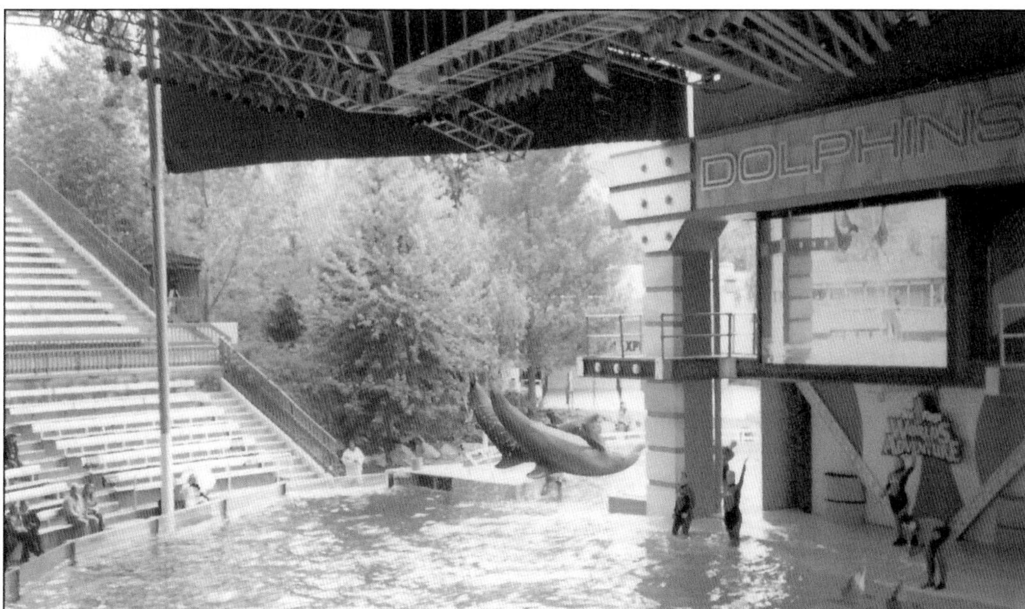

The purchase of the park, however, did not include SeaWorld's headliner attraction, Shamu. The three orcas would be transplanted to other SeaWorld parks along with all of the inhabitants of Patagonia Passage and Dolphin Cove. Four performing dolphins from Six Flags Marine World in Vallejo, California, would be flown in to perform. Stingrays would temporarily occupy the other vacated exhibits. (Sarah Windisch collection.)

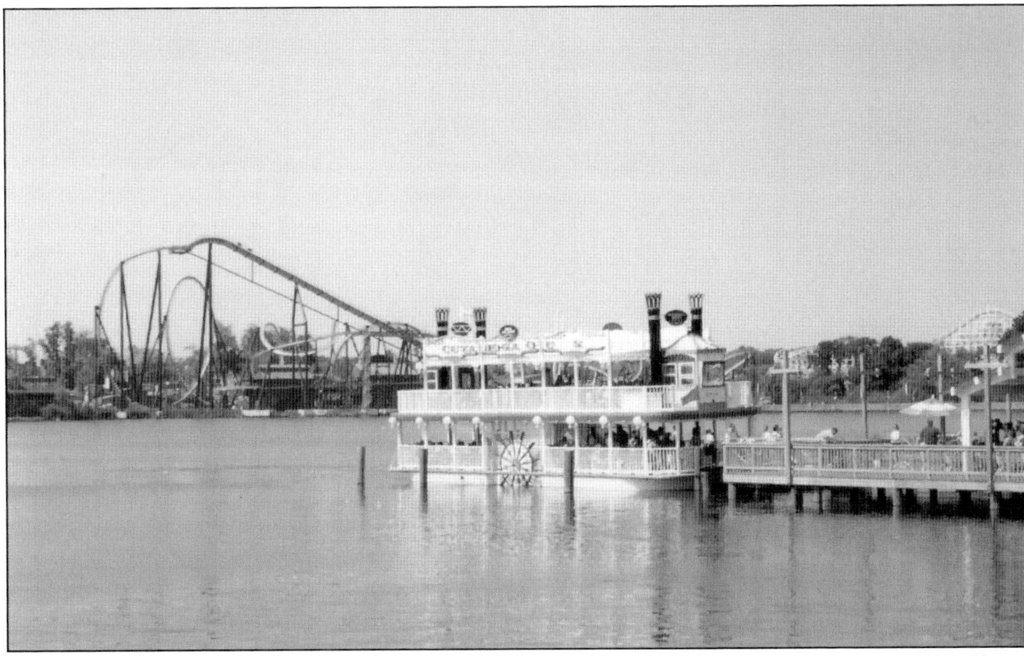

The former SeaWorld area of the park would now be connected by a long, wooded walkway between Raging Wolf Bobs and Happy Harbor. A new floating bridge would also be constructed across Geauga Lake to offer an alternate pedestrian route. Two new ferryboats, *Cuyahoga Queen* and *Aurora Belle*, would also help transport guests across the lake. (Dave Hahner collection.)

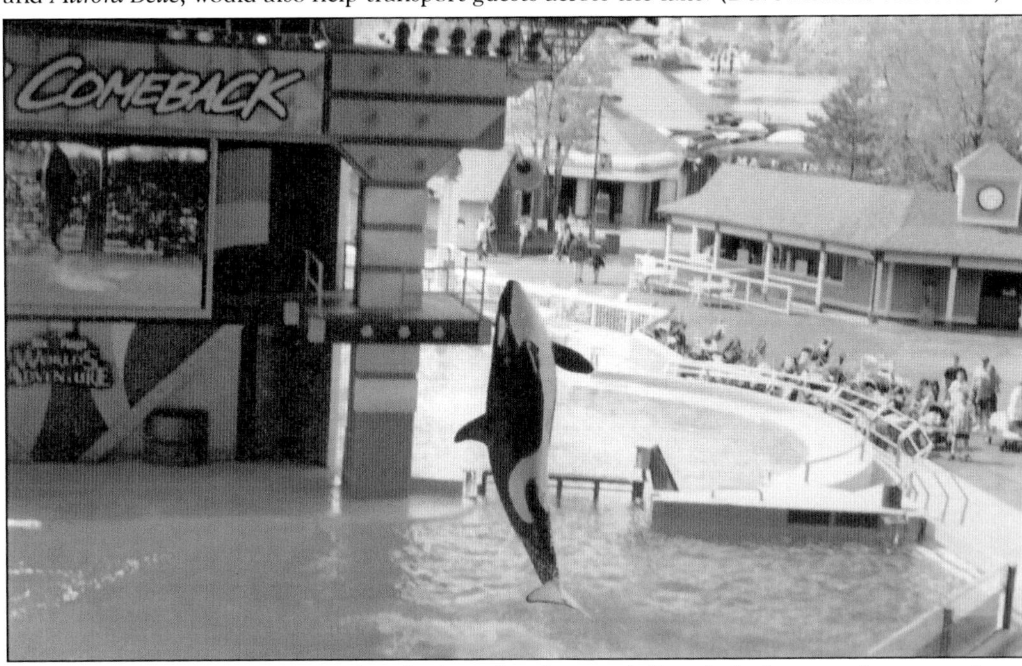

It was clear after the 2001 season that the loss of performing killer whales began to hurt attendance, as sales at the newly combined park fell short of its hoped-for three million. In 2002, the park acquired another orca, Shouka, on loan from a marine park in France. The arrival of Shouka was part of a "Killer Comeback" promotion for the park. (Dave Hahner collection.)

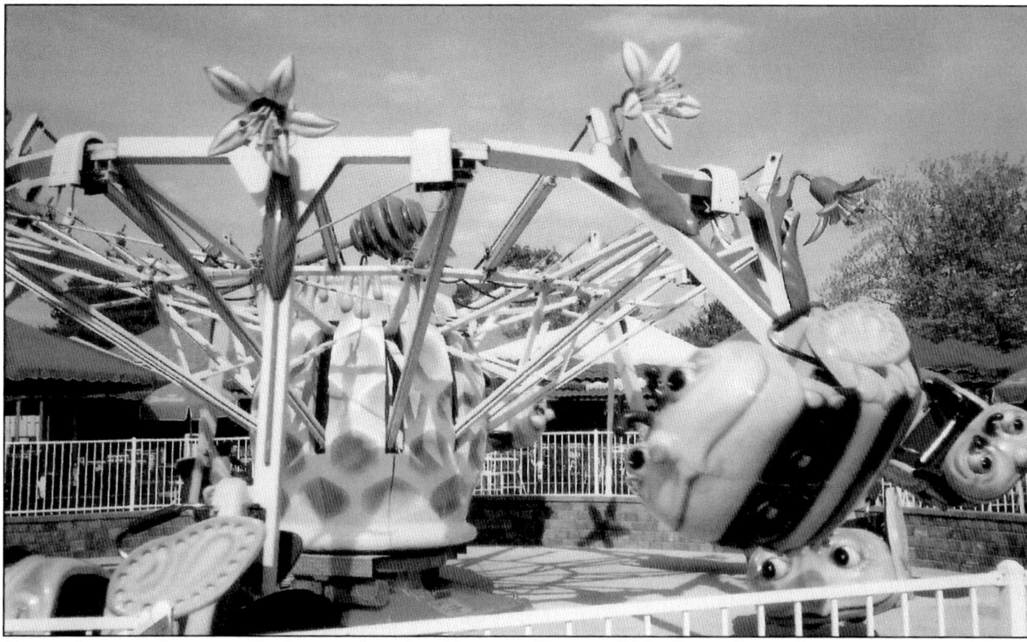

Several new rides, mainly from other Six Flags parks, would be brought in for 2002. Most of these would be added to the former SeaWorld side of the park, including this Thriller Bees ride from Huss. Even with the addition of the new rides and the newly acquired killer whale, attendance still remained disappointing at just over two million visitors. (Dave Hahner collection.)

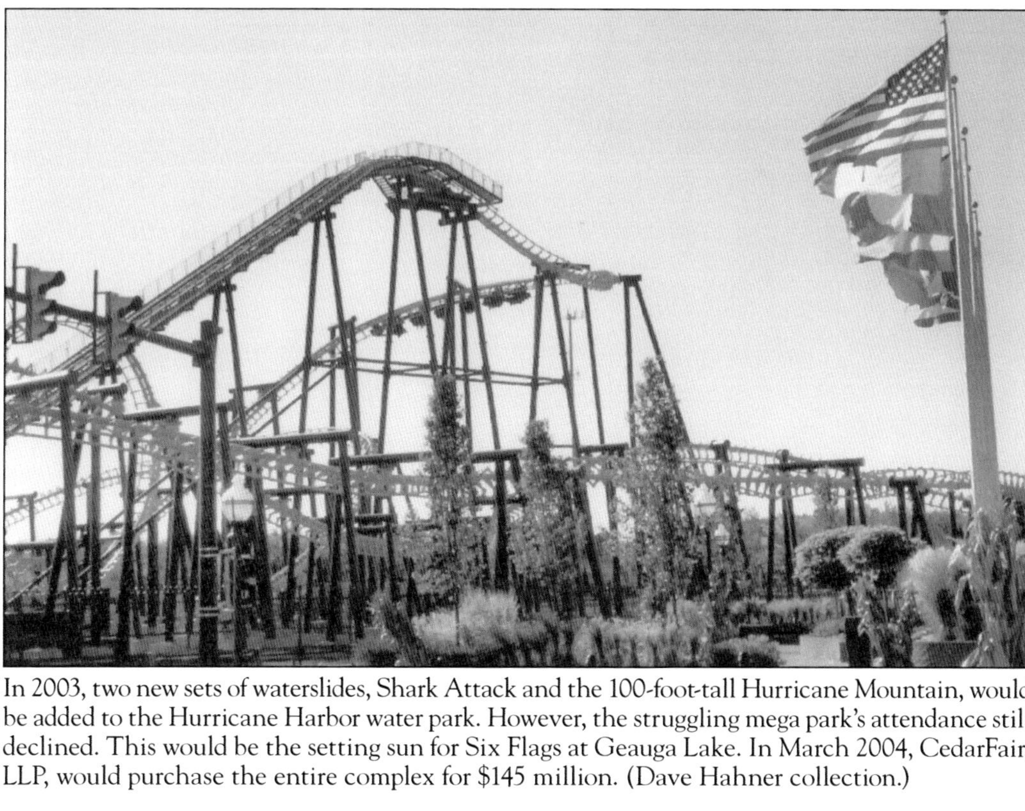

In 2003, two new sets of waterslides, Shark Attack and the 100-foot-tall Hurricane Mountain, would be added to the Hurricane Harbor water park. However, the struggling mega park's attendance still declined. This would be the setting sun for Six Flags at Geauga Lake. In March 2004, CedarFair, LLP, would purchase the entire complex for $145 million. (Dave Hahner collection.)

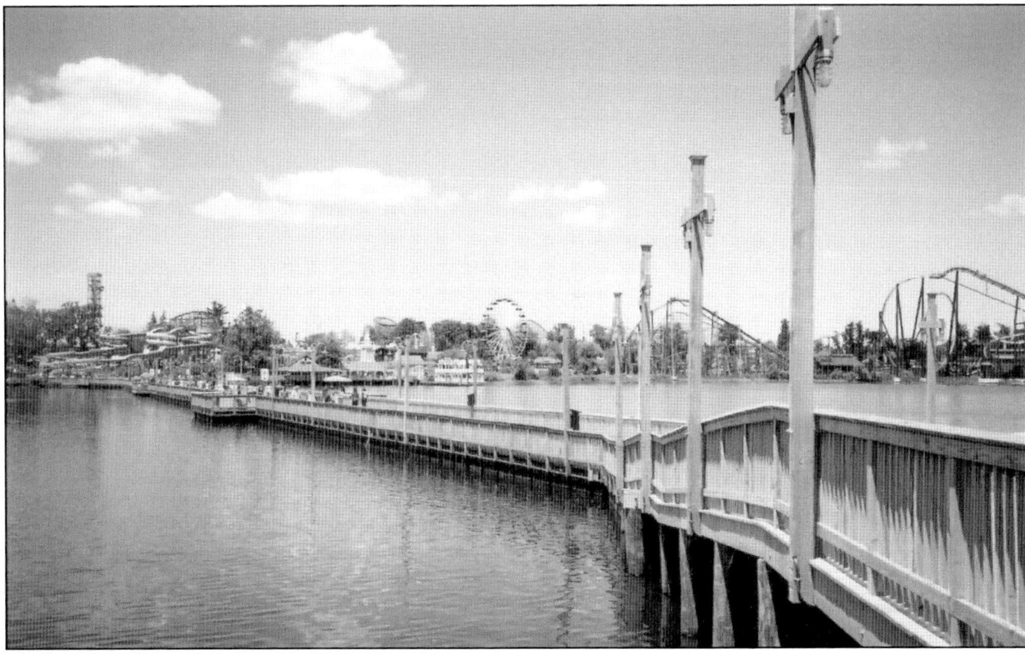

CedarFair renamed the park Geauga Lake and closed the former SeaWorld side completely. Six Flags moved all animals to other homes, and the former SeaWorld Ohio would be gone forever. Many trademarked rides were renamed, and the former marine park was closed off to visitors. Due to these changes, attendance dropped even more than expected. (Dave Hahner collection.)

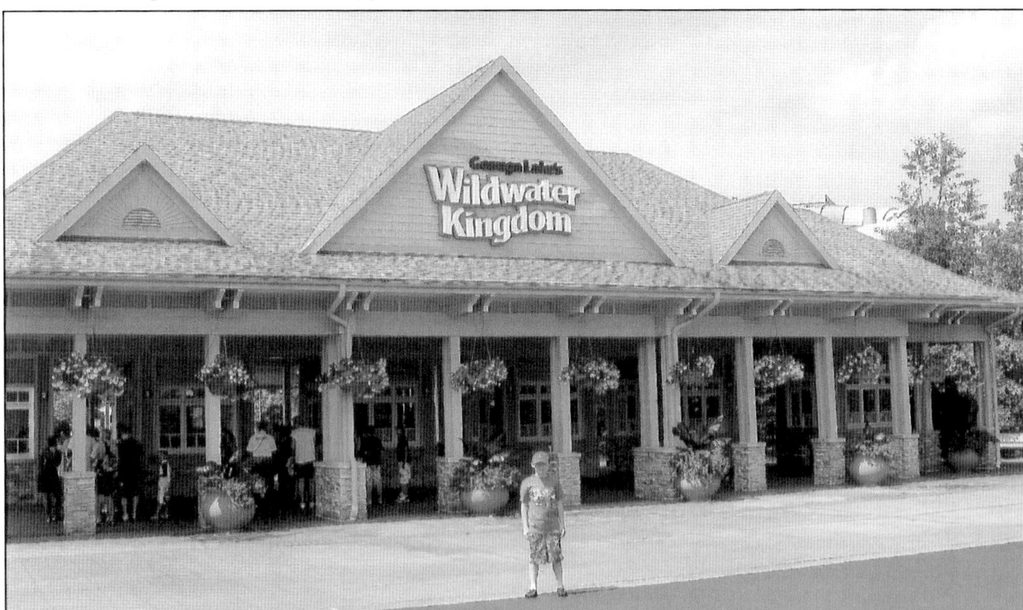

Much of the former SeaWorld would be razed during the 2004–2005 off-season as a new $24-million water park called Wildwater Kingdom would replace most of it. The new water park would open in two phases, with the first part debuting in June 2005. The former Hurricane Harbor water park on the Geauga Lake side was renamed Hurricane Hanna's and remained open during the 2005 season. (Dave Hahner collection.)

The former Hurricane Mountain slides would be moved to the new Wildwater Kingdom area, renamed Thunder Falls. A children's water play area called Splash Landing featuring smaller-sized slides as well as water geysers, and a large tipping bucket would be added. Unfortunately, the once-popular ski stadium remained virtually unused and would eventually be torn down in 2008. (Dave Hahner collection.)

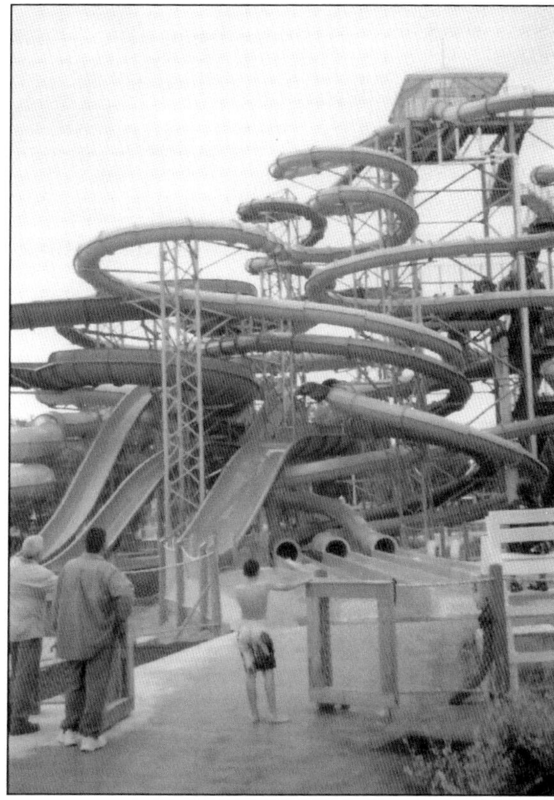

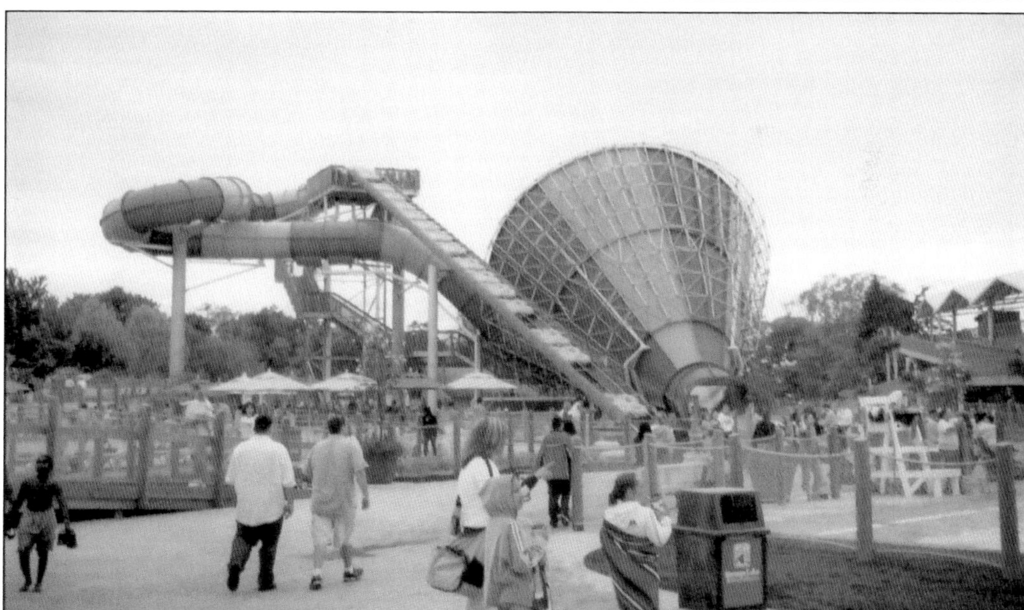

Also included within the new water park would be a brand-new tornado waterslide from Proslide called Liquid Lightning. This large, funnel-like slide features four passenger cloverleaf-shaped inner-tubes that travel down a dark, twisting tunnel, only to emerge in a giant, splashing funnel finale. (Dave Hahner collection.)

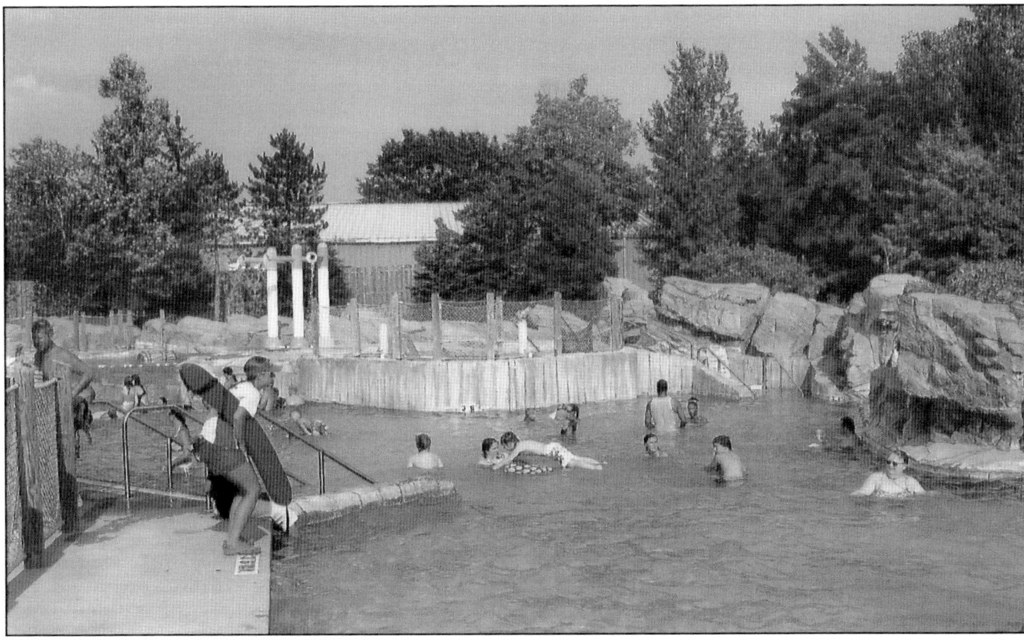

A new water complex called Coral Cove would replace the former Dolphin Cove, with much of the rockwork remaining. It would be a multilevel pool-like area featuring a lazy river named Riptide Run. However, troubling signs were seen elsewhere in the park, as after the 2006 season, X-Flight and Steel Venom were removed and the Bellaire Express monorail scrapped. (Dave Hahner collection.)

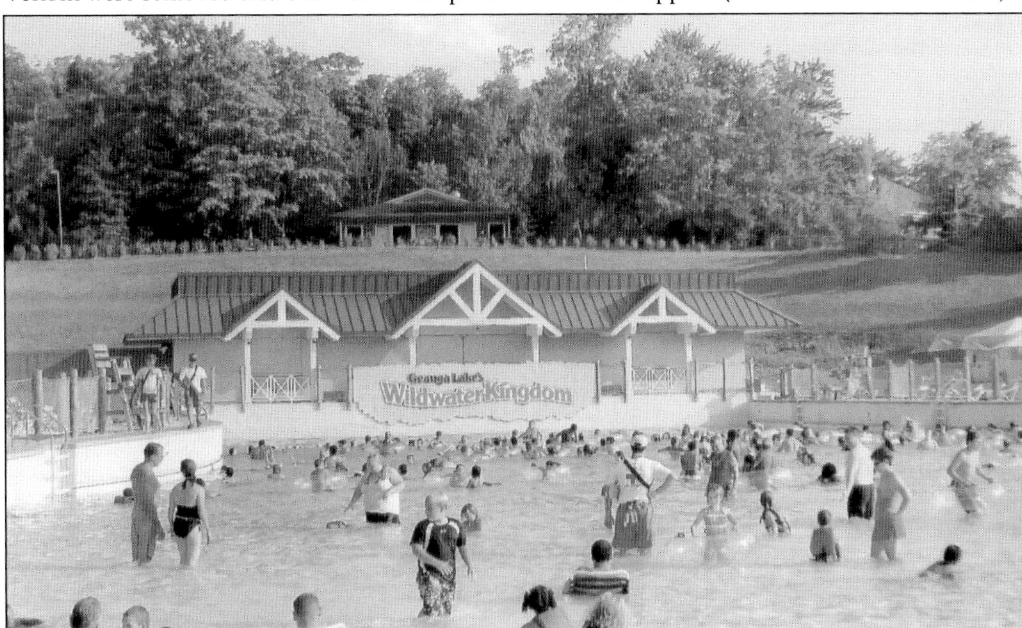

In 2006, the park's third wave pool, Tidal Wave Bay, would be added in the area of the former sea lion stadium. Originally, more was planned for the second phase, but it was scaled back due to disappointing attendance. All of the former water park features would permanently close on the other side. This, along with the other ride removals, left a large empty void in that section of the park. (Dave Hahner collection.)

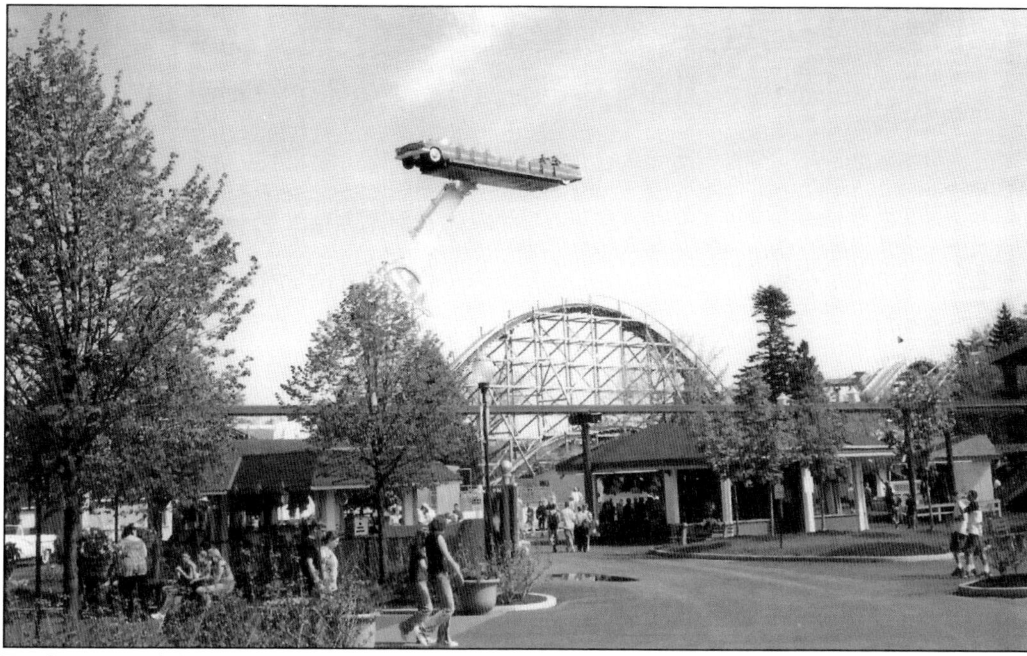

By the start of the 2007 season, it was apparent that the park was struggling with attendance. The new water park became more popular with guests as the ride area had not had any new installments since the sale of the park in 2004. Rumors began to emerge that the park would be downsized even further after the 2007 season. (Dave Hahner collection.)

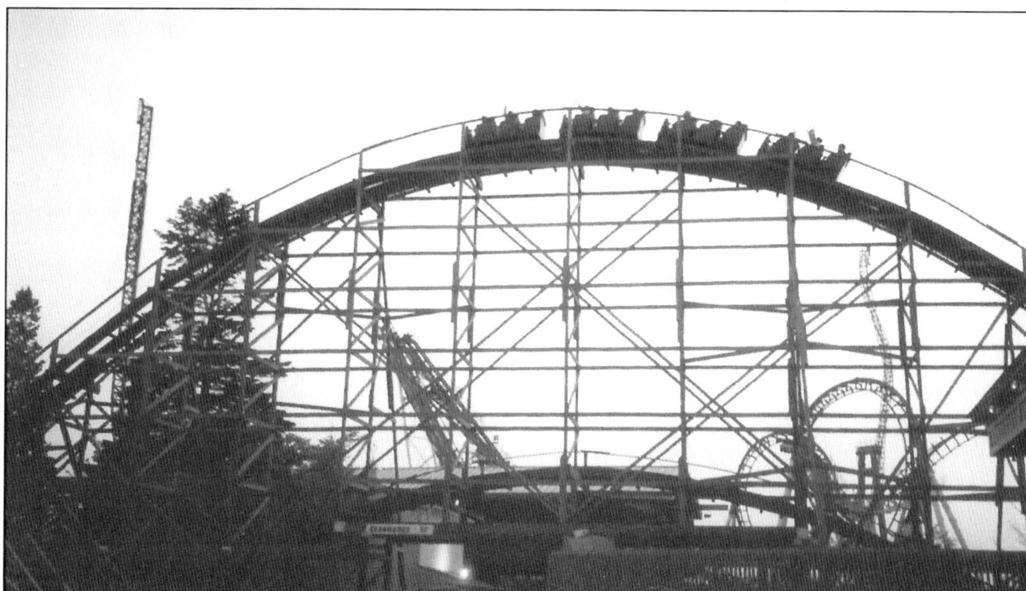

Finally, on September 21, 2007, CedarFair announced that the ride side of the park would close forever, and Wildwater Kingdom would be all that would remain. All rides would be moved, demolished, or sold at auction. The historic Big Dipper, sold to an anonymous bidder in 2008, remains the only ride still intact on the property, a silent sentinel to the fun that once was Geauga Lake. (Dave Hahner collection.)

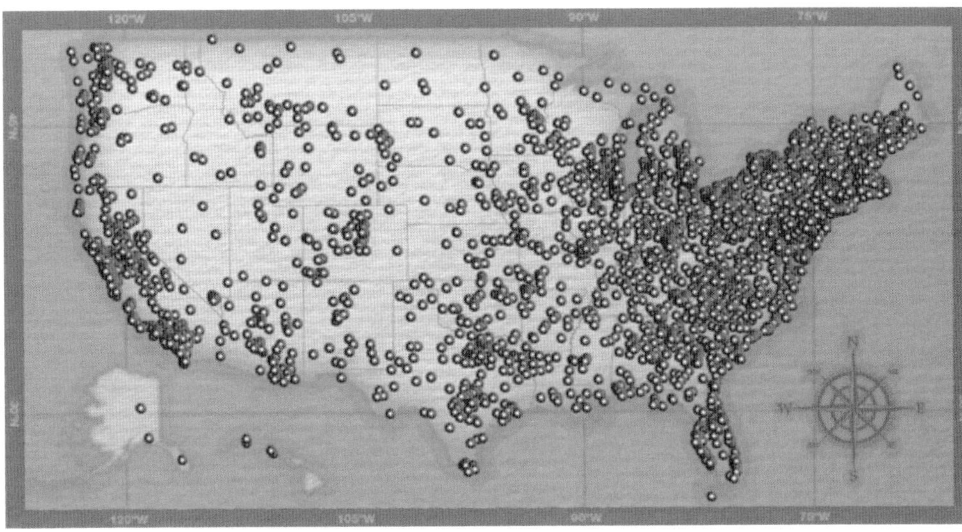